To Ann,

From the day we met
I knew you had a beautiful
heart —
I'm so proud to be a
friend of yours —

Love,
Mary
9/14/04

SOUL SURVIVOR

by

Mary Ross Smith

authorHOUSE

1663 Liberty Drive, Suite 200
Bloomington, Indiana 47403
(800) 839-8640
www.authorhouse.com

First published by AuthorHouse 08/10/04

ISBN: 1-4184-0319-9 (sc)

Library of Congress Number: 2004104947

Printed in the United States of America
Bloomington, Indiana

This book is printed on acid-free paper.

Dedication

This book I dedicate to my son, Julian, who, by the Grace of God, gave me a reason to live.

Also, I dedicate this book to my loving husband, Verne, who is my knight in shining armor.

To my wonderful grandchildren, Jordan and Justin, Grammy loves you very much.

And my daughter-in-law Sandie

And never to be forgotten, my surviving siblings, JS, Arkita, and Abel, whom I dearly love…

Acknowledgments

The writing of this book has only been possible because my husband, Verne W. Smith, gave me unconditional love without judging my past. Thank you Verne, you have been an inspiration, my staunchest supporter, and guiding force in helping me reach and attain my goal to write my story. You gave me all the time and space I needed to write. It was your faith and confidence in me that I could do anything I put my mind to, that kept me from quitting.

I would like to acknowledge the many special people who helped me along the way—through all the tears I shed during the writing of this story.

My first thanks go to Fred S. Sado III, aka Julian Sado, my son, who from the first day I saw his little face, gave me a reason to live. Son, thank you for always believing in me and encouraging me when I was down. You were my defender and helped me keep my focus whenever I became discouraged.

Thanks to Marla Everett, my dear friend who worked closely with me during my first draft. Thanks to Lynda Neely, my dear friend who assisted in the final editing. Thank you, Erick Westcott, Sedona Funeral Home.

Special thanks to Terry Dawson, my agent of The ABACUS Group, and to Jo Ann Krueger who brought my story up to commercial standards. I appreciate all your hard work and thank you for being there for me.

Thank you Lois Mark Stalvey, Author, and mentor, and to the many special people in Sedona, Arizona, who encouraged me in my chosen endeavor.

To the Reader

Just a brief note to clarify the time frame of my story, it takes place during the 50s and 60s.

Please be aware that this story is about the life of a female mortician and the dysfunction in her family life and the lives of her children. I, being the youngest of five, believe I received the brunt of her frustrations and anger.

Some of the names of the characters are fictional; however, the events are real-life, but would most likely be disputed by some who are still living.

I once heard that the mind is its own place and you can make heaven a hell or hell a heaven. The mind of a child will protect the child.

This is where one person chose to break the chain of abuse and give life a chance.

Respectfully submitted,
Mary Ross Smith

1

THEY CALL ME LITTLE MARY; I WAS BORN IN JACKSON, Mississippi, and given the name Mary Eliza Reese, Jr. after my Mother. Our family traveled from Jackson, Mississippi, to Los Angeles, California, in 1947. Dad had had enough of the prejudice of the South and was determined to find a better life. Mother resisted the move but in the end Dad's will prevailed.

I've always been proud of my name for the many admired qualities that my Mother possessed. She was a brilliant businesswoman, who in the early 50's succeeded despite being a Negro female in the competitive Funeral Industry in South Central Los Angeles. She was a beautiful, fair-skinned woman, with black satin hair. She had an engaging personality that caused people to like her on the first meeting. She also had the unique quality of making everyone feel important. People used to say, "That Mrs. Reese can really work a crowd." She loved entertaining; it seemed she was always on stage.

Because of Mother, we were surrounded by important black celebrities of the day, including preachers, politicians, entertainers and even a few ranking officers of the LAPD. Yes, Mother did have admired qualities in abundance, but life for me as a ten year old, the youngest of five kids, four living at home, was sheer hell. Mother's battle with alcoholism tore the family apart.

I remember as if it were yesterday. It was around midnight when Mother yelled to all the kids to get out of bed and come downstairs, and line up from the smallest to the tallest. It was obvious she had been drinking heavily and that she and Dad had been arguing. But what Mother told us, stunned us all and scared me to death, as I knew that my life from that point on was to be very uncertain. She told us to choose whom we wanted to live with, because she was kicking my dad out of the house. Dad

1

was a quiet man who despised smoking and drinking and avoided arguments, especially with Mother whenever possible. Mother's irrational behavior had taken its toll, even for this quiet man.

Willie Jr., named after our Father; at age twelve, went with Dad. Lenore, was sixteen, Ilona, fourteen, so the three of us were left with Mother. JT, my oldest brother was away in the Air Force. Home was becoming a hell; a couple of years later Lenore got married.

Now it was just the two of us, Ilona and me to fend for ourselves.

Without the stability that Dad provided to the family, Mother's behavior grew more and more irrational with each passing day.

After that evening her drinking seemed to increase and her relationship with her married business partner Mr. Hubert, appeared to be more than just business.

Mother was part owner and Funeral Director of the Hubert & Reese Mortuary. She was proud to be the daughter of J.T.Stone, the founder of the famous J.T. Stone Mortuary, in Mississippi.

Her celebrity stature in the negro funeral-home business in Los Angeles, was a big draw for business.

***

The year was 1954; it was an extremely hot day in July. I was sitting on the front steps of the Mortuary waiting for Mother to come out of Mr. Hubert's office. I wondered what was taking Mother so long? I'm bored and wanted to go home. I can hear them talking, but I'm not sure what they are saying… or not saying. Anyway, I spent a lot of time daydreaming about my grandfather. Mother talked about him constantly, what a stern man he was and how admired he was in the South. While I sat on the steps, I thought about this great man that I did not know, the famous J.T. Stone, and wished I'd had the chance to have known him personally.

Mother told me many stories of my grandfather that captivated me, that he was a respected Baptist Preacher in Mississippi, who ruled his family with an iron hand. Despite his reputation of being a strict Father, the five Stone girls and one boy were considered to be spoiled and arrogant. My Mother's brother Nathan died young, in the early 1900's. Nathan, the only son of J.T. Stone, was a free-spirited man. He left Mississippi for the glamour and excitement of Los Angeles. They say he was very handsome, with light-brown skin, and gray eyes. Women found him irresistible.

Unfortunately, at the age of twenty-three Nathan was found dead in an alley in downtown Los Angeles. The exact circumstances regarding his death remain a mystery, but it was widely rumored that his rebellious life style, wealth, and arrogance were factors.

Nathan traveled to Los Angeles, against his Father's wishes. He arrived by train, sporting the finest in fashion, jewelry, and a wad of money. Gambling was one of his faults, and drinking hard liquor was the other.

Upon arriving in Los Angeles, Nathan befriended a group of gamblers and soon he was way over his head in debt. He started wiring home to grandfather in Mississippi, asking for money. After several money wires, grandfather said he'd had enough, and refused to send any more money. Nathan pleaded with his Father stating that this would be the last time he would ask for money, and without the cash his life was in danger. Grandfather stood firm on his decision not to wire any more money, hoping that his son would come to his senses, return home to take his place as the sole male heir to the family legacy and run the Mortuary. Three days later grandfather received a telegram that his son had been brutally murdered. Nathan Stone had been found dead in an alley. He had been beaten with a blunt object and stabbed several times through the heart. He apparently died after the first blow to his head. The killers were never caught and grandfather was never the same. I was sorry I never had the chance to meet my uncle.

***

Mother told me that my grandfather was a legend during his day, known as an intelligent and highly-successful entrepreneur, and a fearless defender of the rights of his people. It was in fact his passion for the well being of the Negro people in his Mississippi town that led him to a close acquaintance with Booker T. Washington, and caused him to establish an ambulance service and Funeral Home in the late 1800's. On several occasions that Funeral Home served as a refuge for desperate or displaced individuals. I heard that he once saved the life of a young Negro man who surely would have been lynched for shooting a White man in a brawl. It was said to be self-defense but in Mississippi, in the early 1900's, that equated to murder. Grandfather shipped the young man to San Francisco, on a train. The young man was put into a plain-wooden casket, nothing fancy so as not to attract attention. It was sealed with a padlock. The interior of the casket was lined with water jars, sandwiches, and apples, just enough to survive the trip. The casket had air holes on the side that were not visible to the eye. He then placed a large sign on the lid that read:

DO NOT OPEN! DEAD MAN IN CASKET

I loved hearing stories of my grandfather and my uncle that were told to me mainly by my Mother. I am sure she may have at times exaggerated, but I believed everything she told me. Often while daydreaming it seemed as though I would travel back in time, watching my grandfather, standing up for what was right and determine to make a difference for his family. I wondered if my Mother was anything like him?

2

I WAS GLAD TO SEE MR. HOLMES COMING IN MY direction.

He was a handsome man with a beautiful smile and a kind manner about himself.

I could daydream later as I loved to visualize what my grandparents were like. But now I have Mr. Holmes to keep me company.

"Hey, Lil Mary, what are you doing?" he asked with a big smile.

"Just sitting here waiting for Mother to come out of Mr. Hubert's office," I said.

"Well, I'm just going to work. Want to come watch me do my magic?" Suddenly energized, I asked, "What magic?"

"You just come with me and I'll teach you some of the business," he promised. In my enthusiasm to follow him I quickly jumped off the step and almost fell but Mr. Holmes caught me and gave me his wonderful smile...I really liked him.

Mr. Holmes was the embalmer for Hubert and Reese Mortuary, while his wife Ima was the beautician and make-up artist. Ima had a wonderful reputation and was in great demand because she was well known for her talent to make the dead appear years younger than their actual age. Her smile would melt your heart. She wore a different wig every day. They were stylish but obviously wigs. When Ima would see me she'd give me the biggest hug. Her large bosom was soft like a pillow and she'd pull my face right into it. I felt like she was smothering me at times, but I felt safe with her. I would have loved to live with she and Mr. Holmes. Once again Mr. Holmes said while reaching for my hand,

"Come on, Little Girl."

I followed him around to the back of the Funeral Home because I was happy to talk with someone, that was better than sitting on that hard step outside Mr. Hubert's office. In the back I saw the hearse was parked in front of the open double doors that led to the Embalming Room. When I

5

hesitated a little, Mr. Holmes gently said,

"Come on, girl. Don't be afraid."

"I'm not afraid!" I adamantly responded even though my voice was slightly shaky. I fervently hoped he hadn't noticed.

This was my first time in the Embalming Room and I was somewhat apprehensive and my heart pounded and my hands were sweaty. As I took my first hesitant steps into the room, I was totally unprepared for the overwhelmingly strong, pungent, and distinctive smell of formaldehyde which filled my nostrils.

My immediate reaction was I started seeing stars, my eyes teared, and the smell nearly overwhelmed me. Taking a minute to adjust, I then slowly walked further into the room where the sight of three dead bodies, two men and a woman, almost made me forget the permeating smell of the formaldehyde. The bodies were lying on tables with sheets pulled up to their necks and it looked to me as if they were naked under the sheets. Before that day, I had never seen a naked person—dead or alive.

Then Mr. Holmes said seriously, but in a kind voice,

"Let me tell you something to remember for the rest of your life, Little Girl. Never forget this. The dead won't hurt you, it's the living that will! This is your first lesson for the day."

In spite of his reassurance, I stood there as if paralyzed. I couldn't seem to make my legs move forward but could feel myself slowly moving backward.

"Come closer," Mr. Holmes kindly encouraged.

"No. I think I should go now," I said, feeling awkward.

"Come on, Little Mary. Nothing or no one in here can hurt you, I promise!"

He walked over, picked me up and then gently placed me on a tall stool next to one of the bodies.

"Now, just keep me company," he said, in the same reassuring voice.

Cautiously I looked around from my high perch and the first thing I noticed was a table located next to one of the bodies. On this little table he had placed all kinds of instruments and tools, just like in a doctor's office. There appeared to be sharp knives, an ice pick and also several tubes and jars.

Even though my heartbeat had slowed a little, I could tell it was still somewhat faster than normal. Trying not to show my fear, I asked,

" Mr. Holmes, what is that tube and what is it for, and how about that one over there?"

"Slow down, little girl!" he calmly encouraged. "Just watch and learn. I'll explain as I go."

"Okay," I said in a small voice, trying not to let him know I was still rather nervous and uncertain about my surroundings.

Next, I became aware that the Embalming Room was very cold and though the smell was still sharp and irritating to my nose, the initial onslaught of the smell had diminished. I continued to look around, not watching what Mr. Holmes was doing at that moment. I was surprised that everything was white. In fact, everywhere I looked it seemed white—white walls, windowsills, cabinets, counters, and chairs. Even Mr. Holmes had slipped into a white coat and white rubber gloves.

"Mr. Holmes, why does it smell so bad?" I asked because the stinking smell of the Embalming Room reminded me of someone sick in the bathroom.

"When people die, everything inside them dies also," he patiently explained.

Fascinated in spite of myself, I watched Mr. Holmes as he inserted a syringe and tube into the dead man's neck and it seemed to work like a vacuum. When the blood started flowing through the tube, which led to the sink, all I saw was red. I suddenly began to feel weak, lightheaded, and then everything went black.

"Little Mary, Little Mary, you okay?" Mr. Holmes voice was frantic as he lifted me off the floor.

As if from a long distance I heard his voice and as I opened my eyes said, "I'm okay." *I sure felt stupid though.*

"I better take you back to your mom," he said as he placed me on my feet.

"Sure," I replied.

Mr. Holmes knew that I was a tomboy, but he always made me feel like a little girl. I was fair-skinned like my Mother and it pleased me when people often said I looked just like her. My long-black hair was usually worn in two braids for efficiency sake, which emphasized my large, black eyes. Even though I was rather skinny, I was as tough as any boy in the neighborhood. My biggest problems were the times I had to wear a dress.

The walk back to the other side of the Mortuary seemed as if it were a mile instead of the short walk that it actually was. As the door to Mr. Hubert's office was still closed, I tried to peak through the lace curtains on the French doors but was unable to see a thing. Just as I turned back to sit on the step, the door suddenly opened with such strong force that it hit me on my butt and knocked me to the ground. Just as quickly as I went down, I jumped back up like a spring as I said, "Hi, Mom, ready to go?"

"What have you been up to?" she asked with a smile, and I wanted to ask her the same question but I knew better.

"Oh, nothing, just keeping Mr. Holmes company," I said with a tentative

7

smile feeling somewhat embarrassed. Whatever she and Mr. Hubert talked about, it put her in a good mood. When Mr. Hubert came out of his office a few moments later, he also was in a real good mood and smiling.

Mr. Hubert was not one of my favorite people; he was a big man, at least two- hundred pounds with very dark- brown skin. Even though his hair was thinning, his thin-black mustache and long sideburns complimented his looks. Usually he wore a half smile as he walked around. Mrs. Hubert seldom came to the Funeral Home.

***

For me, the ride home was long and it usually took forty-five minutes depending on traffic. I was always glad to return home. Ilona, my favorite sister, was then fourteen and I was glad she still lived at home. Our brothers JT, Willie Jr., and older sister Lenore didn't have much time for either Ilona or myself, so we clung to each other. She was my best friend, and protector.

It was around six in the evening and still quite warm, but inside the car there was a distinct chill. "Mother, I can't wait to see Ilona."

"Oh shut up." she said. Just like that, her attitude changed and my mentioning Ilona's name seemed to make her angry.

I didn't say another word, I just sat quietly. Then Mother reached over and took my hand. Her hands were soft and smooth, but as she held my hand she began squeezing harder and harder until tears came to my eyes.

"Stop, that hurts," I said, and I noticed my hand was turning purple.

"Oh, don't be such a baby."

"That really hurt."

"Okay, I'm sorry, I didn't mean to hurt you." but she was smiling.

We drove the rest of the way home in silence, each lost in our own thoughts. Frankly, I just didn't have much to say.

As we pulled into our driveway, I was filled with an overwhelming wish that Dad would be there, but I knew he wouldn't. I missed him so much but according to Mother, he didn't love me. That was what she told me, over and over.

As I glanced out the window of the car, I saw my bike in the back yard. It was a big yard with a huge tree that I climbed quite frequently. I wanted to jump on my bike and ride away, but I needed to see my sister.

Our house was located on the corner of Gramercy and 21st Street, an attractive, upscale, transitional neighborhood. We were one of only three colored families who lived there. The house was a large, older, three-story home with five bedrooms, four bathrooms, a large living room, den, kitchen, a formal dining room, and a basement that gave me goose bumps every time

I went down there. The third floor consisted of one large and one small room and another door that led to the attic, which seemed spooky to me. I refused to go up to the third floor without Ilona.

There was a story about our house that intrigued our family and the whole neighborhood. Supposedly, the man who previously had owned the house had murdered his wife in the house and had also hidden a lot of money somewhere within the walls. The rumor was that one day he would return for the money. Well, if it was true he never returned while we lived there, and we looked and never found the money.

***

As soon as the car had come to a stop in our driveway, I jumped out, slammed the door and with Mother still yelling at me I raced to the backdoor, through the kitchen and up the backstairs which led to the second floor.

"Ilona, Ilona, where are you?" I yelled as I ran to her bedroom door. We called it the Blue Room because it was painted all blue; even her private bathroom was blue. The Blue Room was first JT's room before he left for the Air Force. Only Mother and JT had the privilege of a private bathroom. Ilona had first choice when he left.

Anxiously I called again, "Ilona!" I tried to open her door but it was locked so I knocked with such force I hurt my knuckles. Mother did not like locked doors.

"What do you want?" she said as she opened the door just enough to see me.

"Can't I come in?" I asked.

The door opened and I went in. I was excited to see her, but she had been crying and her eyes were swollen.

"What's wrong?" I asked.

"Nothing," she said.

"Something is wrong. Please tell me," I pleaded with her.

I put my arms around her waist as we sat on the bed, and she began to cry uncontrollably.

Grudgingly she said, "If you tell I'll never forgive you." She was struggling for words.

"What? What?" I kept asking.

"Last night, Mother had a lot of company over, and . . ."

I interrupted, "I heard a lot of noise."

"Be quiet and let me tell you what happen,"

"Ok," I dropped my head in embarrassment for speaking out of turn.

My hands were shaking because I could feel the fear in her voice and that

9

scared me.

"Last night I was in my bed and all of a sudden I woke to some man forcing himself on me. I screamed and screamed and finally Mother came upstairs and started yelling at me, instead of yelling at the man. She said it was my fault."

"Is that why your lip is swollen?" I asked, "It looks like someone hit you!"

"Yeah, he kissed me so hard my lip bled."

"Why didn't Mother believe you?" I asked.

"I don't know!" Ever since Dad and JT and Willie left, Mother has just gone crazy. Little Mary, I'm going to run away," she said.

"No! Please don't leave me." I began to whine and beg her not to leave me. "I'll go with you."

"You can't go! Mother would kill me."

"I don't care, I can't stay here without you, please, please, Ilona don't leave me." I began to cry uncontrollably. I could hear the anger in my Mother's voice, yelling from the bottom of the stairs.

"Little Mary, what's going on up there?" She yelled louder now.

"Nothing," Ilona said.

We could hear Mother coming up the stairs, and Ilona began to shake.

"Don't tell her I told you."

"What's going on?" Mother said, looking down at me. She could see I had been crying.

"Nothing," I said, with my head down,

"Ilona doesn't feel well, and that made me sad."

Mother was angry. She took me by the arm, pulled me out of the door and said,

"Go to your room." I ran down the hallway to my room.

I left Ilona's room with my heart breaking, feeling the fear my sister felt. What could I do? Nothing! That's what hurt. I couldn't go to sleep, thinking about Ilona and Dad.

Ilona was a beautiful girl, with light-brown skin that glowed. Her hair was black and wavy, not like Mother's or mine; she had to use a pressing comb to make her hair straight. She had pretty black eyes, heavy eyebrows, and large breasts for a fourteen-year-old girl; however, she did not think herself to be pretty. Ilona looked so much like Dad I believe that was the main reason why Mother resented her so much. That got me to start thinking about the stories I heard about my Dad while I sat on the bed hugging my pillow...

I didn't really know a lot about my Father. I loved him and tried to hold onto the good memories, regardless of how many times Mother said he hated me. He was a handsome man; he was a little shorter than Mother and that did not bother him. He had been out on his own from the age of twelve. Dad owned an Automobile Service Station not far from our home. He was raised in Louisiana, the grandson of slaves but dropped out of school in the sixth grade in order to work and help his Mother, Big Momma. My Dad's stories always frightened me.

He told Ilona and me that back in Louisiana, Big Momma and her boyfriend Charlie were both alcoholics, and often Charlie would beat Dad just for the fun of it. So Dad ran away from home at the age of twelve. He began working odd jobs, and sleeping in doorways. But even at that early age he was determined to make a better life for himself free from alcohol and abuse.

He was devoted to Big Momma and returned regularly to check on her and to give her money. One evening Dad had an encounter with Charlie that led to a fight that almost killed him. He had worked all day doing odd jobs and came by to give his Mother some money, when Charlie charged out of the back room, cursing and threatening to kill him if he ever showed his face there again. One thing led to another and Dad fought like a man, not a boy. The fight was out of control. Charlie was drunk and not able to get the best of my Dad, so he fought dirty. He picked up a glass pitcher filled with water and hit Dad over the head. Stunned and rather dizzy from that hard blow, the adrenalin, which coursed through his body, kept him fighting with extra strength until he finally knocked Charlie out cold. Barely standing, he stumbled around a bit and wondered why water was running down his shirt.

He hadn't yet realized that his jugular vein had been cut and he was actually bleeding to death right there in his Mother's kitchen. When he touched his neck and saw it was his blood that covered him and not water, reality set in. The last sound my Dad heard as he fell to the floor was Big Momma as she screamed and called for help.

I can only imagine my Dad's thoughts when he awoke and realized he was in the County Morgue. As he was unable to speak or move, he just prayed he would not die.

He lay there and wanted to shout, "I'm not dead" but he couldn't. While the attendant talked and joked around with another man who was in the morgue, he heard the stranger say,

"This boy is not dead!"

My dad could not lift his eyelids as they seemed just too heavy for him to open, but he rejoiced in his heart, as he knew he heard them quite clearly.

11

The stranger who had realized Dad was alive was a doctor.

Just then the coroner came over to examine what he originally thought was a dead boy, "I'll be damn, he is alive! I can't believe it, and his jugular is nearly cut in half." Shaking his head in amazement, the attendant looked around the room and said,

"Oh, Dr. Porter, this nigger be dead in a few minutes, he ain't got no blood left in him."

Not knowing how Dad ended up in the morgue bothered Dr. Porter. "Why didn't they help him in the emergency room? He might have made it."

Dad knew he would probably die; they didn't care he thought, but his will to live was obvious to the doctor.

"I can save this one."

The coroner said, "Why? It's just another nigger."

Dad's heart stopped…

A week later, Dad woke up to find he was unable to move his neck, but he knew he was alive. Cautiously he tried to look around as much as his limited movement would allow and recognized that he was in a basement or storage area where brooms, buckets and all kinds of stuff were kept. Next, he realized he was lying on a cot and then his thoughts began running rampant. *What had happened? Had that doctor really saved his life, and why?*

It seemed as if hours had passed but he had had no way to know the time or day. Finally the door opened and in walked a short, stocky young White man with blond hair and blue eyes. The main thing Dad always remembered after that was the man's friendly smile.

"I see you decided to wake up," cheerfully smiled the doctor. Dad could tell the smile was sincere, but he was unable to speak and to tired to nod his head.

"You had a close call and you checked out, but I fought to bring you back. How do you feel?"

Dad again tried to nod but couldn't as the pain was excruciating.

"It's okay. I know you can't speak just yet, but you'll speak soon enough. The jugular vein in your neck was cut quite severely, and you've lost an enormous amount of blood. By the way, I'm Doctor Porter, and I was in the morgue when you were brought in. Obviously, someone figured you to be dead."

Dad was relieved to know he was alive, and he also knew not to question it, he was just happy to be alive.

"I know the hospital doesn't do much to help Negroes and since it was obvious you were unable to pay for hospital expense, I brought you down here to personally take care of you. I was unable to just let you die…I *had* to make an effort to try and save your life. After all, that is why I became a doctor—to save lives, no matter what color the person's skin. I just had to try and from the looks of you, I did okay."

Dad could feel the tears in his eyes, and Doctor Porter took his own handkerchief and gently wiped my Dad's face.

"You're going to be okay, Mr. Reese. In another week or so you will be able to leave. Don't worry about your strength. It will return but probably more slowly than you would wish. I'll see to it that you have food and I'll get you something to wear at night time, okay? You just rest now, and I'll take care of everything," promised the doctor.

The tears he shed were tears of joy and Dad wanted to say, "Thank you," but the words would not come out. Then again, his emotions were mixed. It was hard for him to believe the compassion that was being shown to him by this White doctor. It was more than he had ever experienced or could have ever imagined. Those remaining days he stared at the ceiling, thinking and thanking God for a White stranger, who called him, "Mr. Reese," not "boy."

Time passed and Dad left the hospital a new man. He had been given a new life, but his anger and hate for Charlie still ate at him every day. As he continued to gain strength and health, Dad had plenty of time to make his plan of revenge. Finally, one evening he put his plan into action.

He had hidden under his Mother's house for three days and during that time the people who knew him believed he had left town, which was what he wanted them to believe. Patiently Dad waited for a time when Charlie was alone and that happened on the third day. Then Dad just walked into the house and calmly shot him dead.

He had planned it all out very carefully and he had an alibi. In Mississippi, it would be hard to prove. *"Anyway,"* he thought, *who cared if a nigger got shot. It was one less for the police to worry about.*

***

Dad met Mother in 1939, at the J. T. Stone Mortuary, on the day he made the funeral arrangements for his first wife. At the time they married he was thirty and Mother was twenty-two. Dad loved Mother and her two children. Shortly after he and Mother were married, he adopted J.T. and Lenore, and gave them the last name of Reese. The use of the word, "stepchildren" was forbidden. They were his kids, and that settled it. Mother and Dad together, had three more children.

Mississippi in the early 1940s had very few opportunities for the Negro. Dad wanted more for his family than he felt Mississippi could offer. It was important to him that his children grow up with a sense of pride, self-worth and dignity. While possible to achieve these goals living in Mississippi, he felt the odds were greatly improved if they were to move out of the South. It was painful to leave all of the relatives behind but to our parents the sacrifice seemed worth it. Perhaps the move was a mistake. It seems that when we lived in Mississippi, the relatives held us together. In California, there was no big family around and our family unit began to fall apart. Dad saw his dreams of a better life for his family evaporate.

Mother began carousing about town with Mr. Hubert. Dad had no patience for anyone who smoked or drank, and Mother did both.

The divorce was bitter and filled with hate, and afterwards we were not even allowed to mention Dad's name without Mother going into a rage. It got so bad that Ilona and I didn't want to be in the same room with her.

JT had already gone into the military service when the family split up. I still remember his homecoming—after all, he was Mother's favorite. I have always felt that Lenore got married at an early age so she could move away from the turmoil and Mother.

Our house was "divided," and also each sibling had been programmed and brainwashed to not trust and even to hate each other.

Ilona and I were left to care for each other and Mother. As the middle child, Ilona was in an untenable situation. Mother treated her like the black sheep of the family, while at the same time she relegated her to the role of being caretaker, housekeeper, and servant.

3

THE MORNING CAME ALL TO QUICKLY AND MOTHER awakened me as she announced, "You're going to work with me today."

I was so excited. It was Saturday morning, and Saturdays were always the busiest day of the week for funerals. Sometimes there could be four or more funerals and everyone was always tense.

As I began to dress, my biggest concern was Ilona. I wondered, *where was she?* I prayed she hadn't run away during the night as she had mentioned the previous night. Quickly I ran to her room—but she wasn't there. Next, I tiptoed down the stairs and checked out the kitchen. *No, not there. Maybe she is in the basement,* I thought. She wasn't there either and then panic began to set in.

Just then I heard a noise upstairs. Not sure what it was, I quietly went back upstairs and as I turned the corner at the top of the stairs, I saw the door to the bathroom at the end of the hall was closed. It was a long hallway, and traversing it on tiptoe made it seem as if it were nine yards in length when actually it was only a few feet.

I moved as quickly and quietly as possible so as not to disturb Mother when I passed her room. Then I softly tapped on the bathroom door. Ilona cracked the door open about one inch and briskly said, "Go away!"

"Please, let me in," I begged.

Silently the door opened and as I slipped in, I had to ask, "Ilona, what are you going to do?"

"I don't know. I can't stay, but I don't want to leave you, she whispered, Mother hates me, you know that."

"No, she doesn't. It's just that she is very angry with Dad, and you and Dad were so close," I tried to help her see the logic.

"It will get better. Please just don't leave me. I have to go to work with her today. I'll be back. Please. I love you," I said as I slipped out of the bathroom and ran back to my own room. I rushed to get dressed because I had to put on a dress for this day at the Funeral Home. Usually I avoided wearing dresses, but as this was a working day, wearing a dress was expected. I had just finished buttoning up my dress when I heard the blowing of a car horn outdoors and knew Mother was ready and I had better get down there quickly.

When I opened the car door Mother gave me a critical look and commented, "Well, at least you had enough sense to put on a dress."

"Yes Mother, " I said, "Do I look ok?"

"Yes you look very nice and I'm proud I didn't have to tell you."

The whole time we drove to the Funeral Home I worried about my sister and wondered if she would be all right. Silence was welcomed and I was pleased the drive did not take too long. When we pulled into the driveway and drove around to the back of the Mortuary, there were four white Cadillac's with gray interiors, all lined up neatly next to the one hearse that carried the body.

Mother was always referred to as "Mrs. Reese" during the funeral services and no one made a mistake and called her by her first name. Mrs. Reese was known to be the best funeral director in just about all of Los Angeles. It was her role to tell people where their places were and what to do next in order for the funeral to progress smoothly. Her confident style was cool and collected and she strolled gracefully, head held high and shoulders ridged.

At Hubert and Reese, it was Mrs. Reese and not my Mother who entered her office.

Mr. Holmes was there to greet her, and Ima was all smiles.

"You'll be pleased with Mrs. Willis' make-up. She looks so peaceful and with the coloring to her hair that I did, she looks ten-years younger." Ima said.

"I hope she can be recognized by her family, Ima," said Mrs. Reese, in a serious tone, but Ima just laughed.

"I'm serious," Mrs. Reese said. "You know, Ima, sometimes you get carried away with your make-up. Mrs. Willis is supposed to look dead, not ten-years younger."

"I'm just doing my work and trying to make her look better," Ima said.

"Your job is to make her look restful, not younger," Mrs. Reese said in her stern voice.

I watched Ima as she turned slowly and walked toward the door. Her beautiful face was now so sad. Mother seemed to be always putting someone "down."

Mr. Holmes knew his wife's feelings were bruised, but he also knew she would get over it. The relationship between Mr. Holmes and my Mother dated back to Mississippi. They had been long-time friends and he had worked for the J.T. Stone Mortuary for many years. When it came to Mrs. Reese, he was a very patient man. After all she was almost like family.

"Mrs. Reese," he said, "We really had a difficult time getting Mrs. Willis' body into the casket. She's a big lady, she must weigh three hundred pounds plus..."

Mrs. Reese laughed as she asked, "She won't pop out when we open the casket for the service will she?"

She was quite aware an oversized casket had been specially ordered which was light blue, with a lining made out of soft white, comforter-like material.

With a smile Mr. Holmes said, "It was still a tight a squeeze, it took three of us to stuff her in there.

"Well, Mrs. Reese, I guess I better get started. It's already nine o'clock. The funeral is at ten and it'll take three of us to roll the casket into the Chapel. Anything you want me to do for you?"

"No," she said, "just make sure the small wreaths go in front of the casket and don't block anyone's view," she reminded. As he left the room, he looked back and was comforted by Mrs. Reese's smile.

The service was about to start and everyone was doing what he or she was supposed to do. I had hoped Mr. Holmes would have time to go and see about his wife Ima, but he didn't. Two assistants, Jan and Sandra, middle-aged ladies who looked quite average and were able to look solemn, had been assigned to help with the families.

All the pews in the Chapel had fans that were advertisements for Hubert & Reese Mortuary, with a picture of Mr. Hubert on the left side and Mother on the right side.

Jan, our in-house driver, had gone earlier to pick up the immediate family members in one of the Cadillacs. The car pulled up about 9:45a.m., with the daughter of Mrs. Willis and two grandsons, ages ten and fifteen. They were escorted by Jan and Sandra into the Chapel and seated in the front pew. Mother stood close by. The Preacher came running in late, but no one noticed except Mother, and she was pissed!

Family members always sat behind the immediate family and friends normally sat on the other side. I knew I wanted to be part of this so I went and stood by the Chapel doors. The doors would close exactly at 10:00a.m., but when latecomers would start strolling in, I would direct them to the family side or friend side to be seated. Mother saw me and looked in my direction, smiling and walking so very graceful.

"What do you think you are doing?"

"Helping. Jan and Sandra were busy." I whispered.

"You should be in the office," she said.

"I like helping. I know what to do," I said.

"OK. Do what you see Jan and Sandra doing. Make sure people have tissue, and if they look like they might faint, call Mr. Holmes over."

She smiled. " If one of those big women faints on you, you'll be in the casket with Mrs. Willis." She had a silly smirk on her face. I guess she thought that was funny, but I didn't. I felt important now that I had a job; I was working for Hubert & Reese Mortuary.

The aroma of flowers was breathtaking; I felt I was in the Garden of Eden. The fragrance of the bouquets gave a sense of peace around me.

The Preacher began the service;

"It's so good to see such a great turn out for Sister Willis."

"Great woman,"

"Godly woman,"

"Loved the Lord."

"Can I get an amen?"

Everyone simultaneously said;

"Amen."

I said, "Amen"

The Preacher said, with his voiced raised.

"Sister Willis is meeting her Master."

" Can I get an amen?"

" Amen, Amen."

I was sitting in the back, looking for Mother. She was standing near the head of the casket and when the Preacher said "Amen," Mother really put emphasis on "Amen." The service went on for over an hour. Then the family was led up to the casket for their final look at Sister Willis. Mother directed and led them in a smooth but orderly manner, pew by pew. Some people were sobbing loudly, others stared and as they got to the casket they would lean over and kiss Sister Willis good-bye. A few ladies fainted.

That was the first time I actually sat through a whole funeral and that also was the day I learned Baptist funerals could go on for a very, very long time. Her family and friends had really loved Sister Willis and the Preacher prolonged his sermon accordingly. People were very emotional and I heard someone say, "They are full of the spirit." That was a term I had not heard before. I didn't get the spirit, so I just said "Amen," a lot. Finally the funeral was over and it was time to go to the cemetery.

"Little Mary," Mother startled me as I had not expected her to be right beside me. "Would you like to ride to the cemetery with me?"

"Oh yes," I said.

"Okay. Go and get my purse out of my office and meet me at the hearse."

I was so excited! Mother always drove the hearse and I knew there would also be two motorcycle escorts waiting outside to conduct the procession.

As everyone left the Chapel, people continued to go to Mother saying, "Mrs. Reese, what a wonderful service." Mother glowed because she loved having the extra attention.

As directed by my Mother, I went and got her purse and then walked over to the hearse, trying not to run as I was nearly bursting with excitement.

People were getting into their cars and getting lined up for the funeral procession.

The hearse always led the procession of cars while the two motorcycle escorts acted like circus performers. They would speed up, and then stand on their bikes, hands off the handlebars, and oh they would put on a show. One rode in front and stopped traffic while the other one would ride at the back.

Even though I knew it was a funeral, still it was an exciting experience for me.

The cemetery we were going to was quite a distance from the Funeral Home and since we drove rather respectfully, naturally it took longer than usual. Nevertheless, the ride was rather entertaining.

After a while Mother said, "Get me a cigarette out of my purse." I reached in her purse and pulled out a pack of Kent cigarettes. "Light it for me," she said.

" I don't know how," I said, surprised she had even asked me to do it.

"Just light the damn thing and keep it down out of sight. Can't let anyone see us smoking at a funeral."

I leaned down toward the floor of the hearse and put the cigarette in my mouth as I had seen her do many, many times. It felt foreign to me but I took the match, struck it, and lit the cigarette. Evidently I breathed in and when I coughed, she laughed at me.

"Sister Willis, you still back there?" she asked.

"Mother, who are you talking to?" I asked.

Just then we hit a bump in the road and the casket jerked. "Sister Willis, be still," she said as she leaned over and took the cigarette.

We were stopped at a stoplight, just as the escort officer was stopping through traffic, to allow our funeral procession to continue, so Mother had a moment to take one giant drag off the cigarette. She seemed more relaxed by the experience.

There was this awful taste that remained in my mouth now. *Why does she smoke, I wondered.* I guess it was cool to do. If it was cool to her it certainly wasn't to me. I was rolling my tongue around and making a weird face.

"What's wrong?"

"Cigarettes are nasty,"

"You'll get used to them,"

We hit even a larger pothole in the road and my heart went thump. I could hear the casket in the back move.

"Sister Willis, you still there?"

I wasn't laughing because it was not funny to me. *Sister Willis is dead; therefore, she should not be moving around,* I thought.

Instead I said, "Mother, the Preacher really liked Mrs. Willis, huh?"

"The Preacher didn't know Mrs. Willis at all—never even met her," she replied.

"But he talked about her so much and how wonderful she was. I thought they must have been best friends and stuff."

"Little Mary, they have Preachers you can rent, and the family rented him. Mrs. Willis didn't belong to any church. She belonged to many organizations, but didn't really belong to one church."

"Oh, I guess this was my second lesson."

"What are you talking about?" she asked.

"Mr. Holmes let me in the Embalming Room and I sort of got woozy."

Before I could say another word Mother angrily interrupted, "Don't let me catch you in the Embalming Room again, do you understand?"

"Yes." In that tone of voice, there was no misunderstanding that she was now quite angry.

We hit another even larger pothole in the road, I could hear the casket jerk again, only this time I knew it had come loose from the track and the fasteners that secured it to the floor. The casket started moving from side to side. Mother looked annoyed and began to speak. "Damn, this road is a mess. I'll be glad when they finish with the repairs." Just then we hit another bump and it was a big one. I could feel the beat of my pulse.

Mother called toward the back of the hearse, "Sister Willis, you still back there?" No sooner had she finished her question, then, all of a sudden the backdoor of the hearse popped open and the casket slid right out and onto the street. All the cars came to a sudden stop and Mother tried to signal to the escort officers on the bikes to stop the traffic, while at the same time maneuvering to try and put out her cigarette without being seen.

I watched in fascination as everything came to a halt and the show unfolded. The officers turned and came back to the hearse. Mr. Holmes, who had been driving one of the family cars, ran over to assist Mr. Hubert who also had been driving a family car. They all just looked at each other and wondered out loud.

"What should we do?"

I was not too young to realize I was witnessing a most embarrassing moment for Hubert and Reese Mortuary. Mrs. Reese hissed to the men,

"Come on. Pick it up."

She whispered for Mr. Holmes' ear alone, "Thank God, that casket has a good lock on it. Can you imagine Mrs. Willis on the street?"

"What a thought," he whispered back.

Ever efficient, Mrs. Reese crisply commanded,

"Okay. Let's get Mrs. Willis back into the hearse."

Watching from the front seat of the hearse and out through the open backdoors, I saw and heard the two escort officers, as well as Mr. Holmes and Mr. Hubert, as they attempted to pick up the casket. They grunted and groaned as they struggled to pick up the weighty casket from off the street. Perspiration began to roll down their faces. After all, Mrs. Willis was three-hundred pounds plus. Finally, Mrs. Willis' casket was returned to the back of the hearse and this time was securely locked in place.

After that everyone involved with the replacement of Mrs. Willis into the hearse tried to walk nonchalantly back to their vehicles, as they wiped their faces with handkerchiefs. The funeral procession was on the move again and I thought to myself, *"Hilton Cemetery, here we come!"*

We entered through the huge gates that were open to receive us and pulled into the wide driveway of the cemetery. I had watched my Mother through all the recent proceedings in awe; as she never lost her composure. It was then I realized why—she couldn't because too much depended on her.

Once inside the cemetery, all the cars led by the hearse, moved at only five miles an hour as the gravesite was approached. We continued on to an open grave with green covering over it and huge brackets to hold the casket over the hole in the ground. As far I could see, it looked like a blanket of headstones, with flowers of all kinds arranged neatly on individual graves. People got out of their cars and waited until the casket was placed above the grave.

The Preacher said,

"It is now time to say good-bye to Sister Willis;

Cause she is gone up yonder to meet with her Lord,

 Amen! Amen!"

I said "amen"

And again, "amen"

The Preacher had most of the crowd in tears. Finally Mrs. Willis was laid to rest.

I looked at the oversized casket above the grave and as I turned to walk away I said, "Good-bye, Sister Willis."

Mother and I returned to the hearse and headed back to the Funeral Home. We were running late due to the unfortunate "mishap." Mother kept a straight face as she steadily drove out the exit of the cemetery and nodded appropriately to those who watched as we left.

Once on the main street, she exhaled as if for the first time all morning.

"I know," I said with a deep sigh of relief.

She looked at me and I looked back at her and we began to laugh, uncontrollably. I couldn't wait to get home and tell Ilona all about that day.

4

SATURDAY EVENINGS MEANT IT WAS PARTY TIME AT THE Reese home. Mr. Hubert, several Preachers, their friends, the organist, gravediggers, anyone and everyone was invited to stop by on Saturday evenings. Because of the prestigious profile of Mrs. Reese, many Black celebrities of the day came to our house.

On Saturday evening following Mrs. Willis' funeral, I avoided the crowd and kept mainly to myself. I was waiting for Ilona to come home. Upon arriving home, Mother grabbed a beer and went to change her clothes while I waited in my room with my door cracked so I could hear when my sister returned. Soon I began to hear people arriving downstairs, laughing loudly, and it sounded as if they were having a good time.

I was very hungry after a very full and stress-filled day at work. Mother didn't cook very often, so dinner was usually not a thought-out event. I hadn't seen Mother in a couple of hours but knew better than to go downstairs for any reason. Ilona came in my room with a bag in her hand and I could smell the onions and fries. Oh, was I happy to see her! She had brought me a hamburger, fries and my favorite chocolate malt. We shared the feast while I told her all about my day.

As the party downstairs grew louder and louder, we tried to guess what they were doing. The living room was very spacious and accommodated fifty people comfortably. We heard Mother playing the Baby Grand Piano and many voices singing, "Oh Danny Boy;" it seemed they were all off-key. Ilona and I laughed and wondered why a bunch of Negroes, most of who came from the South, were singing an Irish song at the top of their lungs.

When Ilona went to the bathroom, I snuck out of the room and tiptoed to the top of the stairs, got down on my knees, and stretched my body toward the stair rail to see if I could get a good look at what was going on.

Suddenly there was a touch on my shoulder. Startled, I jerked and almost slid down the stairs on my stomach and let out an uncontrolled yelp. "Shhh! Quiet!" hissed Ilona, but she was too late because I had been heard.

A shrill voice echoed through the hall and Mother was at the top stair in a flash …and she was drunk! "What the hell are you guys doing," she yelled.

Ilona gave me a hard push and ordered, "Go to your room, hurry!" I didn't wait around; off to my room I went.

From my room I could hear Mother yelling at Ilona, "Bitch! What are you doing?"

"Nothing," Ilona mumbled in an attempt to explain.

Mother continued to yell at the top of her voice. "You make me sick. You think you're smart, make a fool of me in front of my friends."

Ilona was quiet, but I knew she was crying. "I'm sorry, Mother," she said, "I was just playing with Little Mary."

"Be quiet. Mr. Hubert thinks you're so pretty, but you're ugly," Mother said.

I began to cry. The words Mother had said to Ilona hurt me to my heart. Abruptly Mother slammed the door to Ilona's room and my heart skipped a beat because I knew I was next. I was sitting on my bed when Mother entered my room.

"I want you to go to bed. Now! Do you understand me?"

"Yes, Mother," I said and then the door closed behind her.

I wanted to go to Ilona but knew if I got caught, there would be hell to pay. I put on my pajamas, crawled into bed and fell sound asleep. I was soon awakened by loud voices screaming, "Stop! Please stop!"

I got up and sneaked into the hall to see what was happening. What I saw and heard were Mr. Hubert and Mother yelling at each other in Ilona's bedroom. Mother was furious and was calling Mr. Hubert names.

"You bastard, son-of-a-bitch, you were trying to fuck my daughter!"

"No, that's not true." He continued to explain himself and Mother slapped him across his face. By then Ilona was hysterical and then I began to cry in sympathy.

Just then Mr. Hubert pushed Mother against the door of Ilona's bedroom and that was when I ran and stood between them and as I grabbed his right arm, I begged, "Please, please, don't hurt her."

Mr. Hubert's jaws were twitching and his lips were lined with white foam. He was breathing hard and when he looked down at me he just stared at me for a moment before he calmly said to me, "Let go."

I let go, but I did not move from between them. Mother continued yelling and screaming at Mr. Hubert. As he started walking away, Mother tried to hit him in the head with her shoe but Ilona grabbed her hand. Mr. Hubert went downstairs, and slammed the front door so hard it's a wonder he didn't break a window.

Mother snapped viciously at Ilona, "You whore!"

Ilona said, "He just asked me if I was okay because he heard you yelling at me earlier."

"You're a liar!" Mother said in a hateful manner.

"Mother, please believe her, please just stop." I was crying so hard I hadn't noticed that Ima and Mr. Holmes had come upstairs.

"Come on, Little Mary," I heard Ima say. As I turned around she opened her arms, and I just fell into them.

It was 2:00 a.m., and things had quieted down. I had climbed back into my bed, feeling very tired but sleep wouldn't come. I just lay there and stared at the ceiling and asked myself, "*Why? Why is Mother so mean? Why doesn't she like Ilona?* No answers came, just more questions such as, *Was it because she looked different than Mother and me?*"

I remembered thinking of what my Dad had told me before he and Mother divorced. He was trying to explain to me why each of his five kids were a different color. He began by saying, "JT is the first-born, and he has the darkest skin. Next comes Lenore and her skin color is a little lighter. Ilona has, milk-chocolate, brown skin, while Willie Jr.'s skin is even lighter than hers. Little Mary, you're the last born and we just ran out of color," he explained.

"But Dad, what about Mother? I look just like her," I reminded him.

"Yeah, you're both pale," and he'd smile.

I remembered that Dad liked showing my picture off and would brag, "This is my little White child."

The next morning came too quickly and my first thoughts were of Ilona and wondered if she was okay? Our friends and neighbors often teased us saying that I was, "Ilona's shadow". She could not move without me bumping into her. I just loved being with her. Later as I was brushing my teeth, anxiety rushed through my whole body. I couldn't help wondering, *what was this day going to be like?*

Every Sunday Mother always slept late. We didn't attend church, because Mother said every funeral was a church service for us. But whenever I heard our resident Preacher's sermons I'd think, *what a phony*, because on Saturday evenings he would be drinking, smoking, cursing like a sailor, flirting with Mother and talking nasty to her. I hated him. He was tall and slim. His hair had been treated with chemicals called process, which made his hair look like wax—straight with big waves all over his head. Most of the time, he had a scarf tied around his head to keep his hair flat. Another thing he did was smile all of the time and show off a distinctive gold tooth in the front of his mouth. I didn't care for his little beady- black eyes either. I didn't like him, but Mother loved him, as he knew how to stroke her ego and make her feel good. Mother surrounded herself with people like that.

I traveled down the hallway, making sure I did not make any noise so as to not wake Mother. Ilona still slept, I climbed into bed with her, jeans and all, and in the process I awakened her. She turned over and smiled when she saw me. I melted and her smile let me know everything would be okay.

"What am I going to do with you?" she asked.

"Keep me," I said and we laughed softly and just lay there for awhile. It seemed like an eternity, because we had each other, and we knew without ever speaking a word that no one would ever be able to separate us. Then we discussed our plans for our future—she wanted to have lots of kids while I didn't intend to have any.

Suddenly I said, "Ilona, what if we end up like Mother?"

"Never," she said with a sad voice, "I'll love my kids no matter what."

"Will you still love me?" I asked.

Ilona rubbed my forehead softly, brushing my hair back. "Little Mary, we are more than sisters. You are my heartbeat, and my heart beats for you. I'll always take care of you."

5

DAYS, WEEKS, MONTHS, TWO YEARS PASSED QUICKLY. during summer vacations Ilona and I began going to work with Mother. We both really enjoyed working there. Ilona answered the phones, took messages, and ran errands for Mr. Hubert and Mother. The Embalming Room became my playground, I also played in the Display Room (Casket Room).

Many evenings Mother would stay at the Funeral Home late at night. The Funeral Home business thrived! They could not keep up with all of the funerals. Business was booming with five and six bodies at a time, two or three funerals a day. Three or four bodies would be placed in the Viewing Room. It was cramped at times, because the Embalming Room didn't have enough space or tables.

Mother drew in business. People knew she was the daughter of the great J.T. Stone, of the well-known Mortuary in Mississippi, and that meant quality service. Mother really knew how to run a Funeral Home. She was known as the "Queen of Mortuaries." She had been featured and recognized in many Black-owned newspapers and magazines. She was asked to speak at conventions and church programs. Her name and face had become so well-known in Los Angeles, virtually every African American knew of Mrs. Reese. Reverend Miles had a Sunday radio program, and she would often appear as a guest speaker. Whenever she did the program, listeners were known to increase dramatically.

Mr. Hubert knew that Mrs. Reese was the reason for their success and they fought constantly about everything, but he could not ignore how people would admire her. She had won the respect of the Black Community and he became increasingly more jealous.

To make matters worst, Mother had other men-friends and she would flaunt them just to make Mr. Hubert jealous. That really irritated him. Every

27

day became a new episode in the relationship between Mr. Hubert and Mrs. Reese. People whispered behind their backs and waited to see and hear what they would fight about next.

Summer vacation ended and we returned to school. I hated being separated from Ilona, I was only in the sixth grade at 24ᵗʰ Street School, and Ilona was in the ninth grade at Mt. Vernon Junior High.

Soon life really began to change. Mother had met a man named Norman at a funeral. Norman had lost his older sister and Hubert & Reese Mortuary handled the arrangement for her.

"Are you married?" Mother asked Norman.

"No," he said.

"Are you dating anyone?" she asked.

"No," he answered.

"I would like you to meet my daughter, Ilona. She is gorgeous, and not dating."

Mother was well aware of his financial status, which she learned while assisting the family with the funeral. Norman was fourteen years older than Ilona, but that didn't matter. Mother was tired of the responsibility of us and here was someone who would possibly like Ilona, marry her, and she would be out of the house.

Norman met Ilona and he fell madly in love with her. Ilona was in no way ready for marriage, but what was she to do? With the nights at home, taking care of Mother after she would get drunk, and being cursed out on a regular basis, what options did she have? Mother would arrange for their marriage when she finished Junior High. Norman Wilkins was tall, dark, and handsome, and he loved to talk. He was an expert on any subject you mentioned; he knew it all. Everybody loved Norman and Ilona was lucky she had a good man.

* * *

Soon my days and nights got longer and longer and I became more and more lonely because I was usually alone most of the time. Although there was a house full of people downstairs in the evenings, I would sit in Ilona's room waiting for her to come home, trying to stay awake. I sensed life would be changing and taking on new meaning for me; yet, I had no idea what the future held. The fear of not having my precious sister around both saddened and worried me. Mother was occupied with Mother and I knew I was really in her way.

I had to admit that Ilona seemed to be happier than I had ever seen her and Mother was quite pleased and happy when they had finally set a wedding date—

August 13, 1957. It was planned that the wedding and reception would be at our home and Mother intended to have everything catered. Top musicians would entertain, the newspaper would have a full-page article, with a front-page headline that stated, "Wedding: The daughter of Mrs. Reese, of the Hubert and Reese Mortuary…" and it would tell of the elaborate wedding, and would follow up with all the details on page 7A. Also, the Mayor of Los Angeles would most likely make an appearance and so it was planned, that too would be included in the lengthy article.

One night when I had fallen asleep on Ilona's bed I woke up when I heard the door open. I looked at the clock and it was 1:30 a.m. but when I saw Norman and Ilona standing at the door whispering to each other, I pretended to be asleep.

"The date is set," he said, and in a sudden move she turned his face and pressed her lips firmly on his.

I stirred around a little, ruffling the covers, rubbing my eyes and face as if they just woke me.

"Ilona, is that you?" I croaked.

"Yes," I heard her whisper. "Hush," she said as she gestured with one finger to her lips.

"Walk me to the door," Norman said.

"Go back to sleep, Little Mary. I'll be right back!" Ilona said softly.

While I waited for her to return it seemed like time had stood still. All I could think about was losing her to Norman and it made me afraid. *How can I get her to take me with her?* I wondered.

Ilona quietly came back into the room, turned on a lamp, and I could see how her face glowed, she was so happy. "Norman gave me my engagement ring tonight," she told me all excited as she explained that even though the date had been set, he had not picked up the ring until that day.

As I looked at how her eyes lit up like stars when she talked about Norman, I envied her. "I'm so happy for you," I whispered, but at the same time my heart was breaking because I would be losing the only person in the world who truly loved me.

Then I asked her, "Ilona, how did you get in without Mother seeing you?"

"We came through the side door—too many people in the kitchen," she replied. "There must be at least twenty people down there."

"I know, and they are really loud. Oh, I'm so glad you're home!" I said hugging her. I could clearly hear the sound of my insecurity in my voice.

"Go to sleep, Little Mary. We'll talk tomorrow," Ilona promised and she leaned over and kissed me on my forehead.

I felt safe that night because Ilona would not let anyone hurt me. The noise downstairs was irritating, and I just wanted it to be quiet so I could go to sleep.

We lay there in bed listening to Mother and her friends laughing and talking loud. It would take awhile before we would fall asleep. When I closed my eyes, I visualized Ilona's wedding day. Everyone would be happy and having lots of fun celebrating with Mother and Mr. Hubert at the fabulous wedding and then Ilona would leave with her new husband…leaving me behind.

I knew my fears of being alone were escalating and it was frustrating for me that there was no one with whom I could share these fears. All I seemed to be thinking about was being alone with Mother. We had never been alone together for long periods of time, except at work, and then I was usually on my own. I could feel tears running down my face into the corner of my mouth and tasted salt. Silently I wept, not wanting Ilona to know how sad I was.

***

Things were slowly changing in my life. Ilona was not going to work with us anymore. I began working on more funerals, learning more and more about what people needed to hear at the time of their sorrows. It was difficult to talk with Mother. We found ourselves lost for words and she seemed angry most of the time.

There were many days I would go and talk to the bodies when no one was around. The Viewing Room would usually have two or three bodies lined up against the walls with long ivory-lace curtains hanging from the ceiling to the floor. Floral arrangements gave the smell of being in a florist shop. The caskets were always open and only showed the deceased from the waist on up for the viewing. The lights were always kept dim and gave a sense of quietness in the room, so I felt the need to whisper. I walked to each casket and took my time until I felt comfortable with whom I would talk with that day.

That day it was a seventy-five year old woman, resting peacefully. I thought, *She has strong features that showed signs of wisdom, knowledge, and strength that most likely had kept her family together.* Looking at the nameplate I read out loud,

"Sara Jones."

"Beautiful casket, Sister Jones," I said. As I observed the all-white casket, with gray-metal handles, and pink-satin cushions.

"Well, Sister Jones, you're looking good today. That Ima did a good job on your make-up. Not too much—you look beautiful. Oh, you don't have to thank me," I said.

"You know Sister Jones, I wish I could have lived with you,"

"Do you have time to listen?" Then I laughed to myself. She'll listen and won't talk back.

"I wish I could cry for you, Sister Jones, but you're in a better place." I reached over the casket and touched her hands placed neatly on top of each other. Even though she had dark skin it looked gray and her hands were hard and cold to the touch, not soft like Mother's. Mother's hands were soft, but she always held my hand too tight. I did not like holding Mother's hand.

Sister Jones lay so still, so quiet, with no emotions, no feelings, no breath left in her. But she had a look of serenity on her face. I stood staring so closely to see if there was any movement. I thought when staring at the stars they twinkle, maybe Sister Jones might twinkle just a little. I wanted so much for her to sit up and take me in her arms and say, " I love you baby, and I'll protect you." But the longer I stared at her face; I knew she would not come to life for me.

"Sister Jones, I know you can't hear me, but I like to talk and when I try to tell anyone what goes on at night, they push me away. What should I do? I'd rather stay right here with you, I hate going home, I'm afraid all the time. I think about running away, but I have nowhere to go. I'm afraid of Mother's men friends. They come into my room and touch me where I don't want to be touched, I fight them, and sometimes they fight me back. I tell Mother and she says I'm lying. I want to run away Sister Jones, if you were alive, I'd run to your house. Why did you have to die? I bet you were a kind and loving Mother. I have nowhere to go, even my Dad doesn't want me and Ilona is leaving me. I sometimes want to kill myself, but I'm afraid to do it. I'm taking some of Mothers' sleeping pills and I'm saving them for the day I get the nerve to do it.

I hope I'm not rubbing your hand too hard? Sister Jones, I wonder if Mother would love me if I died, or miss me. I love her so much, and I try so hard to please her, but nothing pleases her. I keep the house clean and wait on her hand-and-foot. I rub her feet at night when she doesn't have company and that does please her. I wish I had the peace you have. You rest now, I'll see you in the next life, and I can't wait. Oh well, I guess I have talked your ears off." I gently rubbed her hands in gratitude for listening. When leaving the Viewing Room, I felt like I was leaving a friend. But that was OK, tomorrow I'd have a new one to talk to.

6

ILONA'S WEDDING DAY WAS QUICKLY APPROACHING AND my fears began to escalate. When Lenore had been married it had been a big deal too, but I hadn't paid too much attention to the activities because I wasn't very close to her. This time was different. I spent endless hours alone in my room because just about every conversation in the house and around the Funeral Home was of Ilona's wedding and only served to remind me of the loss I would soon be experiencing. Plans were constantly being changed, re-arranged and changed again. How many bridesmaids and groomsmen? Who would be the flower girl? What would be the appropriate song to sing and who should sing it? Day after day the house was filled with excitement and there were parties almost every evening.

Mother was in her element and basked in the spotlight of being a celebrity. She determined that her daughter would have the most talked-about wedding the Negro community of Los Angeles had ever seen. It was even planned that a couple of magazines would send out their reporters in order to get the inside story as to who would be attending the big event. The local Negro-owned newspaper ran a weekly update on the plans of the upcoming wedding.

There was so much traffic in and out of our house during that time that I never knew who were the reporters, or who was part of the wedding party. Basically, I was ignored and left to my own devices and kept out of the circle of planning. I just sat at the top of the stairs and watched through the banister as people scurried around, brought in plants, rearranged the furniture, installed new carpet, and placed and secured the tall, ornate candle stands. The windows, walls and floors, were not forgotten either as the window washers and a cleaning crew washed, polished and scrubbed, until not a spot had been missed. I was afraid to walk across the floor for fear of slipping it was so shiny.

During this time I had a lot of time to think and try to sort things out, and one of the puzzles I couldn't find an answer to was: "If Mother didn't like Ilona very much, why was she putting on this huge wedding and making such a fuss?"

As things escalated they got out-of-hand and pretty soon the plans changed again. After all the work on the house had been completed and it had been spiffed up to Mother's satisfaction, it began to dawn on her that the house was big, but not big enough to hold all two-hundred people who had been invited. The original plans had to be scrapped and then she faced a real challenge—finding the right place to hold the wedding and reception. However, Mother had a lot of well-to-do friends and she intended to use her persuasive means.

Again the Hubert and Reese Funeral Home was in the news: "Wedding change: home not big enough."

During all the upheaval in our lives, Ilona did not seem to be affected by all the attention, but I was miserable because basically I was ignored and was not getting any attention at all. At times I wanted to shout, "Does anyone know I'm still around?"

Early one morning I overheard Mother talking with Mr. Hubert on the telephone and they were discussing a time and place for a meeting to wind things up. I remember thinking, *"Good, then things will quiet down around here. But what am I thinking? Things are never quiet around our house. A wedding should be a time to be happy—so why am I so sad?"*

Our sister Lenore started coming over more often and helped Ilona with ideas for the bridesmaids' dresses, flowers and colors. This was the first time I had seen them act as if they were sisters, and friends. That was great except there still was no place for me. I just sneaked around and listened to their whispers. Once I heard them as they quietly discussed sex and Lenore, with a big grin reassured Ilona, "It only hurts the first couple of times, then it's easier and lots of fun."

* * *

Even though Ilona was about to be married, it should be remembered how young she actually was at the time. In the fall she would only be in her first year of high school while I would be going into junior high, a big transition for me. Another thing about which I wondered was: *"How would Ilona go to school if she were married?"*

During that busy time of the wedding preparations, all seemed to go well. I'll always be indebted to Lenore that she found a way to bring me into the sisters' circle, even though she was constantly telling me, "Close your ears." For the first time three sisters had something in common. I remember how we talked and laughed together...especially about what Ilona's new husband Norman would be expecting from her.

About a week before the wedding I wandered into the kitchen to find Lenore and Ilona seated around the kitchen table. The minute Lenore spotted me she quietly told Ilona to change the subject. Now I was more curious then ever and wondered, *"what was so secret they couldn't talk about it with me?"*

I plopped onto an empty chair and asked one of the questions that had been going around and around inside my mind, "Ilona, what about school? Will you still be going to high school?"

"No, I'll be a housewife," Ilona said with great pride. "Norman works two jobs and he wants to start a family, so I won't need to work. He'll take care of me."

I noticed how Ilona glowed whenever she told Lenore and me how her future was so secure. How this man would love her, and even though she hadn't fallen in love with him yet, she knew she would. Norman had told her he loved her enough for the both of them.

One good thing that came out of all that wedding business and that really surprised me was, Lenore became a close friend to me, not just a distant sister. Those days together were filled with rushing around, going shopping, and finding sexy nightgowns for Ilona, with Lenore giving advice.

I had tried to keep up a good front and smiled my approval of the wedding and all it entailed, but inside I felt as though I were drowning. The thought of being alone at home with Mother after the wedding scared me and I worried more and more each day. In fact, it bothered me there had been no further outburst of anger towards Ilona on Mother's part—on the contrary, she had actually been kind to her. Personally, I felt Mother was delighted she would be getting Ilona out of her house. After all, Norman had been her idea and things had worked out just as she had planned.

Mother basked in all the attention she received from everyone and never tired of being told again and again, "It is so wonderful of you to be giving your daughter such an elaborate wedding!"

But I felt that inside, Mother was thinking to herself, *"Yes, but as soon as Ilona is married, she will be Norman's responsibility and not mine! Just a little longer and I will be rid of her!"*

Ilona's wedding gown looked fit for a queen, and the credit went to Mr. Hubert, who had been ecstatic when he had been asked to give the bride away. After that, he personally had taken Ilona to purchase the most expensive wedding dress you could imagine.

Those last few days before the wedding Ilona and I had taken some time to sneak away up to the third floor where no one would hear us and we would not hear them—especially Mother. If accused, we could just tell her we didn't hear her up on the third floor.

The third floor was not my favorite place but during this time it was the only place undisturbed by the turmoil going on all around us. In the past we had spent many hours hiding away from Mother and her friends up there, secretly making plans for our future. Ilona did not share my discomfort of the undisturbed third floor and in the past had spoken of secret hauntings, and of ghosts that she claimed to have seen. *"Did she imagine them or was the third floor really haunted?"* I always shivered at the thought. Ilona had taken great pleasure whenever she had told me the stories and I had personally believed she loved to watch me squirm.

Whenever we were up there we would say it was "our time." Ilona and I had our own world on the third floor and I absorbed every word she would say. In the past I had known she loved me and would always be there for me...but then...she would soon be leaving and starting her own family. *Where would I be in this picture?* I wondered.

* * *

Time passed quickly and before we knew it, the wedding day had come upon us. One would have thought with all the thought and planning that had gone into the plans, things would have run smoothly, but everyone was stressed to the max. Since Mother had to have everything perfect, she just pointed her finger and yelled at anyone in her path.

"Do this, do that," as she fired off her orders to all. I don't think anyone escaped her delegating. She allowed no room for mistakes and constantly reminded all of that fact.

My dress for the wedding was a beautiful light-blue chiffon and with it I wore white patent-leather shoes, white lace socks, and white gloves. In my hair were woven tiny, baby's-breath flowers.

The bridesmaids' dresses were gorgeous light-blue dresses, to be worn off the shoulder, with shoes that perfectly matched, and there were white roses which were artfully worn in their hair. A pearl necklace and matching earrings, gifts from the bride, completed their ensembles so that everyone matched to the max.

After I dressed, I hurried to Ilona's room to find it was overly crowded with all the bridesmaids, plus a few friends who had gathered to watch Ilona and assist her in getting dressed. Ilona had so many people around her she could not see how I was desperately trying to squeeze in closer to her to let her know I was there. The laughter and talking in the room was loud. But my only thought was to be with Ilona. My heart pounded so hard I could almost hear it beat in that noisy room. This would be our last day…only there was no place for me and it was obvious she did not need me now because she had a whole room full of people making over her. They worked on her hair, her nails and make-up, but she had not yet put on her dress. I watched as one of the bridesmaids produced a garter and Ilona dutifully sat down while Lenore slipped the garter over her foot and up her leg right above the knee. It was made with beautiful white lace and had a few little flowers around the edges. Ilona had always had beautiful legs, but now in her wedding undergarments she looked so sexy, like a woman, not like my sister who was only seventeen.

I stood there feeling helpless, useless, and so lost and in my mind I was silently screaming, *Ilona, please don't leave me! Take me with you!* But not a word passed my lips.

Just then Ilona glanced in my direction and noticed I was standing in the doorway. Immediately she gave me a beautiful smile, opened her arms and simply said, "Come here." Oh, how my heart leaped with joy and I could not push the girls out of the way fast enough as I rushed into her loving arms, not caring if I messed up her make-up. Suddenly the room became quiet and it seemed as though the clock stood still for a few minutes as I held onto her for dear life and she held me so tight I thought I had hit my windpipe and couldn't breathe. Finally I gasped and choked on my words as I tried to plead for her not to leave me. My tears rolled down my face and fell onto my beautiful dress.

Quietly Ilona said, "Someone get me a Kleenex." Someone immediately handed her a few from the box on the dresser.

It stayed very quiet and no one in the room moved or said a word. They just stared and there was not a dry eye as all who witnessed the scene realized the seriousness and poignancy of the moment.

Slowly Ilona released me and softly promised, "My Little Mary, I will come back for you, just trust me. I'll always be with you and remember, no one will ever be able to separate us—not Norman or Mother, not anyone. You must believe that. I will convince Norman that you should live with us. He is a good man."

I could not seem to stop my crying but Ilona took the Kleenex, which had been given to her and gently wiped my tears and she crooned softly, "Please don't cry, Little Mary. I will come back for you, I promise."

Selfishly and childishly I wanted things to stay the same but in my heart I knew things would never be the same for me. Because I loved Ilona so much, I was truly happy for her that she would now be out from under Mother's cruel tongue and rule and sincerely wished she would be happy with

Norman. So, as was my habit whenever I would become overloaded with emotions—good or bad—I withdrew into myself. Gradually my crying and tears subsided and like the man who has fallen overboard and reaches for the flimsy lifeline thrown his way, I clung to her promise and determined to wait for Ilona to rescue me. I accepted that first she would have to leave and be happy with Norman.

The three freshly washed, and shined white Cadillacs from the Funeral Home, picked up the bride and bridesmaids and took them to the church. Mr. Hubert strutted around like a peacock in mating season in his tux. He was as proud as if he were Ilona's real Father…but I still did not like him.

Because Mother was used to making sure that everyone was in the right place at the right time at her Funeral Home, it served her in good stead for her daughter's wedding, and the wedding started right on time. While I waited for my cue to be seated, I stood towards the back of the hall, looking at all the people sitting and talking in the church and wondered just who they all were. I hardly recognized anyone that we knew.

From my location in the front pew and next to the isle, I had a good view as first the groom and then his groomsmen took their positions on one side of the front of the church. Next, the bridesmaids walked down the center aisle to the music with precise movement and took their places at the front of the church, opposite the groomsmen.

After that, the little flower girl came shyly down the aisle and was dressed in a child's complimentary version of the bridesmaids' dresses. Her dress was light-blue satin, with ruffles around the bottom, and she wore white-lace socks, with new shiny black patent leather shoes. As she slowly and methodically dropped the rose pedals down the aisle, her confidence grew until she was gently gliding like a little angel. A boy of about four followed in his black tuxedo and carried a small, white-satin pillow, on which the rings were attached. Nervous at all the eyes staring at him, he stumbled and fell to the floor. Quietly, a woman close to where he fell gently helped him to his feet, whispered a few words of encouragement in his ear and then headed him in the direction towards the front where the proud and beaming groom was standing. The people had been so thoroughly entertained by the incident that it was hard for them to settle down.

After a moments pause, the bridal march began to play and everyone stood and turned their attention toward the back as they waited for the bride to enter. The stirring, loud music, brought the hair on my arms to attention, and just at that moment I could see Mr. Hubert in his black tux with Ilona holding his arm. They walked and paced themselves to the wedding march as they walked down the white- linen runner. To me, Ilona looked just like an angel walking on a cloud. I was so proud of her and overcome with emotions that words could not describe her beauty at that moment.

I stared in awe at my sister. My eyes were stuck in position and I don't think I even blinked. Oh, how beautiful she looked! Even though the veil covered her face somewhat, I could see her glowing smile through the veil and it seemed she just lit up the whole church. The photographer was all over the place, flashing his camera like shooting stars, and people seemed not to notice as they were so spellbound at how gorgeous a bride she was. To me, she was an elegant, royal princess.

The reception went on until late in the evening and then Norman and Ilona departed for their honeymoon. My heart sank as I watched their limo driving away.

* * *

For a week after the wedding there were nightly parties at our house with people stopping by with bottles of whiskey and beer, still celebrating. Any excuse to party.

Naturally I stayed out of the way and usually that was upstairs in Ilona's room, wishing she were there but knowing she was having a good time with Norman. I also wondered where they had gone on their honeymoon and didn't know why it was such a secret. The only thing I knew for sure was that I felt miserably alone.

A month had passed and I had not heard from Ilona and I was afraid to ask Mother. But finally my need to know *something* reluctantly drove me to approach my Mother in her bedroom where she was resting after she had had a hard night.

Quietly I entered her bedroom and trying for an air of nonchalance, so she wouldn't suspect my true feelings, finally asked,

"Mother, have you heard from Ilona?" There was no reply so I repeated myself, "Mother, have you heard from Ilona?"

As Mother lifted her head off the pillow, she was wild-eyed and my tongue literally seemed stuck in my throat and I swear I felt my blood turn cold.

"I have *not* heard from her," she said in a very aggravated voice, "and I don't want you talking to her anymore!"

"Why?" I blurted out before I could stop myself. She was upset with me, but right then my need to know where Ilona was, and when I could see her, was stronger than my fear of Mother.

Mother sat up in the bed and with an evil-looking face looked me straight in the eye and with malice dripping off each word said,

"You will *never* see her again. She's married now and she won't have time for you or me. Anyway, the last time I talked with her she said she was sick and tired of having you hanging around her all the time."

"I don't believe that!" I shouted. "She loves me, and she's coming to get me so I can stay with her!"

Mother laughed out loud and snarled, "You're so stupid!"

My whole body reacted as I began to tremble; my heart literally hurt as if a knife had pierced it.

"Go to your room, and I don't want you to ever talk about her again. She's out of our lives now and you and I will do just fine." As I turned to leave the room, Mother said in a calmer voice, "You can go to work with me, okay?"

"Okay," I answered dejectedly. As I walked down the long hallway I did not have the strength to hold up my head, so I just looked at the floor and hoped it would open up and swallow me. *Oh, how I missed my sister, but what if Mother was telling the truth? Was it true Ilona was sick of me?*

7

WHENEVER I HELPED WITH A FUNERAL IT WAS NOT unusual for me to receive praise for how well I worked with people. Even though I was quite young, I had been blessed with the gift of empathy and seemed to naturally know just what to say or do to calm grieving parents, spouses, family or friends. I didn't have to wonder or think because I just *knew* what they were feeling and did what came naturally. Another reason I think I was so comfortable with the people was that the Mortuary had become more of a home to me than was my own. For this, I freely give most of the credit to the hours I spent in the Embalming Room with Mr. Holmes and Ima.

There was one funeral in particular where all the details of those few days still remain quite vivid in my memory. The deceased was a Mr. Calder who had died in a motel while in the act of having sex. The problem was, he had *not* been with his wife—but with a prostitute.

His widow was made aware of the circumstances under which he had suddenly died of a heart attack and passed on, but what really bothered her was that she felt certain all their friends and family knew as well. In light of what happened later, it was not surprising that the Widow Calder was very upset. She probably dwelled on all the gossiping and murmuring she imagined must have been going on about her husband and it probably made her not only uncomfortable, but feeling very humiliated by the actions of her thoughtless husband who had truly betrayed her.

Many evenings when Mother and Mr. Hubert stayed late at the Funeral Home, I hung around downstairs in the office and usually during those evenings Mr. Holmes and Ima would keep me company as long as they could, but they had family waiting for them at home. After they would leave and while waiting for Mother and Mr. Hubert to come down from the upstairs apartment, I would usually wander from room to room visiting the deceased, playing with the caskets, and arranging and fluffing the shiny-satin comforters.

On that particular evening as I made my usual rounds, the serene silence was suddenly interrupted by a loud commotion at the front door of the Funeral Home. First, I heard banging on the door and then a woman yelling and cursing at the top of her voice—it was Widow Calder. "Let me in so I can cut up that son-of-a-bitch!"

It was obvious she was drunk and not making much sense as she continued her tirade from window to window, then back to the front door and finally to the outside door to Mr. Hubert's office. In my fear and state of near panic I wondered, *why don't Mother and Mr. Hubert come out and stop her?* Suddenly, I heard a loud crash like glass breaking but didn't know what to do. Widow Calder had thrown a huge rock through the office window.

About then, Mr. Hubert *finally* came running down the stairs. If I hadn't been so scared, I would have laughed at the comical sight he made as he was trying to pull up his pants and button his shirt, all at the same time, with Mother a few steps behind him. Her hair was messed up and her own clothes were barely half on. I always had known what they were doing and that was the main reason I hated Mr. Hubert.

As he hurriedly came down the stairs, Mr. Hubert kept yelling, "What the hell are you doing? What the hell are you doing?"

"Let me in, I want to cut that son-of-a-bitch up!" Even though her words had been badly slurred, I definitely got the gist of her meaning.

Mother yelled out, "Mrs. Calder, Mr. Calder is already dead. Go home before you get in trouble."

But trouble was already coming around the corner. I heard the police sirens and they were within a few blocks of the Funeral Home. Naturally curious, people were out standing in the street as they watched the entire disturbance. They weren't about to miss the excitement and I saw that some laughed while others looked to be shocked. The traffic had stopped in front of the Funeral Home and the police cars aimed for our place from two different directions. For the number of police cars that arrived so quickly and so furiously, it was obvious someone must have called the police and told them they had heard gunshots. In an all- black neighborhood, that always brought the police in numbers and in record time. It seemed that the police cars had hardly been stopped before the officers were out and running with their guns draw towards the now suddenly subdued and frightened Mrs. Calder.

By then, Mother had regrouped and collected herself and when she regally came outside she immediately took over by saying with one of her special smiles, "Officers, everything is under control. I'm Mrs. Reese, one of the owners here at the Funeral Home. Mrs. Calder has just lost her husband and is having a difficult time with her loss." So saying, Mother put her arm around Mrs. Calder and said, "Come on dear, it's going to be okay."

The police put their guns back in their holsters but one of the police officers asked, "Mrs. Reese, I see a broken window, what happened?"

"Oh it's nothing," Mother said matter-of-factly. "It was just an accident. Please, everything is alright here."

The police did not look convinced, but there were no guns around and they seemed to have respect for the Funeral Home and maybe for Mrs. Reese.

The next morning came with the sun shining brightly into my window. I strained to open my eyes and rubbed them because I really did not want to get up, but I had heard Mother calling me so I forced myself out of bed. I hated the way I felt—as if I had been drugged. Then I remembered it had been a long night and today Mrs. Calder would bury her wayward husband, without cutting him up, thank goodness. I may have been young but not too young to understand and empathize with her grief, hurt, and humiliation.

Since Reverend Miles was out of town, I heard Mrs. Reese call "Rent-A-Preacher" and request they send a Baptist Preacher to do the service. Mr. Calder had not been a man for church going. "Please have the clergyman arrive at least thirty minutes before the service starts," she requested. "No later than twelve thirty."

The funeral was to start at one o'clock. Mrs. Reese and I both glanced at the clock simultaneously. Mr. Holmes and Ima looked at Mrs. Reese. It was then twelve forty-five, the Chapel was full and Mrs. Calder, her children, and her Mother had all been seated in the front pew. The casket, half open, showed the torso of Mr. Calder directly in their view. Mrs. Calder held her head down and sobbed softly, and I could feel her sorrow. Then, the soloist began singing, "How Great Thou Art."

Mrs. Reese looked at the clock again; it was now twelve fifty-five, but still no Preacher. She stood up from behind her desk and began to pace the floor. Then she said, "Well, let's do it! The show must go on!"

No one said a word. Mr. Holmes, Mr. Hubert, Ima and I, just stood up and followed her to the Chapel and took our places, as usual. Mrs. Reese walked from behind the curtains that hung near the pulpit, ready to preach this service. She calmly began,

"I want to apologize for starting a little late, but our clergyman has run into some traffic, so with your permission I will give the eulogy." She began, "I have known the Calder family for some time..." but before she could finish her sentence movement from behind the curtain startled her.

Mrs. Reese turned to see the clergyman as he hurriedly took his place. "I apologize for being so late...caught up in traffic...my last service went on a little longer than planned," he explained breathlessly. "I'm Reverend Hargrove, please forgive my lateness." He gave a slight bow and continued, "Mrs. Reese, my apologies to you and the family. If it's okay with you, I'll take it from here?"

Mrs. Reese had specifically requested the Preacher be there early so she could discuss with him how Mr. Calder had died. This was not the usual situation and so it was not something you could just wing. She politely said, "Let's take a moment please, Reverend Hargrove, to go over the eulogy."

"Oh, no," he quickly replied, "I've done hundreds of funerals, and I can see here that Mr. Calder died suddenly...a massive heart attack, is that correct?"

"Yes, but let me explain," my Mother firmly insisted.

"It's okay," he, too, insisted.

Still, Mrs. Reese tried to be diplomatic with the Reverend and gestured for him to come behind the curtain with her for a moment. She had tried to be very careful so as not to alert the audience that there was a problem.

He blithely brushed her off when he said, "Oh, I want to thank you for your concern, Mrs. Reese. I'll take it from here."

I think that was the first time I had ever seen my Mother actually stunned and at a loss for words.

Reverend Hargrove said to the audience, "Let's take a moment for silent prayer. Close your eyes and thank the Lord for another day." He was charming, with a strong masculine voice. A few moments passed in total silence and during that time Mrs. Reese prayed he would look down at the note she had placed on the pulpit for him, that briefly explained how the deceased had passed.

Reverend Hargrove raised his head and with a loud shout startled everyone by saying, "Praise the Lord who has risen!" He had slammed his hands down on the pulpit, and then his voice went to a whisper, "I want to talk to your hearts today, my beloved people. We don't know when our time will come, do we?

No, we don't know, and I don't know if I want to know!" Suddenly he shouted again, "We want to be ready! Don't we?"

The Chapel was so full that some people had to stand. Mrs. Reese and Mr. Hubert were extremely nervous and kept looking at each other, not knowing what to expect from this Preacher. I stood there, watching Reverend Hargrove as if he were a performer who was there to entertain us. His showmanship was exceptional and I could not stray from his words;

they were sharp and cutting to the heart, and I could see he was reaching the emotions of everyone in the Chapel by the outbursts of "Amen's."

Every few minutes you'd hear from the crowd, "Amen! Yes, brother, tell it like it is!"

The sobbing throughout the pews was muffled by, the Preacher's, "Amen! Amen! Can I get a witness? Amen!"

The people responded, "Yes, Reverend," as they fanned themselves from the heat they had worked up. The emotions were high and the Reverend Hargrove was being fed by the responses from the crowd.

The service continued and Reverend Hargrove's ego was visible. "My sisters and brothers, I want to close this service with a thought you can take with you today. You may not know the hour!" He hit the pulpit so hard most of the people jumped in their seats. "But, let me say this to all God's children." He was on a natural high now, and his voice could be heard all through the Funeral Home. The Reverend stood up tall and looked out into the many faces, and with his fiery voice said,

"Brother Calder died suddenly! Yes, he did," as he lifted his hands to the sky. "God don't make no mistakes! No. No. No. He had a plan for Brother Calder and **I want to go the same way!**" he said with loud and strong conviction as his words echoed out.

The look on Widow Calder's face was as if she had been bitten by a snake. Mrs. Reese and Mr. Hubert only looked at each other in shock and amazement.

"Oh, no!" Mrs. Reese said out loud.

Ignorantly, the Reverend Hargrove continued on and on, **"Yes, I wanna go the same way. Don't you?"** he shouted and hit the pulpit at the same time. **"Brother Calder had no pain. I believe Brother Calder had a smile on his face! What a way to go! Quick, sudden, just snapped up by the Lord! What a way to go!"** he said again, repeating himself. "Amen! Praise the Lord! Amen! Can I get another Amen?"

The crowd began to move around restlessly in their seats and murmur because everyone knew that Mr. Calder had died in a motel while having sex with a prostitute. Even I knew it!

Widow Calder stood up and screamed. The sound was so chilling I could have sworn my heart skipped a beat. Then the good widow yelled to the Preacher, "How dare you make a fool of me?"

Her Mother and kids also jumped up and started yelling at the Reverend Hargrove. The mood in the Chapel had changed drastically. No more "Amens." Now there was trouble in the air.

Mrs. Reese and Mr. Hubert quickly rushed over and tried to hold Mrs. Calder and her family who were moving toward the Reverend with the intention of punching out his lights.

Within a matter of minutes the Chapel emptied. The crowd had been shocked and amazed by what they had just heard. I heard people complaining and someone said, "I'm just disgusted." Another asked, "What kind of fool was that Preacher? Why would he do that to the Calder family?" Mr. Calder would be buried later that day without a Preacher.

Finally Mrs. Reese told him the whole story, and the Reverend Hargrove, defeated and ashamed of himself had tears in his eyes as he left the Mortuary. He did not look back.

Mrs. Reese said his response to her had been, " I'm giving up preaching. I do not believe this was my calling."

There's an old saying, "Promise a lot, deliver more!" Well, the Reverend Hargrove delivered too much that day.

* * *

For the first time the Hubert and Reese Mortuary had received bad publicity and it would take time to rebuild their reputation. The good thing was, Mrs. Mary Reese had a great reputation from being the daughter of J. T. Stone of the famous Mortuary in Mississippi, and that would keep her in good faith with the people of the Black Community in South Central Los Angeles.

8

FOR ME GOING TO SCHOOL WAS A KIND OF HIT OR MISS situation. I enjoyed going to school, but Mother did not care one way or another if I went. Surprisingly, I somehow managed to keep "A"s on my report cards.

* * *

Mr. Hubert and Mother began having serious problems when Mother had started seeing another man who lived across the street from our house— Tom Thomas, a postal worker. He was shorter than Mother, which didn't seem to bother either of them, baldheaded, skinny, and he was also a heavy drinker. Like a servant, he waited hand-and-foot on my Mother, and I disliked this man even more than I did Mr. Hubert.

Usually when Tom Thomas was there, I spent the majority of the time in my room. As Mother didn't allow locks on any doors, it was not easy for me to have any privacy. I soon discovered a chair wedged under the handle gave me a feeling of some security.

Mother had a TV in her bedroom and the other TV was located downstairs in the den. Since too many people might be downstairs at any one time, for me, the TV downstairs was out of the question. So, some nights when she wasn't in her room I would watch her TV, until I felt sleepy.

The news was usually pretty depressing, except for all the excitement over Sputnik, a satellite that might possibly be seen streaking through the sky. Somehow I missed it.

Other things in the news were: Congress had approved the first Civil-Rights Bill for Blacks to protect voting rights; Black students were barred from entering an all-White high school in Little Rock, and President Eisenhower sent Federal Troops to enforce court orders to remove the National Guardsmen. Segregation was also the big topic on the news. I didn't fully understand why Blacks would be barred from any school. TV brought the outside world into my Mother's room, and it made me fearful to think I could be hated for my color. Although I looked White, I knew I was colored.

One night the party downstairs was getting out of control. When I heard loud voices and glasses breaking, Tom and Mother screaming and cursing at each other, I went and sat at the top of the stairs to listen and hoped they would not see me. It was only the two of them, but there was so much noise it sounded like a crowd.

"You can't go out like that!" Tom yelled. Evidently he was pissed and his anger seemed to provoke Mother even more.

She snapped, "Get the hell out of my way you dirty, lowdown nobody!" As she continued putting him down, the glass in her hand seemed to fly through the air and hit Tom on the chest. Even though he had seen her intention and tried to move out of the way, Mother had been quicker. "You don't tell me what to do! Fuck you!" The words she used made me flinch each time she said them. She had a way of making curse words sound positively degrading.

Tom leaped at her and not able to control his anger, grabbed her by the arm and pushed her away from the front door. Toms words slurred as he yelled, "You are not leaving this house like that!"

"Kiss my ass!" Mother defiantly screamed as she turned back to the door. Her reply only pissed him off more and soon they were in each other's face, their saliva spitting as they yelled.

I couldn't take any more and my heart pounded as I ran down the steps, taking three at a time, and jumped into the middle of them screaming "Stop! Get your hands off my Mother!" By then my whole body was shaking like a leaf in a storm.

Tom backed off for a moment, but Mother continued calling him names and saying anything nasty she could think of about his Mother, his kids, or anything she hoped would hurt him. Evidently it hurt him enough for him to reach over me and slap her face.

At that moment, the anger inside me caused me to react. It was as if I could not control myself and I hit him in the chest with my fist over and over again as I yelled, "Are you crazy? Stop! Please stop!" Tears coursed down my face and I was scared; but I couldn't let him hurt my Mother.

His breathing was hard and fast, he had beads of perspiration on his face, and it appeared as if he were almost foaming at the mouth. Through gritted teeth Tom said to me, "Just look at her!"

I did look and noticed my Mother had on her full-length sable fur coat with house slippers on her feet.

With one sudden move, Tom yanked her coat at the back of her neck and it fell to the floor. Mother stood there naked. He explained, "I won't let her go out like that!"

"Mother, where are you going?" I wanted to know.

"None of your damn business. I do what I want and to hell with the both of you!" she spat at us. The alcohol had given her the personality that I hated.

"She's going to see Mr. Hubert," Tom said with tears in his eyes.

Just then there was a hard knock on the front door and a constant ringing of the doorbell. I peeked through the lace curtain on the door and saw two policemen standing there. Since they had seen me, they said harshly, "Open the door!"

Quickly Mother picked up her sable coat and put it on in a hurry. When I opened the door, the policemen entered the living room, looked around and took mental notes of the broken glasses and overturned chairs.

"What's going on here?" asked the tall, blond officer.

Having calmed himself down, Tom went into a long explanation of a domestic quarrel.

The policeman replied, "The neighbors complained about all the noise, and said that it is an ongoing, nightly thing. If we get another call, someone is going down to the police station, do you understand me?"

The other policeman patted me on my shoulder and gave me a look of pity as he asked, "Are you all right?"

"I'm fine and thank you for coming," I replied.

With no other choice, the two policemen then left and I saw them helplessly shaking their heads. Tom and Mother went upstairs, arm-in-arm, once again all lovey dovey. Me? I was left in the entryway, forgotten and with only my shattered nerves for company. Slowly, I dragged myself up to my room, climbed into my bed and just lay there. I was unable to sleep as my system was overcharged by the latest confrontation and my thoughts kept running around and around as if I had no way of stopping them. *I ran down to save her, and she turned on me. Why did she hurt me like that? Why?*

9

I LAY THERE IN BED AND FOR SOME REASON BEGAN thinking of the photographer my Mother had insisted take pictures of me. *Why couldn't I forget what happened? It had been years ago and I had never told anyone, not even Ilona.*

The first time I met the photographer was when he came to our house to take pictures of me to put on the front cover of a Black magazine. The daughter of Mrs. Reese was a cover girl and that truly made Mother proud of me...at least for a short while. It caused Mother to receive attention, and so did I.

The photographer had me stand outside in the front yard of our house in a yellow raincoat, with a yellow matching rain hat. A man stood over me with the water hose to make it appear rain was falling on me and the bright yellow umbrella protected my face from getting wet. The photographer must have snapped at least a hundred pictures as he would say, "Turn this way. Turn that way. Smile. Look off into the distance." He gave me orders as if he were directing a movie.

"You could be a movie star at ten years old," Mother had told me proudly.

I did what I was told, and Mother was pleased at the outcome. The magazine cover was great and again the Hubert and Reese Mortuary was in the spotlight.

Mother and the photographer then decided I should have more photos taken so my visits to the photographer's home became frequent. Each time while she drove me to his house, I would plead with Mother not to take me. Her reply always was, "How many kids can make the money you're making?"

That always puzzled me because I had heard people say we were rich and so, wondered, *"then, why did the money matter?"*

She would reach over to hold my hand as if to assure me it was okay. Holding my hand was not what I wanted from her because she would squeeze so hard that tears came to my eyes.

With my eyes still closed as I lay in bed, I could visualize the time I walked through his back door and upon seeing that short, gray-haired White man with his nasty smile, I had chills go up my spine. He had taken my hand tightly, led me through his backyard, and then we crossed a small bridge over a pond where yellow, orange, and dotted fish swam leisurely around.

Then as we walked slowly towards his garage, he told me, "What a pretty girl you are."

Chained to the side of the garage was a large dog and when he started to bark, the man became irritated and just pointed to a long, two-by-four piece of lumber. I didn't understand what it was for.

He yelled at the dog, "Shut up, Mute." Then he looked at me with his beady eyes and said, "I call him Mute 'cause I wish he couldn't bark."

"Pretty dog," I said. "I like dogs, can I pet him?"

"No!" and with a sharp jerk of my hand he led me into the garage. Mute kept barking, and the disgusted photographer finally said, "Come with me." Then leading me back outside to where Mute was, he reached over, picked up the two-by-four, and viciously hit Mute on his back. Mute yelped with such pain that I felt as if the man had hit me.

"Please, don't hit him. Please," I begged.

"Shut up! You see what happens when you don't do what I say?" Then he squeezed my hand tightly, like Mother. By then I was very fearful and wondered, *what would he do to me?* I worried about Mute as he took me back to the garage.

I remember thinking, *How can I get out of here?* I looked for a way to escape, but there was only one door and he had blocked it. Another question that plagued me was, *If I get out, where would I run? Mother has always dropped me off and I don't know where I am.* So the man would not catch me off-guard as he had Mute, I just stared at the man and watched his every move and the whole time my insides trembled and my teeth chattered.

The photographer began setting up his camera and lights, straightening out a big black sheet hanging from the ceiling. I watched him closely, fearing his every move.

"I really want to go home," I said with a shaky voice, as if crying would be next.

He turned to me and without any warning slapped my face—not hard enough to bruise, but hard enough to bring tears to my eyes. "I won't have any crying, and you'll not go till I say so!" he angrily hissed at me.

Shocked, I replied as if I had power, "My Mother will be angry!"

"No, *I'm* paying your Mother, and you're going to model for me. Now just be quiet and put this on."

It was a flimsy see-through nightshirt and I told him, "No, I don't want to."

Quick as lightening the photographer grabbed me by my hair, pulled me into his face, and his breath made me want to vomit. The feelings of desperation and helplessness were overwhelming and I tried to push him away, but my strength was no match for his. He yelled and spit in my face and then dragged me by the hair out the door to where Mute was and I could see Mute was still wounded. His tail tucked. Suddenly, he let go of my hair, picked up the two-by-four again and started beating Mute. The yelping and crying was deafening to my ears and poor, helpless Mute, was tied up so he couldn't get away from that maniac. That man continued to beat Mute mercilessly until there were no more yelps, no more cries. Mute was dead. I was hysterical and petrified with fear and every part of my body was trembling uncontrollably because of the brutality I had just witnessed, and because I fully expected that crazy madman would begin to hit me next.

Once again the photographer grabbed me by the hair again and pulled me back into the garage. As frightened as I was, all I could see and hear was Mute. Branded into my mind was the image of that poor, abused dog lying there, his blood soaking the ground, his eyes protruding out, and his once beige coat matted with his blood. It made me sick to my stomach. My ears rang with the sound of his painful cries.

"Sit down till I'm ready for you and put this on," he demanded me to obey.

I sat there looking at the nightshirt, afraid not to put it on, and feeling so afraid of being treated like Mute. Slowly, I took off my blouse and slipped the nightshirt over my head. "My Mother is really going to get you for what you're doing," I said as I cried and talked at the same time, while I changed into the nightshirt.

"Your Mother won't know. If you don't want to end up like my dog, you will shut up, or you know what will happen to you."

Oh, God, please help me! I remember repeating over and over in my mind.

"Okay, Little Mary, let's get started," that horrid man said as if nothing unpleasant had just happened.

I froze and then begged, "No, please. I don't want to do this, I don't want to take pictures." I was more frightened than I had ever been; I had no way out.

By then the photographer had lost his patience with me. He grabbed my arm and threw me on the floor and even though I struggled with him, I could not win against his strength. I wanted to die, and in some small way, I believe I did.

For a long time after that experience, I seemed to relive everything nightly, and in the mornings when the alarm sounded at 6:00 a.m., I would jump at the sound. My nightclothes would be wringing wet, and I always worried I had wet the bed but that wasn't why I was wet from head to toe. I still see Mute.

After that I was never the same. Something had happened or died inside me and since I was basically alone and had no one to talk with about it, I began to lose interest in school and my friends became boring to me. No longer was I an "A" student. From then on, I only did enough to get by.

* * *

Next, my thoughts jumped to when I was in junior high school. It was rather awkward at times as I no longer was a child, but a teenager. My friends had already matured in their bodies, but I was slow in developing so I began wearing a bra and had to put socks in my A cup. Actually, I had to cut one sock in half and put only one half in each cup.

Monthly periods were something all the girls talked about, but I had no idea what to expect, so I finally got up enough courage and asked Lenore what to do when it happened. She was so understanding and went out and bought me a box of sanitary napkins. Then she kindly took the time to show me how to put on the belt and pad.

Although it was embarrassing to me, I was able to feel I fit in with my friends. Even though my periods had not yet come, I had lied and wore the napkin once a month just so I could also complain about having cramps.

That reminded me of how good Lenore had been to me during that terrible time. She was aware of and knew a lot of the dirty secrets between Mother and her friends, and she had also been aware that Mother had continued to take me to the photographer.

I overheard her telling Mother, "Mother, don't take Little Mary to that nasty man. I know how nasty he is. Remember, how I refused to go back?"

"Stay out of my business!" she had snapped, irritated at Lenore. "I'm not going to take her anymore because he didn't pay me, so I told him, 'Go to hell!' Anyway, he wouldn't let me see the pictures either."

I was thankful to Lenore, especially because I hadn't realized that she really cared for me. Lenore had no idea what had happened to me, but she knew what she had experienced. Evidently, she had a choice not to go again, but I had no choice. She must have thought she could protect me from that horrible man, but she didn't know it was too late.

10

EVEN THOUGH LENORE WAS MARRIED, SHE CAME around often and began working some funerals once in a while. She had many friends and one of them was a young man by the name of Johnny Cochran and he was Mother's favorite. "That young man is going to be somebody big one day," she'd say. At the time Johnny was in law school and doing very well. Whenever he came over to the house he was always kind to me, and I thought he was pretty cool.

Lenore's husband hardly ever came around and I often wondered why not. Since he did not drink or smoke and everyone at our house did, I assumed that might be the reason. But her brother-in-law Daniel came by often and I thought he was so cute. By then being a tomboy was not cool anymore and I had a crush on him, and to my surprise he started noticing me. I combed my hair in a different style and put on a little eye pencil around my eyes. Then I started staying downstairs more and our attraction to each other became evident to others. Lenore teased me and reminded me he was too old for me. Mother did not want me to like him, and told him in no uncertain terms that he was not to mess with me.

But Daniel and I always found a way to meet and when he kissed me for the first time I melted, left this world and entered the world of ecstasy. Daniel knew our age difference would be a problem, but we were in love and secretly made plans to be married when I turned eighteen, five years away. That was intolerable for me and I often wondered, *How can we wait that long? I'll will not survive in this house!*

Daniel knew of the problems I was having with Mother's friends constantly coming on to me, but was not in any position to change things. He would graduate from high school that year while I was still in junior high. Our plans for a white house, with a picket fence and a dog, would have to wait but we still dreamed of how happy we would be.

I loved Daniel more than I ever thought anyone could love another person. Our age difference was only four years and I didn't understand why others thought it was such a big deal. Daniel never disrespected me and we never went "all the way." He told me he could wait until we were married. With all the ugliness that was going on at home, it was Daniel that was my salvation and my way out, so the negative things didn't seem to matter as much.

* * *

It was after Ilona married and moved out of the house that Lenore and Mother seemed to have grown closer. On the surface it seemed as if Ilona had deserted me and Mother took every opportunity to remind me that I had been a burden to my sister and she had been glad to get away from me. Mother never tried to hide the fact that she was glad Ilona was gone. I was unable to let her go and still missed her so much, but I had to keep that to myself.

Mother and Lenore would often sit in the kitchen drinking beer. Mother drank Budweiser as if she were drinking water on the desert and dying of thirst. Sometimes, after they had put away a couple of six packs, they went upstairs to Mother's bedroom in order to be closer to her bathroom. Sometimes she and Lenore just stayed in the bathroom because the beer worked on their bladders and with the frequent need to go, being right there made it more convenient.

One evening when there was the usual "party" going on downstairs, Tom became impatient while waiting for them to return. Mother was always the life of the party, and she had been gone too long to Tom's way of thinking. Instead of going upstairs he yelled at the top of his voice, "Big Mary, you have company down here! Get your butt down here!" The Preacher, Reverend Miles had come by to visit and since there had only been two funerals that day, they had all started drinking earlier than usual. It was then around ten o'clock in the evening and Tom just continued to holler up the stairs for Big Mary.

After several yells I came out of my room and yelled back down to him, "Why don't you come up here and get her?" He got under my skin and my resentment for him was obvious in my tone of voice and attitude.

Reverend Miles never looked anyone in the eye when he spoke to them and that always bothered me about him. Personally, I thought he was a phony and had expressed my point of view to Mother several times but she always defended him. He always preached as if he personally knew God, but my feelings were that I didn't want to know God if he knew him.

Many times when the Reverend, who favored his own bottle of Jack Daniels, had been imbibing for some time, he would get into a heated discussion with Tom on the subject, "Is God real?" He and Tom could debate for hours and the more they drank, the louder they got. For me to try and sleep was out of the question, so I would sit at the top of the stairs and listen to the crazy folks downstairs.

Countless times I wished they would all go home and had wanted to shout "Go home!" but knew I could never get away with doing that. So I just kept it all inside and listened to the nothingness those drunks would talk about. Reverend Miles and Tom could be heard for blocks as they argued over God and the Bible.

One night I heard Tom, in a superior and accusing tone say, "You sleep with men, Reverend Miles."

"God loves everybody," the Reverend had said in a raised voice, as he tried to sound as though that was the point.

Upon hearing that, my ears perked up and I wondered, *how could he sleep with a man? He's married to Eva.*

By then, the argument had escalated and everyone else was listening. When Mother and Lenore saw me on the steps, Lenore yelled at me, "Go to bed, now! It's got to be one o'clock in the morning."

She had been a little upset, but I knew it was not at me but about what was going on downstairs. I knew from past experience that things would only get worse, and I wanted to hear it all. What Tom had said to Reverend Miles was in my mind and it wouldn't leave, *"You sleep with men!" I had never heard of anything like that. Was he just being mean? Maybe I heard him wrong.*

Then Mother jumped into the fray and began talking down to Tom by asking, "How can you insult my guest like that?"

"It's the truth and you know it!" Tom was shaking he was so angry. Mother had taken sides with Reverend Miles and Tom didn't like it.

A friend of Reverend Miles had also been there; a young fellow about twenty-two years old named David, and from what I heard next of the argument, it sounded as if the Reverend Miles and David were lovers.

Lovers? That was confusing to me. *How could they do that? They had the same body parts. How could they fit?* I just could not picture two men together and thought about all the dead bodies I had seen in the Embalming Room, but that was a new concept for me. In today's vernacular the expression, "Doesn't compute," would aptly explain my feelings.

Tom and Mother's arguing had escalated from angry, hateful words to dishes and glasses being thrown at each other. From my experience with the two of them, I had learned to stay completely out of their way and if Mother did not scream in pain, I knew she was the one that had inflicted the pain on Tom.

I sat on the step, and leaned over the banister and tried to see who else was there. Reverend Miles and David yelled at Mother and Tom to stop, while at the same time she called Tom a son-of-a-bitch. Mother defended Reverend Miles and David's relationship to the end. Lenore somehow was able to calm them all down somewhat, and soon Reverend Miles and David left together.

All I could think about was trying to visualize the two men together and it just didn't fit in my mind. I wasn't sure how I would react to Reverend Miles now that I knew he was weird. Liking another man was sick to me.

The next day Mother acted as if the world was fine again and everything was normal., but I still puzzled over the new revelations that had been exposed the night before. During the ride to the Funeral Home, I could not hold it in any longer and asked, "Mother, how can Reverend Miles and David be lovers, like Tom said?" I felt stupid, but just had to have some answers.

Turning, she looked me in right in the eye and was serious for the first time as she answered, "They just are. Sometimes nature gives people the craving for the same sex. Remember the body we had a few months ago?"

"Which one?"

With the sound of a lesson being given, she said, "The man that Mr. Holmes was showing me, the one that had a penis *and* a vagina. It's a freak of nature, and that poor man didn't know if he was male or female."

"I didn't see that body!" I said, knowing I had missed something. "Why didn't Mr. Holmes show me?"

"Are you crazy? You're too young to know about this kind of stuff."

"But I work there too."

"I don't know why he didn't show you, Little Mary, but you'll see enough, the longer you work there."

"Mother? Does Reverend Miles have a vagina *and* penis?"

"I don't know, and to tell you the truth, I don't care," she answered.

"Reverend Miles likes young boys, I know that and I know it is going to get him in trouble one day. "Why do you defend him, Mother?" I asked, hoping she could make me feel better about why she liked this evil man. To me the Reverend Miles always seemed to bring darkness into a lighted room. "Men wanting to be with men, and women with women, I have never been so confused."

"Little Mary, you must keep this to yourself," Mother insisted. "That is why they use the phrase, 'He's in the closet.' "

"Huh? What does that mean?"

"It means he only does things with men behind closed doors. It's his secret."

"That's awful, their parts don't fit!" I blurted out. I was trying not to sound like an idiot but had to ask, "But why?"

"I don't know, Little Mary, it just is. You just keep quiet about it, okay? Reverend Miles can't let this get out. He has a big following at church."

"I know, that's why I don't understand him doing stuff like that."

The rest of the ride we didn't talk. I felt sad at what I had just learned and had knots in my stomach. It was a secret and I didn't know why.

Entering the door to the Funeral Home, Mother grabbed my hand and held it tight as she reminded me, "Remember, it's a secret."

"Okay, I won't tell anyone," I promised as I pulled my hand away before she could squeeze too tight.

Mr. Holmes was waiting for Mother to go over some funeral arrangements. I was glad to see him and ready to help him clean and sterilize his tools. While I sat in the Embalming Room looking over the tools, I saw some S-shaped needles—one big and one little. The door opened while I was holding one of the needles.

"Little Mary, put those down before you hurt yourself." Mr. Holmes was like the Father I wish I'd had.

"What do you do with these?" I asked.

He picked up the big S-shaped needle and gently rubbed his finger over it and outlined the shape. "This one you sew up the stomach." Then he picked up the small one and explained its purpose, "And this one we use on the mouth."

I had a frown on my face and Mr. Holmes asked, "Hey, Little Mary, not getting woozy on me are you?"

"No." I smiled at him and all was okay.

I watched as Mr. Holmes started to embalm a man of about sixty-five years old, his body was wrinkled and gray, and the huge veins in his hands looked as if they had collapsed. Mr. Holmes inserted a tube into the old man's neck and began draining the blood from his body.

I thought I was used to observing this procedure and turned my head. But as I watched the blood flow into the sink, it made me nauseated, only I didn't want Mr. Holmes to know. Seeing the blood flowing reminded me of the poor dog Mute, and I was just unable to watch. I felt a stab of pain remembering and knew I could never tell a soul, especially my friend Mr. Holmes, because he might think I was a terrible person. He'd hate me; I just knew he would.

Abruptly I said, "Mr. Holmes, I'm going to the Front Offiice. I'll see you later." I felt as if Mr. Holmes could see right through me.

"See you later, Little Mary. Stay out of trouble," and he grinned at me.

I walked in at the wrong time as Mr. Hubert and Mother were in the middle of an argument, but they continued as if they hadn't even seen me, though I knew they had.

"I want out!" Mother said maliciously.

"You can't leave. We're partners," he pleaded with her.

"I'm going home, back to Mississippi. My sister needs me there."

"That's ridiculous," he said, getting close to her face.

Oh, no, I hope they don't fight, I thought.

"I'm leaving in two weeks. You can find a buyer to buy me out."

"Make me an offer."

"You know it's my name that made you rich!" She was being very sarcastic and mean. "I'm going home. I hate it here! I just want away from you!" she all but yelled. There were tears in her eyes, not of sadness but tears of bitterness. Mother's wrath was evident to Mr. Hubert and me. She wanted to hurt him, destroy him because he would not leave his wife for her and now she would not leave Tom. She also still wanted to destroy my Dad Willie.

Mr. Hubert was fuming. He knew he could not lose control because his reputation was at risk. I didn't know what to think. *What was going to happen? Were we really going to Mississippi? I can't even remember the place.*

Sliding into a chair near the door, I was frightened by what my Mother had just said about leaving for Mississippi. I had just started school and now she said we would be leaving.

Mr. Hubert looked at Mother with hate in his eyes, too angry to cry, but if he had a gun I believe he would have shot her. Speechless, Mr. Hubert walked out the door, slamming it hard enough to rattle the windows.

I looked at Mother, and she was smiling with a look of pleasure on her face because she had succeeded in hurting him. "Get out of here, Little Mary."

Quickly I jumped up and moved out the door. I sat on the steps where I had so often sat while Mother and Mr. Hubert had been in the office together with the doors locked and curtains closed. Then I sat thinking about moving to Mississippi. *Two weeks. I can't believe I would be leaving in two weeks.*

Soon Mother came out of the office smiling and asked, "Where is Mr. Holmes?"

"In the Embalming Room."

"Go and get him. Tell him to come to my office, now," she all but demanded.

Running around to the back, I could smell the embalming fluid and I called out, unaware I had actually yelled, "Mr. Holmes! Mrs. Reese wants to see you, now." I was out of breath and hoping Mother would change her mind about leaving.

"What's going on, Little Mary?"

"Just come now, please!" I told him.

We walked at a fast pace and could see Mrs. Reese at the door of the office waiting for him. As we reached the steps, she said, "Little Mary, go play or something while Mr. Holmes and I talk."

They closed the door, and I sat down on the steps, as I had nowhere to go. My heart was racing and drops of perspiration formed on my nose. I hoped Mr. Holmes would be able to talk her out of this latest idea. Holding my head up with my hands on my chin, my heart was full of sadness. Then my thoughts turned to Ilona. *Where was Ilona and why hadn't she come and got me like she had promised? Where was my Dad? Why did he hate me? What had I done to him? He loved Ilona and Willie Jr., why not me?* I could feel the tears building in my eyes and fought to hold them back.

The meeting between Mr. Holmes and Mother lasted quite a while and I wished I could have known what it was they had talked about.

On the way home I looked out the window and watched cars passing us. I found myself looking into the windows of cars, and homes wondering what it would be like if they were my family. I did that a lot, wondering what it would it be like to have nice parents. Parents that cared if you lived or died. I wished Mother loved me, but I knew in my heart, she wanted me out of the way. I reminded her that she was a Mother, something she did not want to be.

The atmosphere was solemn and the presence of trouble was in the air, but I dared not ask questions now. I knew there were times when I should keep quiet or I would get Mother started and her outbursts would then go on and on.

11

SOMEHOW, MY MOTHER HAD FOUND OUT THAT MY DAD had a new girlfriend and that she was White. This really had her upset and so Mother became angry with everyone. That night she decided to go over to Dad's house and give him a piece of her mind.

I had gone to sleep in Ilona's room, as I did sometimes, when I was suddenly awakened by Mother saying, "Get up, girl."

Startled, I looked at the clock, saw it was 12:30 a.m., and asked, "Why?"

"Just get up and dressed. Hurry up damit!"

I got up, frightened, not knowing what was happening.

"Come on!" I heard hear calling me as she headed for her car in the driveway.

I went through the kitchen and out the back door to her car and I was shivering, but not because it was cold. Fearfully I asked, "Mother, where are we going?"

"Just wait and see."

"Mother, please. I hope you're not going to Dad's." Somehow I knew that was where she was going, "You said he hates us."

I hadn't seen my Dad in over three years and I realize now that I was still quite naïve for a thirteen-year old. So many thoughts and questions raced through my mind as I wondered why we would be going there now. Since my Dad and Mother split up, I had never once been over to his house. I knew it was on a large lot; his house in the front, and behind it was a duplex—there were three houses on one property. It was located on the South Side and was considered to be mostly an all- Black neighborhood. The West Side, where I lived with my Mother, was mixed.

I could smell alcohol on Mother and knew she was drunk as she was driving crazy, speeding, and talking out loud. "I'll fix him," she muttered.

"What are you talking about?" I asked.

It seemed like a demon was talking instead of my Mother when she said,

"You think I don't know you're fucking Daniel!"

Shocked, I said, "What? That's not true, I have not!" I was so frightened; I thought she was going to kill me.

"I swear, Mother, I haven't done anything with Daniel, I swear!"

Her anger escalated, and she screamed, "You're a whore! God's going to punish you!"

"I haven't done anything, I swear!" The fear of what she was going to do to me was unbearable and I thought about jumping out of the car. I thought, *Run away or she's going to kill you.*

"I'm taking you to live with your Father!" she announced.

"Why? I haven't done anything."

She wouldn't listen to me and just kept cursing me and calling me terrible names.

"It's the middle of the night, Mother. Please, I don't want to go. He hates me. Please, Mother, don't take me. I love you, I want to stay with you."

My pleading did not faze her and she continued with the hate statements and accusations,

"You make me sick! You're nothing but a whore! Let him have you!" At that minute I knew she hated me just like she had hated Ilona, but I didn't know why. I had never been on a date with Daniel and saw him only when he came to our house. I had never done any of the things that she was accusing me of, and Daniel and I had only kissed. Nothing I said mattered, she was crazed with hate and it all came down on me, and whoever got in her way.

Hysterical and crying, I kept insisting that I had never had sex with Daniel but she just ignored me. Before I could move, she took one hand off the steering wheel and slapped me across the face as hard as she could. The car swerved and almost hit another and I could taste the blood in my mouth.

"No, you're going to stay with him and his White girlfriend. I hate that motherfucker so much! I wish I could kill him," she screamed with rage.

"What did I do?" I insisted.

She began rambling, "I didn't want you in the first place. He wanted you, not me."

The words were cutting me to pieces and I continued crying and pleading and trying to hold her hand. I begged her, "Please, Mother, I'll do whatever you want me to."

She continued driving like a maniac and after turning the corner on two wheels, she pulled into a driveway and onto a front lawn. Instinctively, I knew this had to be my Father's house but I didn't want to see him—not this way.

"Mother, please, let's go home," I begged with every inch of my heart. But the more I begged, the more she pushed on the horn, blasting away.

Before the car had completely stopped, Mother tried forcing the gears into "Park," meanwhile opening the car door and jumping out while it was still moving

I saw the lights go on inside and there stood my Father, in his pajamas, at the front door. I sat there frozen, not sure what to do. It was dark and I didn't know where Mother had gone until suddenly she appeared in the headlights.

Just then I saw Ilona running around from the side of the house in her nightgown and robe as she screamed, "What's going on?" When she saw us, fear shown immediately on her face. "Mother, what are you doing here? It's one o'clock in the morning."

Then I saw Mother rushing towards Dad with a huge silver trashcan that had been sitting at the curb. I knew she was strong, but this was like superwoman. It only took a moment to see it was empty, as she lifted it high above her head and threw it at my Dad. He moved quickly out of the way and darted back into the house.

I was hysterical and Ilona was screaming, "Stop! I'll call the police on you!"

Mother shouted back, "Call the son-of-a-bitches!"

I jumped out of the car and ran over to Ilona and as we embraced, Mother was on her like black on coal. Ilona ran into Dad's house and Mother was at her heels. I was right behind her pleading for her to stop.

Mother then screamed, "Willie, you bring that White bitch out here so I can kick her ass."

When Ilona picked up the telephone to call the police, Mother leaped across the room, snatched the phone from her hand and proceeded to beat her with it. Dad grabbed Mother from behind and held on tight while she struggled with what seemed like the forces of hell.

My heart fell when I saw he was going to hit her, and I screamed, "Please don't! Please don't!"

I was choking on my own tears and I knew I had to get out of there. Panicking, I ran out the front door as though being chased by bats-out-of-hell. The speed of my feet amazed me and I just kept running, not knowing where I was going. Finally, I ran out of steam, and leaned against a street sign to catch my breath. I looked at the street sign to see where I was. The sign said 95th Street and Central—not a good place to be, especially late at night.

I was exhausted, wet with sweat from head to toe, and I was getting cold. I had no coat, no money, and had on the blue jeans and shirt that I had thrown on in a hurry.

My senses came back as I caught my breath. *What had I done? I was lost!* Scared, I looked around at my surroundings as I tried to figure out in which direction to go. I was so confused. *What was I going to do?*

I prayed I would see a policeman. I knew there was no God, but I was hoping if there was maybe he'd help me out. There were none in sight, only a few winos hanging around, drinking bottles of wine in brown paper bags. Terrified as I was, I knew not to act scared but just keep walking. My only thought was how to get home and how to get some help. It was dark and cold, and I didn't know my Dad's phone number, or address. If I had the number, at least I could have called collect. I knew I was in trouble.

I told myself to stay calm, but felt as if I were in the middle of hell and did not have an exit. So I started walking, hoping that I was heading in the right direction. I could feel the eyes of the people on the street watching me and I desperately tried not to show that I was frantic inside. What I wanted to do was run but didn't know where to run. Then I saw a liquor store on the corner, directly across the street, but when I got closer I saw that the sign said, "Closed." There was an older man standing alone near the store and then I realized he was leaning on a phone booth. "Thank goodness, a phone," I said aloud and the thought of help at my fingertips surged through me. "I'll call the operator and she'll send a policeman to get me." For a few moments I felt hope.

I ran across the street and as I approached the man I could see he was a shady-looking character. Nervous as I inched closer, my heart was pounding as I said, "Excuse me, Sir, I'd like to use the phone." I did not want him to see me shaking, so I held myself tight.

He moved aside, glaring at me and with his movement, his body odor wafted towards me and it was disgusting. He reeked of alcohol and an unwashed body. I wanted to turn my head, but I did not want him out of my sight.

I reached for the phone and found just the cord dangling down. It was broken and I felt as if I were sinking. Then, even though I had no desire to talk to the man, I realized I had no choice and asked, "Sir, could you help me? Which way is 75th Street?" Actually, I didn't think he would know which end was up and I was afraid of getting too close to him. But I was desperate, even though he smelled awful.

He pointed into the alley and said, "I have a phone back here that you can use."

"No, thank you," I said as I ran away from him. I may have been stupid but I wasn't crazy, so I ran as if being chased by the law—only I really wanted so much to see the law.

Then I saw the 96th Street sign and thought, *Oh, no, I have run in the wrong direction, but at least now I know I just have to turn around and go the other way.*

In my desperation and looking for a phone, I even thought that if I could call Daniel he would help me. But then I knew I would be accused of sleeping with him.

Deep in my thoughts, I did not notice that I was being followed. Then suddenly I had a sense of fear and knew someone was directly behind me. I should have never looked back. But I did, just as a tall Black man, dressed all in black, grabbed me by the arm. I pulled away so I could run, but he picked me up and held me in a bear hug. I kicked and screamed but there was no one around. "Shut up bitch" he slurred.

"Please, let me go!" I begged and he only laughed and laughed as if this was funny to him. I could not get my arms free and as suddenly as he had grabbed me, he opened the door of a car and threw me into the front seat He struggled with me fighting and kicking, but he pushed me so hard my head hit the steering wheel and I saw stars. He was drunk and strong. In fact, the alcohol seemed to be coming through his pores causing him to smell so awful that even in the middle of the struggle, I could not ignore that odor.

Things were happening fast and I was fighting with all my being, when I heard him say, "Bitch, I'll cut your throat!"

I stopped fighting when I felt the cold blade on my neck and I froze. I knew I was going to die and I didn't have time to think of what to do next. When I stopped fighting, the man relaxed for a minute, putting the knife down on the floor under the steering wheel.

Laughing again, he said, "You a pretty little bitch, and you mine tonight." He continued to laugh as he was pulling at my shirt, then reaching his hand down toward my personal parts. I was thinking that I had to do something, so I pretended to give in. Then while his attention was concentrating on his conquest, I let my left hand slowly slide down to the floor where I felt around for the knife. Fortunately, I was able to grab it and then when he wasn't looking, I stabbed him in the shoulder, again and again.

"What the fuck!" he shouted in pain and shock, as he grabbed his shoulder.

Then with all my might, I pushed him off me enough so that I was able to get out of the car and with the adrenalin flowing through my veins, I ran like hell. Shortly I became aware of some wetness on my arm and on my chest and realized that he had cut my neck. The pain was like a bad bee sting, but the cut was minor. He was a lot worse off than I was. I knew that.

Everything happened so fast. It was dark but when I held up my hands, I saw blood all over me. I wondered if I had killed the man and then fear ran through every part of my body as though I was trapped in a casket, and the feeling of being buried alive washed over me. I began shaking. What had I done. I had just stabbed a man. I could still feel the knife cut through his skin. I felt so bad that I had hurt him. I could not stop the vomit that came out of my mouth right there on the street.

I wanted to stand in the street and scream as loud as I could. "Somebody help me please!" But I would have been afraid of anyone who might have come to me.

I ran till I could no longer run and then hid in the bushes until I caught my breath. Then I proceeded to run some more and I had thoughts of the night never ending. Finally I saw a tree that was easy to climb and I climbed the tree and sat there, trying to think of a way to get help. Maybe if it were daylight, it would be safer to try and run some more. It probably was only a few minutes, but it seemed like hours when I saw a police car turning at the corner and coming towards me.

Jumping from the tree, falling and then rolling on the ground, I yelled, "Help! Help!"

The police saw me, stopped the car, and both policemen jumped out and came towards me. I had never been so happy in my life.

"What happened? Are you okay? What are you doing out here at this hour?"

So many questions, and I had no answers. *How could I tell them I had stabbed a man? They'll take me to jail,* I thought. One officer had a blanket and placed it around me then led me to the back seat of the car where I collapsed in his arms.

"Little miss, are you hurt?" he asked. "You're covered with blood."

"I must of cut myself when I fell out of the tree," I told them because I did not want to go to jail.

"Here, let me take a look. " He was being so concerned.

The buttons on my shirt were gone except for the one remaining that held it closed.

"It looks like you're cut," they said. I felt the pain on my neck so I was sure he saw it.

"No, I'm fine. Please just take me home."

"Not that easy, little girl. I have to know what happened, and why are you out here all by yourself. Where are your parents?"

"I ran away," I said.

The policeman had gentle eyes and spoke softly to me. I was so tired and just wanted to go home. "My name is Mary Reese Jr." When I told him that

I saw a look of surprise in his eyes.

"Are you the daughter of Mrs. Reese, with Hubert and Reese Mortuary?"

"Yes. Please take me home." With not an ounce of energy left, I broke down and cried uncontrollably.

"Sir, I was trying to find my way home, I didn't run away."

Since the Black officer had shown real interest and care in what had happened to me, I told him everything. Finally my tears dried up on the outside, but inside I was drowning in them.

"Let's go." He gently took my face in his hands and said, "It's not your fault, Mary. If the guy was shouting and yelling at you, he's not dead. We aren't going to take you to jail, but we will take you home."

Someone cared, even if it was a stranger, and for those few moments I felt safe.

It was five-thirty in the morning when we pulled up in front of our house. Mother never called the police when she realized I was missing, and when they found me they called and told her. She stood waiting in the doorway as we got out of the car.

Reaching to hold the policeman's hand, I whispered, "Please don't tell her."

He looked down at me and said, "I have to. It's not your fault. She'll understand."

"You don't know her like I do," I said under my breath.

"Are you sure you're okay? I can take you to the hospital and tend to that cut if you want." The policeman had given me his handkerchief to put on the cut, to stop the bleeding and then again said, "Let me look at it to be sure." After checking it he said, "It's okay. Not deep enough for stitches."

Thank goodness, I thought.

I walked past my Mother and went up to my room while the two officers talked with Mother. Feeling filthy, I ran the bath and only thought of getting clean; getting the smell of the drunks off me. As I passed by the mirror I caught a glimpse of myself and it startled me. There were splatters of blood on my face and my shirt was covered with blood. My neck was red and down my chest and around my breasts I saw splashes of blood. Running the water in the bowl, I washed my face, just wanting to get clean. As the water turned red in color, it brought the tears back. As I cried I kept asking myself in a broken voice, "Why? Why didn't Mother open her arms when I got out of the car? Why didn't she take me into her arms and tell me she was glad to see that I was all right?"

Then I answered them myself, as I reclined in the tub of hot water. *Silly questions,* I thought. *She has already told me she never wanted me—right from the beginning.* I lay in the tub, having to fill it twice in order to feel clean. *What would happen next? Was Mother going to be angry with me?* I was afraid to think what she would do to me.

The door to the bathroom opened—she didn't knock. The draft from the open door chilled my naked body and I said, "Please, close the door."

"Are you okay, baby?" she spoke as if she were sincere.

"Yes," I whispered. I'm really sorry, Mother." My tears came unbidden and seemed to have a mind of their own.

She walked over to me, leaned over the tub and rubbed my forehead. "I'll put some medicine on that cut and alcohol on the bruises."

"Okay."

"You clean up and we won't talk about this at all," she decided.

"Okay," I mumbled, a little surprised and yet somewhat disappointed at the same time. I was surprised she was not angry. I didn't want to talk about it either, I decided. I just wanted to fall sleep and wake up and find that it had all been a bad nightmare. Lying in the tub, I kept wondering, *what had happened at my Dad's after I left. Was Ilona all right? How badly had Mother hurt her?*

These thoughts and more raced through my mind. Uppermost was, *what had happened to the man I stabbed? If he weren't dead, would he come after me?*

I told myself I would never let myself get that emotional again, to run away in blind darkness. I could imagine how an animal feels when being hunted. There are no words to describe the feeling of such fear. Since Mother said we would not talk about it, I would probably never have all the answers to my questions. When Mother said, we would not talk about it; that settled it. So trying to stop myself from thinking was as impossible as trying to stop an oncoming train. I had seen Ilona only for a few minutes and wondered if she still loved me. The void in my life was something I was just learning to live with.

From then on, I began to fear the night as soon as the sun began to set. Even with a chair wedged at the door and double checking the windows, I still could not sleep. There was nowhere I could go and feel safe. My nightmare even followed me during the daytime and I found myself constantly looking over my shoulder. For a long time, there was no rest or peace of mind for me as the vision of the knife and all that blood stayed vivid in my mind.

My dreams became my enemy and I hated to close my eyes. I learned to sleep after school so that I could be alert at night and it seemed I was always wondering if he would come after me. Dying was not my fear. It was the pain that I feared.

12

THE DAYS AND NIGHTS SEEMED TO RUN ONE INTO another and the television kept me informed about what was happening in the South. Now that Mother was making plans to move there, I had an interest. With all the racial issues going on, President Eisenhower was trying to do a good job for the Blacks in the South. He seemed to be fair. At least that is what I heard Mother say. The world was changing all around and I had a front-row seat as I watched. All of the stories I heard about Mississippi were scary to me. I had trouble visualizing that I could not ride the bus unless I sat in the back of it, or go into a restaurant and eat…the food would have to be "Take Out." And then there were the drinking fountains marked, "White Only," or "Colored." I could not imagine this, and why?

And the All-Colored school I would be attending, *How would I fit in? Would I be liked?* My fears were real, but what I wanted did not matter. The world revolved around Mother and I did not have any choices.

I loved Mr. Holmes and Ima and I didn't want to leave them. I enjoyed school even though I did not give it my all. It was my escape from home, and the Funeral Home was my security. It was difficult to imagine leaving and starting over. All I thought about was, *Where was Ilona? Why didn't she come and get me? She had promised that nothing would separate us. But she never even called or came to see me.*

Maybe I would be safe in Mississippi, as the man in my nightmares was in Los Angeles.

I was sitting on the steps outside the Mortuary while Mother packed the last of her belongings, when Mr. Holmes walked up and looked down at me with sadness written on his face.

"Hi, Mr. Holmes," I said, glad to see him.

"Hi, Lil Mary. What are you doing?"

"Nothing, just hanging around waiting for Mother." I guess I looked like I had lost my best friend. I was losing the only people that cared about me: Mr. Holmes, Ima, and all my dead friends who came and went.

"Can I come with you?" I was asking to be rescued from that step.

"I have two bodies back there waiting to be embalmed. You know they can't wait long."

His smile always made my heart happy.

"Can I come help you?"

"Don't need help, Lil Mary, but you can come watch."

"Ok." I walked beside him. I was too big to hold his hand anymore and knowing this would be my last time here, my heart became sad.

The closer we got to the Embalming Room, the more I thought of all the fun I had had in there, talking to the dead people, combing their hair, helping Ima with filing their fingernails and most importantly, talking to the dead people, telling them my stories of how one day I would be somebody really important. I remembered how many times I envied the dead bodies, for they were at peace and I wasn't.

"I guess you guys will be leaving in a few days for Mississippi," Mr. Holmes said by way of making conversation. There was sadness in Mr. Holmes' voice, and I think I saw his eyes getting teary. He would not make eye contact with me. A slight sniffle let me know he was hurting as much as I was. While Mr. Holmes was putting on his white coat and gloves, I walked around the slabs looking at the bodies and thinking, *They don't have any troubles.*

Dragging my hand around the slab as I moved slowly about, I looked into the face of a corpse lying there—it was as if he were sleeping.

"Mr. Holmes, what's this one's name?"

"That would be Mr. Johnson. Young man, heart attack. Died in his sleep. We never know when, do we? Here today, and gone tomorrow," shaking his head as if he were teaching me a new lesson.

I only wished it had been me lying there. Standing there, I wondered what kind of life he had before, and if he had ever done anything as bad as me. I picked up his hand from his side and gently placed it over his chest and then put the other hand on top. I thought I heard a noise, but it was probably my imagination. Then I heard it again. It sounded like someone had passed gas. I turned and looked at Mr. Holmes.

"Did you do that?" It had startled me because the sound was so close to me.

He was smiling and then he started to laugh.

"Ooh Mr. Holmes, did you break wind?"

Still laughing, he said, "No!"

"Yes you did." I was looking at him very seriously, embarrassed that he thought it was me. "I didn't do it! It wasn't me." I was talking fast to protect myself.

We were the only two living people in the room. Mr. Holmes was holding his stomach, laughing from his gut, trying to talk. Unable to form a sentence, he became hysterical with laughter.

"Come on Mr. Holmes, I didn't do it." His laugh was so funny that I began to laugh as hard as he was, holding my stomach and trying not to wet my pants.

"That was Mr. Johnson over there. We just got him from the morgue this morning.

He's the one who passed gas."

The look on my face made him laugh even harder than before. "No way. You're putting me on aren't you?"

Our laughter was heard outside the Embalming Room doors. Ima came in from the side door that led directly into a hallway, which went past the Casket Room and the Viewing Room to the Front Office.

"You two are making too much noise. We can hear you all the way to the Front Office." She was serious but her smile let us know she wasn't angry. We were making a disturbance, and Mrs. Reese had sent her back there to tell us to be quiet. This was a Funeral Home, not a comedy club.

"What is so funny in here?" Her curiosity made Mr. Holmes and me crack up more.

"Ima," Mr. Holmes was stammering, "the body passed gas. I wish you could have seen Lil Mary's face. She's already light, and she turned white as a ghost." Mr. Holmes could not stop laughing.

"Get a grip, Mr. Holmes." Trying to be stern, Ima called him "Mr. Holmes." Come to think of it, I had never heard her call him by his first name. I didn't even know his first name.

"Okay, okay," he said, wiping the tears of laughter from his eyes.

Mr. Holmes walked over and put his arms around me and gave me the biggest hug. His warm body made me realize how lonely I was for affection.

Standing by the door, Ima gestured for me to come to her. "I'm going to miss you so much, Little Mary." I knew by the look in her eyes that she loved me. I let go of Mr. Holmes, and quickly found myself smothered in her large breasts, my pillow of security.

"Little Mary, you are very special. You light up our lives around here and I believe you could make a dead person talk." Her smile had the warmth of sunshine. When Ima loved you, you knew you were loved.

I could not fight back the tears and I didn't care if the world saw me cry; I had never felt so loved as I did at that moment. "I'll miss you too," I mumbled.

"You're going to be okay," she promised.

"Yeah," I was choking and my throat seemed to have closed.

Saying good-bye was so hard to do. Ima had been there so many times to comfort me and calm my Mother down. I would miss her and Mr. Holmes more than they would ever know.

Ima left Mr. Holmes and me alone after we promised to be quiet.

Trying to change the mood, I asked him the question I knew sounded stupid.

"Mr. Holmes, how could that man pass gas? He's dead."

"Lil Mary, when people die, remember what I told you, everything stops. But his bowels still had air trapped inside and it must come out. Sometimes, it takes time to pass, but it gotta pass."

Still trying to understand exactly what Mr. Holmes was saying, out of the corner of my eye I saw movement. Turning suddenly, I saw the body's arm slide from his side and hang off the table. Immediately I started to run out the door.

"Stop!" Mr. Holmes had grabbed me by my collar.

"Mr. Holmes, I gotta get out of here." I was scared and not ashamed of it. I had never experienced this in all my days spent in the Embalming Room, and it scared me.

"Dead people aren't supposed to move, Mr. Holmes." I was frantic, thinking I had seen a ghost.

"Come on, Lil Mary. You been around a long time, you don't have to be scared."

"Why then is this body moving and farting?" I was dead serious and trembling.

"Because this man hasn't been dead twenty-four hours. His body is still warm. Come here." Mr. Holmes reached for my hand. "Touch him."

"No, I don't like this body." I was afraid for the first time in years.

"Come on girl. I can't let you out of here being afraid. Remember your first lesson I taught you?"

"Yes, I do!"

"The dead won't hurt you, but the living will."

"Yeh, Yeh, I knew that, but..."

"Calm down, okay," he said patiently.

I began to relax. Mr. Holmes was right; the bodies had never hurt me. It was the living that I was afraid of.

"Touch him." Then he took my hand and gently placed it on Mr.

Johnson's arm.

"His body is still warm," I said in surprise. "His skin feels like ours."

"But he won't feel like that when I finish embalming him."

Mr. Holmes was proud that he had taken away my fear, and I was relieved I now believed that the dead man wouldn't hurt me. Thus, I spent the rest of the afternoon watching Mr. Johnson get embalmed. But I found I was still keeping my eye on him and knew in my heart if he moved, I would run out of there.

That evening I tried to call Daniel because I had been wondering if he had heard about what had happened to me. He didn't answer and naturally I wondered where he might be as I had called him at least three times that day, and each time there had been no answer.

Mother and Tom were planning the trip to Mississippi and figured the drive would take at least three days and four nights. While they planned, I sat on my legs at the foot of Mother's bed with the TV blasting. I eagerly waited for the news to come on. The "Late Night News" came on at 9:00 p.m.

Finally the news reporter said, "What a night! Wilt Chamberlain is joining the Harlem Globetrotters!" I thought, *Big deal. What's happening in the South? I want to see how the White people were treating the Blacks.* But the news was mainly all about sports, and I had no interest in that.

The news reporter went on, "Floyd Patterson knocked out Roy Harris in the twelfth round, and he remains the Heavyweight Champion…"

Ok, this is good, but…

Then he started on Khrushchev and the tension in the Middle East. I had no understanding of world issues, or how they would affect my life.

My only concern was my present living issues, and what to expect when going to the South. I was told that a Black man would be killed just for looking at a White woman. That's what I was interested in.

"What's happening in the South?" I heard myself asking out loud. My patience was running out as I insisted, "Get to the important stuff, will you?"

Mother and Tom walked in just as the news began to air what was going on in Little Rock. Immediately, Mother said, "Go to your room."

"I'm watching the news."

"Too bad. Go downstairs." So, I reluctantly left her room, but didn't go downstairs as I didn't like to be down there by myself. I felt much safer on the second floor.

13

J UST AS I WAS GETTING INTO BED, I HEARD THE PHONE ring and rushed to grab it before Mother did.

"Hello?"

"Little Mary, it's Daniel." I quickly turned my back to Mother so she could not see the look on my face.

"Are you alone?" he asked.

"No. You must have the wrong number." I said trying to sound believable.

"Meet me outside at eleven o'clock tonight, okay? In the back driveway."

"Okay. No problem. Hope you find who you're looking for," I said as I hung up the phone and started to walk out, hoping Mother would not be able to read my face.

"Who was that?" Mother asked as if she knew I was up to something.

"I don't know. It was a women looking for a Dennis, or something like that." I lied as I closed Mother's door behind me and hoped this night that she and Tom would go to sleep without a fight or argument.

Back in my room I looked into the mirror and checked my face. The bruise on my cheek was still slightly visible but I couldn't do anything about that. Then I washed my face and combed my hair just the way Daniel liked it. Putting a little rouge on my cheeks hid the bruise well, and the black eye pencil added the magical touch.

I was smiling when I looked in my closet for the red and white blouse that was Daniel's favorite, and realized that just the thought of Daniel made my eyes sparkle. I was ready in no time but then had to sit and wait until 11:00 p.m., and that seemed like an eternity.

With nothing but my thoughts to keep me company, I think I was ready to explode from having so much "stuffed" and not discussed. *Would Daniel understand all the things that had happened? Would he hate me? Would he take me away, so that I would not have to go to Mississippi? Maybe he would marry me. I love him so much. Daniel will help me; we can marry and be happy forever. I just know it.*

Finally, after pacing back and forth for almost two hours, it was 11:00 p.m. Very quietly I sneaked out of my bedroom, looked down the hall towards Mother's room, and stopped and listened for voices. Thank goodness it was quiet and I hoped they had fallen asleep. My heart was racing as I moved slowly down the stairs, praying the steps would not creak, then through the kitchen and out the back door. By then I was nearly panting with fear of being caught. Mother would kill me for sure if she knew I was sneaking out to meet Daniel. I softly closed the back door and the screen door without making a sound.

Standing on the top step, I said to myself, "Where is he?" Then in the driveway, I saw a light come on inside Daniel's light blue, 1958 Chevrolet. What a wonderful sight. I ran over to the car and Daniel opened the door just as my hand reach for the door handle. Getting into the car I felt embraced by the feeling of safety. Daniel had the radio on and "Catch a Falling Star" was being sung by Perry Como. We didn't listen to White music too often, but that one was nice. We held on to each other tightly; a crowbar could not have separated us.

"Daniel, I need you. I need you to take me away," I said urgently and then began telling him all the gory details of what had happened to me the night Mother had flipped out and how sorry I was. "It was all my fault," I said.

"No, it was not your fault, Little Mary. Oh, how I wish you were older; then we could run away and get married. I should be able to protect you," and I saw there were tears in his eyes.

Putting my hands on his face, I held it very close, kissing him on the cheeks and softly on his lips. "Please, Daniel, its okay. I'm okay. We can run away now!" I knew I would go with him anywhere and that as long as we were together, everything would be all right.

"Little Mary," Daniel said very seriously as he removed my hands from his face and put a little distance between us. Suddenly, to me the atmosphere in the car seemed to cool and a sense of "something not right" was in his voice. With his head held down, he struggled for words. My fear was that Mother had cursed him out and forbidden him from seeing me. He leaned over and turned off the radio but when I tried to pull him close, he pulled away.

"Little Mary, I have to tell you something, and I want you to know how sorry I am. I would never hurt you intentionally. You have to know that I would never hurt you on purpose."

My heart began to slow down and it seemed I could hardly breathe. I knew I did not want to hear what he had to say but told him, "Daniel, it's okay. We love each other. Nothing or nobody can stop that." I was trying to have enough strength for the both of us.

"Little Mary..." With tears in his eyes, his nose started running and I fumbled around my pockets looking for a Kleenex.

"I have a handkerchief," he mumbled as he reached in his back pocket. "Little Mary..."

"Stop calling me Little Mary. Tell me what's going on, Daniel. What is wrong?" I demanded because I was getting frustrated.

"Men have needs, you know that."

"Yes, I know that. So what are you saying, Daniel?"

"I have been having sex with a girl that graduated with me. We have been sleeping together for the past six months."

My heart stopped. I swear I heard the last beat! "Daniel, why? Why? You said you loved me. You said how we would make love. How could you do this to me?" I was crying and the sound of my crying was deafening to me. Then I was lost for words. All my dreams had just evaporated in front of my face and I now felt I didn't have anything to live for, and I wanted to die. I actually pictured in my mind the casket closed and my body buried in the dirt. I was devastated. My life was over and there I was alone again, with nothing to hold on to.

He tried pulling my face towards him to kiss my tears as he said, "Little Mary, I'm so sorry. I never meant to hurt you, but she was easy. It was just sex, not love."

"Daniel, why not me, why didn't you have sex with me?"

"You're too young, Little Mary. I respect you too much. You're not that kind of girl."

He was right about that; I had been saving myself for him, and only him. I loved him so much I probably would have had sex with him if he had only tried. As I held him I thought, *I can forgive this. I love him.*

"Little Mary..." Daniel was still struggling for his words, and I sensed there was more and sure enough there was when he said, "She's pregnant."

My mouth dropped open and I had trouble breathing. I felt as if he had stuck a knife in my heart, as I said, "No. No. Pregnant. Pregnant." I must have kept repeating the word, hoping I had heard him wrong.

"I'm sorry," he was crying, and I was crying, "I'm sorry, Little Mary. I love you. Please forgive me."

"Sorry? You're sorry?" I said angrily. "Daniel, how could you do this?" If I could have climbed into a dark hole, the darkness was nothing compared to my feelings at that moment.

Daniel went on, giving me the details of how many months pregnant she was, and now that he was going to be a Father, his parents were making him marry her.

Numbly I sat in his car, unable to speak. The shock was more than my heart could handle and as the reality of what he had just said hit me, all I could think was, *Now, too, even Daniel has betrayed me and is going to marry someone else.* The pain was so tremendous I thought I would be sick.

Daniel kept saying, "I love you, Little Mary. I'm sorry. If I don't marry her, my family will disown me."

At a loss for words all I could say was, "I understand," when actually I didn't.

Nothing in my life mattered anymore. Before that night, every breath I took had been with the hope that Daniel would someday take me away, love me, and protect me. It had always been my dream that he would keep me from harm. That night, my dream had forever been shattered.

I don't remember walking back into the house or up to my bedroom. What I do remember was just lying on my bed, staring unseeingly up at the ceiling and wishing I could die. Something had truly died inside me that night—my will to live.

14

MOTHER INFORMED ME THAT OUR MOVE TO MISSISSIPPI might just be a temporary one—just for the Fall semester. She wasn't sure she really wanted to live back there again, but I knew Mother; she changed her mind as often and as easily as she changed clothes.

That drive back to Mississippi was far worse than living in the house with Tom and Mother. They had gotten married just before the trip, but that hadn't changed their relationship. The car became a prison for me as I was trapped in the back seat while they argued the whole trip. In order to avoid any possible conversation with them I had decided to sleep as much as possible, but the closer we got to our destination the more anxious I became and couldn't wait to get out of the car whenever possible. We had stopped often to get food and drinks, and for Mother to use the restroom at just about every truck stop. Tom complained of how frequent she had to go, but what did he expect - she was drinking beer while he drove.

One time when the car was going at a good speed and we were making nice progress, Mother suddenly yelled, "Pull over! I have to go!"

Tom had been getting more and more upset with her needing to stop so often and responded, "You'll have to wait till we get to a truck stop or gas station."

"Stop now!" she demanded.

"There's a gas station a few miles ahead. Just cross your legs," he retorted.

As usual, whenever her will was threatened, Mother became verbally abusive and called him every name she could think of. But this time Tom did not react and just kept driving. Soon I heard him say, "There, it's over to the right."

I had been lying on the back seat and so decided to go with her as it had been hours since I had last gone. When I sat up and looked around to see where we were, my worst fears of the South became a reality. Tom had pulled the car up to the gas pump, and on the front of the service station there was a big sign that read, "Clean Restrooms" and another smaller one that said, "Whites only."

Mother got out of the car and said, "Come on, Little Mary."

"I'll hold it," I said because I was too afraid.

"Come, on, there's a restroom around the side we can use."

I followed her around the corner of the service station, my eyes moving back and forth as I looked at my surroundings, feeling tense. Sure enough she knew exactly where to go.

"There's the restroom for us," Mother said as she pointed to a sign on a door, only there was no closed door. It was open and a huge sign read **"Colored"** in big bold letters.

I thought that was awful and did not want to go in. There was a smell that made me hold my nose and only one toilet for both men and women and flies were buzzing around. It was not only disgusting, but also unsanitary.

"Oh, Mother, I can't go now," I said and headed back to the car, sickened by the reality I had just seen.

At the car a White man was pumping the gas for Tom and looking at him with resentment. When the attendant saw me, his eyes fixed on my face and then he looked at Tom and then back at me.

Tom quietly said, "Little Mary, get in the car." I didn't question him and did as I was told.

Tom paid for the gas, and Mother came from around the side of the station walking gracefully. I watched her come toward the car with her head held high, all dignity, no matter what the circumstance. She feared no one.

Tom drove off with a sigh of relief—in fact we were all relieved. Mother laughed aloud, and then Tom began to laugh.

"What's so funny?" I asked because I was not amused; I hated what had just happened.

"This is the South, Little Mary," Mother informed.

"I don't like it already." I deliberately was being nasty, but I meant it. "Tom, why was that man looking at us so funny?"

"Little Mary, look in the mirror."

I sat up and leaned to the front, looking in the rear view mirror. "Okay."

"What do you see?" Tom was getting on my nerves; I just wanted him to get to the point.

"I see me! So what are you saying?"

"Look at me, Little Mary, then look back in the mirror again."

I went along with it. "I still see me."

"Yeah, and you look White! You could pass for White."

"No I don't! Why do you say that?" He had really ticked me off besides hurting my feelings. I didn't want to look White. I was a Negro, not White. White people hated me because I was a Negro; at least that is what Mother had told me often enough. The news reporters also had told me that.

Tom laughed because I was upset. "Girl, look in the mirror again. You know you're Negro, but when White people look at you, they see a White girl." It seemed he was enjoying telling me how White I was.

"Look, there is no mistake when they look at me. I'm Black, that's what they see. But you and your Mother, well, all they see is White."

Mother said, "Yeah, he's right, so we can use that for our benefit."

Why did I have to look White? I was a Negro, and proud of it. I sat back in the seat with nothing else to say. Right then I hated everything and everybody; my world had been turned inside and out. I was tired of living and all I wanted was to escape into sleep.

I lay down in the back and thought and thought. I could not stop thinking about Ilona, the Photographer, Mute, Daniel, and the man I had stabbed. Also, I thought about Reverend Miles who liked young boys and what a phony he was by always telling people about God, and here he was a sicko monster.

I remembered back a few years to a time when Ilona had been angry with me, and I didn't know why. We had gone shopping at the May Co. Department Store located at the corner of Crenshaw and Santa Barbara Blvd, where a White lady had made the remark, "How nice to see a Negro girl taking care of a little White girl." Ilona had grabbed me by the arm and we left the store in a hurry. After that Ilona did not speak to me for weeks and wouldn't let me go anywhere with her. At that time I had not understood her reaction, but now I did. I looked White and she didn't. We were different colors and she resented me for that, as if I had a choice.

Suddenly, it registered in my mind that I was different. I really did look White but on the inside I was a Negro. People did not see me as I saw myself. As I listened to Tom, I became more and more miserable as he went on and on about how he could be lynched for just being with us.

As our trip continued on and on, it became almost unbearable for me. Tom talked so much I wanted to scream. Even while Mother slept Tom talked to her as she snored. Also he kept turning on the radio because he was looking for a station that didn't sound like hillbilly stuff. He'd grumble, "Got to have soul music in the South."

Suddenly I heard something I liked and said, "There, leave it there, Tom, please." It was the first time I heard Mahalia Jackson singing, "How Great Thou Art." It was the sound of heaven and the hairs on my arms stood straight up. When she hit a high note I got chills and all my anxieties seemed to disappear, and I had tears of joy in my eyes. One thing I knew, if there really was a God, then Mahalia Jackson knew Him.

Her singing had not touched Tom as I had been, and he quickly turned the station again. "I'm looking for some soul music, not gospel," he grumbled.

Sam Cooke came on and that made Tom happy for the moment, but when James Brown followed, (he screamed when he sang) he made us move to the beat.

I saw Tom frequently looking in the rear-view mirror, watching for Whitey—that's what he called the police.

"Little Mary, we're almost there,"

Thank goodness, I thought. *One more day in this tomb with him and Mother and I would hold my breath till I died. Mother's snoring may not bother Tom, but it bothered me.*

After the song Tom casually mentioned, "You know your Mother knows Sam Cooke."

"No, I didn't know that. Why haven't I met him yet?"

"You will." Tom was proud he knew something I didn't.

I was deep into my own thoughts, when the song, "For Your Precious Love," sung by Jerry Butler and the Impressions, interrupted my train of thought. That had been Daniel's and my song and the words were branded on my heart. "I would do anything for your love…" The words filled my eyes with tears but I managed to say, "Turn up the volume, please."

Tom asked, "Feeling lonely for Daniel?" as he turned the volume up a little. "He's got someone else I hear." There was pleasure in his voice and it was then that I realized he had known before I did that Daniel had gotten a girl pregnant, and was being forced to marry her.

I ignored his comment because I didn't want to give him the satisfaction of knowing that he had hurt me.

"Did you tell him about that night?"

"It's none of your business, Tom. It's over between us, and that's that."

Tom had a grin on his face and if I had been a man, I think I would have punched him. *Why did he keep reminding me of that night? It wasn't a secret anymore. I hadn't killed the man; I don't think, he had tried to kill me.*

I listened to the last of the song and silently cried to myself. I had not only lost Daniel, but also everything besides and I hurt more than words could say.

Just then Mother awoke and asked, "When will we be there?" Obviously she, too, was tired of the car. "I'm hungry."

"Almost there, Baby. Hold on, we'll be at your sister's in another hour, no more."

Petulantly she insisted, "I want something to eat now. I can't wait that long. If I do I'll get sick. Stop at the first restaurant you see."

"Big Mary, this is a White area. We can't stop. I don't want to go through another situation like at the service station."

"Oh, stop at the restaurant coming up," she demanded. She was frustrated with Tom being afraid. Then she shocked me when she said, "Little Mary, you can go in and get the food."

"What? Why me?"

"Because I said so! Tom can't and I don't feel good. I'll write down what we want and you just give it to the person at the counter."

"I'm not pulling up there, Big Mary. They're going to think I'm with a White woman," Tom stated.

"Then pull around the corner, Tom. Little Mary can run around from there and no one will see her with either you or me, and they won't know she's Negro."

"I don't want to go in there. They'll know I'm Colored," I replied nervously. I remembered how the service station man had looked at us.

"Go on, here's what I want," Mother insisted.

I took the note, and money out of her hand and got out of the car. I looked around to see if anyone was watching us.

They weren't, so I walked around the corner of the building holding my breath and my hands trembling. *Would these people really hurt me because I was Negro? I'll just give them the note, pay for the food, get out of there, and all will be okay.*

Slowly I walked through the doorway and tried to act normal. The first thing I saw was a sign above the counter that said, "Whites Served Only." Thinking of my Mother, I held my head high and walked over to the counter where I handed the note to the lady standing there. She was wearing a pink, low-cut dress that showed her cleavage, with a little white apron.

Looking at me curiously, she asked, "You new around here, honey?"

I just looked at her. The words would not come out of my mouth because I was afraid to talk. The only White people I had known had been teachers at school and I had never been afraid of them. But this was different, this was the South and their hate was out in the open.

"My family, we're just passing through." My voice had trembled and I thought for sure she could see right through me.

She looked at the note and said, "This gonna take a few minutes. Ya'll sit over there."

Then turning in the direction of the kitchen, she yelled out, "Three ham

87

sandwiches to go!"

Looking into the faces of those sitting and eating, I stood there patiently and thought, *If they knew I was colored, they would run me right out of here. But they don't know.* Then I sat down at a table as if I were one of them. With a smirk on my face, I thought to myself, *I have fooled these White folks!*

When I walked out of there with the food and my back to the restaurant, I wore a big smile as I had just pulled the wool over their eyes.

As we continued to drive and eat our sandwiches, we all laughed when I shared how I froze when the lady had asked me if I was new in town. I mimicked her Southern drawl and it felt good to know that she had no idea she had served a Negro. The joke was on her.

Then, in a quiet moment in the back seat, I felt uneasy about having fooled someone and having deliberately pretended to be someone I was not. I wondered, *Was that the right thing to do? Pretend to be White in order to get service at a restaurant? If the White man didn't want me in his place, why should I go?* There were so many things I did not understand.

15

MY AUNT NORMA LEE AND HER HUSBAND JOHN WERE waiting on their front porch when we arrived at their home. I don't know what I had expected, but when I looked at their house I was truly amazed at how big it was.

Aunt Norma Lee ran to me with open arms and as she hugged me said,

"Darlin', my Little Darlin', you jest as pretty as your Mom." I liked her drawl because it made her words sing with feeling.

My Mother and aunt Norma Lee did not look alike, or even sound alike. Mother's diction was perfect and she did not have a Southern accent. But one thing they did have in common were their eyebrows—they didn't have any. They just used an eye pencil and drew them on.

Not knowing these people made me feel a little awkward at first. I had never met my aunt but she radiated so much warmth and passion, that I knew I loved her at first sight.

All of a sudden, children came running out of the house and over the steps—all ages, from sixteen-years old to six. The strange thing was, they were all different colors, just like my sisters and brothers. They were all talking at the same time, excited about us arriving, and I began to relax and fell right in with answering their questions.

"How old are you?" "What is Los Angeles like?" "Are the schools really mixed?"

I thought I was a celebrity with all the attention. They seemed to look up to me as I had lived in a place where I was free to go and come as I pleased. I could eat at any restaurant, or go to a movie and not have to sit only in the balcony. Also, I had the liberty of riding a bus and being able to sit in a front seat. I could go downtown in Los Angeles. to shop, and go into any store without fear. All the things I had taken for granted, were privileges my cousins had not known.

The excitement of the day wore down as my cousins and I sat on the front porch talking. The tension of the past three days in the car faded with the sunset. Comparing our lives was informative. I had so much to be grateful for, living in a place where I was not judged by my race, at least to my knowledge. I had not witnessed the discrimination in California or at least to me it had not been as apparent as in the South. However, I had heard that it would surface its ugly face sometimes when Blacks applied for quality jobs, or for a loan to buy a home, or if they wanted to buy a home in an all-White neighborhood.

The next day I awoke hearing a child crying. I had tossed and turned all night because being in a new place, it would take a little time to get adjusted. I had to share a room with my cousin Etta May, who was as fair-skinned as I. She had already gone downstairs and I was going to be labeled as being lazy if I didn't hurry.

I rushed around trying to find my clothing and personal items, feeling the urgency to hurry.

The kitchen was huge, and there sat Etta May and her little sister, who was still crying.

"Sorry I overslept."

"That's okay. I have to see to it that Little Sister eats her breakfast." Etta May called her little sister, "Little Sister."

I thought that was odd and asked, "What's her name?"

"Mary Jane. But she likes to be called Little Sister."

"What do I call her?"

"Little Sister," she said as though I had asked a dumb question.

"But she's not my sister."

"No matter. She only answers to Little Sister." She sounded a little annoyed.

"Okay," I said, feeling stupid. "I'll call her Little Sister." That ended that conversation.

Etta May spent the whole day showing me around the big house and the Mortuary, introducing me to all my relatives. The huge plantation-style home was two-stories high, with four bedrooms, three bathrooms, and a large kitchen and dining room. I found that I was related to everyone in the neighborhood. It seemed as if everyone I met was an uncle, aunt or cousin. In order to not go crazy remembering names, I called all the adults either auntie or uncle, without using a first name.

I noticed right away that there was a difference between my cousins and me. They talked differently, and walked slower than normal, whereas

I walked fast. I was always in a hurry. Nothing appeared to be important enough for them to rush.

The big house was directly behind the J. T. Stone Mortuary, located on the corner of Texas Ave. I had no memory of Mississippi, so it was like my first visit. Etta May took me on a tour of the Funeral Home and there I felt like I belonged.

Visiting the Embalming Room, I met a man named uncle Bud. He was not my uncle, but I was told that if I did not refer to him as uncle, his feelings would be hurt. Uncle Bud looked older than dirt with his big belly and toothless smile. He moved like a turtle and talked even slower. His strong face portrayed all the wisdom and knowledge of the past.

I heard that he loved to talk about the past and he was willing to talk, if you had the time to listen. I wanted to sit on his lap but there was not much room to sit, so I pulled up a chair and prepared to spend the whole day listening to him.

Uncle Bud had all the history I wanted to hear. He had known J. T. Stone, my grandfather, all his life.

Each day there was a new lesson in life and death. I spent most of my days listening to uncle Bud. His stories of the past fascinated me. I listened and soaked up the information like a sponge taking it all in, listening for any similarities that we might have. He had the strength and courage to live and raise his family, with so many obstacles to overcome.

Uncle Bud started with the story of how my grandfather, J. T. Stone, had been reared as a White man, finding later as a young adult that he was not all White.

I had to be patient to hear the whole story.

16

I WAS GLAD WHEN I SAW UNCLE BUD REACH INTO HIS pocket, pull out his teeth and put them in his mouth, because that meant he was going to tell us a story. We went out on the front porch, where he sat most of the time, if he was not in the Embalming Room. The porch ran the whole length of the front of the Funeral Home and had a long bench for sitting, and a big rocking chair for uncle Bud. The day was pretty, neither too hot nor too cold, and a certain calmness hung in the air. The weeping willows stood tall and still.

As we walked to join uncle Bud, Etta May and I chattered and laughed about the White lady in the restaurant, and how I had been amazed she had not known that I was a Negro. Hearing this uncle Bud nodded his head in agreement and said, "Your aunt Sadie passes for White now and don't have much to do with us. She lives in New York."

I had not ever met aunt Sadie, and from what I had heard, wasn't sure I wanted to. Uncle Bud talked so slowly, with his Southern drawl, he had my total attention. I didn't have to ask him to repeat himself.

Getting comfortable in his big chair, he leaned back and said,

"Did you know that J. T. Stone was a real patriarch? Yes, he was, and your grandmother Nellie, she was a matriarch. Yes. They were somethin'." Uncle Bud shook his head in adoration, praising my grandparents, who I had never met.

I knew this was going to be a long story, so I sat on the steps and leaned my back against a post. As I glanced at the street, I couldn't help but notice that the traffic on the street moved slower, nothing like the traffic in Los Angeles. Here, people seemed unconcerned, as though they moved to a different clock.

"Come on, uncle Bud, why was my grandfather raised White?" My curiosity was at its peak, and I was getting impatient.

"Little Mary, didn't Big Mary tell you the story?"

"She told me a little, but never the whole story. I have heard a lot about grandfather but nothing of grandmother. Why is that? You say she was a matriarch, or something like that."

"She was! She was the light of his life, Little Mary. Oh, how J. T. loved his Nellie. She worked with him, shared his dreams and ideas, which were founded on Christian beliefs. Your grandfather became an Ordained Minister. Did you know that?" There was compassion in uncle Bud's voice, and I could tell he had loved grandfather like a brother.

"No. I didn't. But I knew he was a Preacher." I wasn't sure if that was the same thing. "Tell me more," I begged because I wanted to hear more and more.

"Did you know that your grandparents died seven days apart? They just couldn't live without each other. Yeah, that was a sad time for all of us. J. T. really lost something after Nathan was murdered. He was never the same."

"I know that part uncle Bud, but that's about all I really know. Mother only tells me what she wants me to know." I felt strange telling him that, but it was the truth.

"This is the story," he said, letting me know he shared only one story at a time.

"Well, your grandfather was born in a rich family in Louisiana. The plantation belonged to Mr. James Morris and his brother Tom. They was rich White boys, they was. James Morris was a married man at the time and wanted children real bad.

There was a pretty little servant girl and James visited her a lot, but what he didn't know was that his brother, Tom, was also visiting her. Well, strange as it may be, Mrs. Morris became pregnant and around the same time, so did the little servant girl. Somehow, James found out about his brother Tom and the servant girl, and it started a big mess between the two. Yes, it did."

I sat holding my hands, twisting my fingers back and forth, just hanging onto each word and eager for his next words. Then uncle Bud stopped talking, like he had forgotten the next word he wanted to say.

"Uncle Bud. Then what?" I asked, trying to help him move on.

"Oh. Where was I?" The look in his eyes said his mind had gone somewhere else.

"You said Mr. Morris had found out about his brother Tom sleeping with the servant girl. You said it was a big mess. So what happened?"

He moved his mouth around, pushed his teeth back in place, and then started again "Oh, yeah. Well, James was so upset with his brother that they fell out for awhile, 'cause Tom said the servant girl was pregnant by him and James was sure it was his. They didn't know whose it was and that was the problem."

"That's awful," I said, shocked. I had never heard that story.

"Little Mary, the two brothers fought all the time, and when the baby came it was a boy, and he looked White. To add coal to the fire, Mrs. Morris had her baby a week later, and it was a girl. Well, James was happy, but a boy-child would have been better to his way of thinking.

"Anyway, the two brothers could not come to an agreement and they really had no way of knowing which of them was the baby's real daddy. Every day they argued. Finally, after weeks of quarreling, James said, 'Tom there is no way we can tell by looking at this boy whose child he is. Let's say he is both ours and call him J. for James and T. for Tom and we'll call him J. T. Morris.'

Most of the people were shocked over the fuss; after all, he was the child of a servant girl. But he *was* a boy, and that is what James Morris had wanted, and he *was* White. Tom was angry, but what other solution was there? He agreed to the name, but later left the plantation for good. The brothers never were able to reconcile their relationship.

"Mrs. Morris knew how much her husband had wanted a boy and decided to take the child and raise him as her own. After all, he was as White as any White child could be. The servant girl remained a servant; only now, she moved up to the big house and became J. T.'s Nanny. They threatened her that if she ever told she was his real Mother, she would be hung."

The look on my face must have reflected my feelings and uncle Bud said, "Little Mary, it sounds like a sad story but Mrs. Morris really loved J. T., and reared him as if he were her own child."

Uncle Bud looked at his pocket watch and announced, "It's four o'clock. You better go now, and I'll tell you the rest another day."

I hadn't wanted to leave because I wanted to hear the rest of the story real bad. But what I had learned so far about uncle Bud was that things would come to me in bits and pieces. When I looked in his eyes, I could tell he was real tired. Talking and telling the stories seemed to have drained him of what little energy he had. I surely hadn't wanted to drain him or cause him to move any slower so I said, "Uncle Bud, I'll come back tomorrow. Okay?"

"Okay, Little Mary."

I really had liked being around uncle Bud because there was a sense of security, as if he were the grandfather I never knew. As I walked down the steps, I looked back at uncle Bud, now taking a nap where he sat.

Mary Ross Smith

I was learning about my roots and I wanted to understand my Mother's roots; who she was, and who was I?

17

ETTA MAE HAD BEEN READY TO LEAVE BEFORE UNCLE Bud had even looked at his watch. After all, she'd heard his stories hundreds of times, whereas I was anxious to hear everything.

We started out walking slowly, but as we got closer to the house Etta Mae began walking briskly. I knew it was close to dinnertime and I asked, "What's the hurry?"

"It's my turn to help with the dinner, and I'm late."

I had forgotten what it was like to sit down at a table and eat dinner with family. When my Dad had been home, we had eaten many meals together as a family but now Mother only cooked when she felt like it, or on Christmas when J. T., Ilona, Lenore and I, all helped in the kitchen. Actually, we did all the work and Mother took the credit.

After the family split up, our refrigerator was only filled with Budweiser beer. The majority of the time I had eaten at school. It usually was a Snickers Bar for breakfast, but I would have gladly traded it for eggs and bacon.

Then, at my aunt's house each day, I found a full-course meal ready for everyone at dinnertime. Never before had I seen so much food on a table, except at Christmas. There were collard greens, black-eyed peas with rice, yams, cornbread, potato salad, ham and chicken. To me it looked like a feast fit for a king. Also, we sat down at the table together, like real family.

When aunt Norma Lee started blessing the food, I wondered if she had forgotten that she was at the kitchen table, not at church. She could pray like a Baptist Preacher and many of her prayers went on for over five minutes.

More than once Little Sister had fallen asleep at the table. I would hold my head down with my eyes only half-closed as I watched the food, and prayed she would stop and say, "Let's eat." It was wonderful with the family all together, laughing, talking about things that had happened that day. It made me ask, *Why couldn't I have a family like that?*

Table conversation usually centered on the Funeral Home, school and friends. Even though I was an outsider, I had loved every minute of the family connection. It was obvious my aunt loved her family and that is what kept them together. If they fought, she made them make up before they went to bed. Her theory was, "Never go to bed angry." Many times I can remember hearing her remind someone that it was written in the Bible.

One night, halfway through our dinner, Tom started arguing with Mother over what, no one knows. It was just their way. Aunt Norma Lee had tried to calm them down but finally the kids were told to go to their rooms. Quietly I finished my meal and then went to Etta May's room.

"Lil Mary, are they still fussing down there?" Etta May asked.

"Yes, they are." I was disgusted and it showed.

"How can you stand it?"

"I hate it, but what can I do?"

Her concern was sincere, but Tom and Mother argued all the time. Sometimes they would fight but that night it was just arguing, for which I was grateful. I had realized that Etta May had been trying not to show that she felt sorry for me.

"Are you going to go to school here?"

"I guess I will, but Mother hasn't said anything. She doesn't care if I go or not."

"Well, my mom will make you go," she said as if she were sure about it.

"I'll wait and see and if I have to, then so be it." I had been flip with her because I really was afraid to go to a new school but dared not tell her. You see, Mother had taught me not to ever let anyone know when you are afraid, or they will take advantage of you.

That night I lay in the bed, listening to every noise of the old house, wishing I were back in Los Angeles with Ilona.

Aunt Norma Lee came into the bedroom around six in the morning and with a smile said, "Wake up, y'all. It's time to get up."

I tossed around and thought, *Why do I have to get up? I don't go to school, yet.*

"Come on Little Darlin'. You goin' to get registered today." She was all cheery. *How could anyone be that happy at six o'clock in the morning?*

"Is Mother going with me?" I asked, rubbing my eyes, trying to focus on the cheery voice.

"No. Etta May will take you with her and if she needs me, I'll come up there."

"Aunt Norma Lee, what time do you get up?" I was curious and wondered if maybe she hadn't been to bed yet.

"Darlin', I'm up at five, every mornin'. I go to my prayer closet and meet with the Lord. Yes, I do, Darlin'. I meet him every mornin'."

I thought she was going to preach again, and she did. Southern folks seemed to repeat themselves a lot.

Etta May and I walked to school. She was so sweet that I really liked being with her and felt maybe things would be okay. When I walked up the steps at the front of the school, I felt like an unwanted stranger. Kids stopped and stared at me as if I were an alien.

I asked, "Etta May, why are they staring at me?"

"They'll get used to you. They not sure if you White or not."

"Oh, come on, Etta May. They know I'm Colored. No Whites go to this school."

"They don't know. I'm serious; they don't know Lil Mary. I grew up with most of them, but you Whiter than me."

My heart was pounding so hard I thought it could be heard. I walked with my head up. That was another thing my Mother had taught me—walk tall.

After getting registered I was sent to a classroom, and Etta May went another way. Holding my breath without showing any signs of being different, alone and afraid, I walked in with thirty eyes watching my every step. I sat down at the first open seat and let out a silent sigh.

The teacher began, "Oh, we have a new student."

It had to be me. I slid down a bit in my seat in the hope she would not call on me to introduce myself. That's what they did at church and I hated it.

"Miss Reese. Stand up, please," she said politely. "Tell us a little about yourself."

Standing there, I knew it better be good or I'd never live it down. "My name is Mary Eliza Reese, Jr." Some of the kids laughed when they heard "Jr". Evidently they had never heard of a girl being named Jr. Proudly, once again I repeated, "My name is Mary Eliza Reese, Jr...." I paused to see if they would laugh again. "I was born here, but up till now, I have lived in Los Angeles, California, where people are free." With pride in my voice, I looked around the room to see their reaction.

The teacher had lost her smile but politely said, "Okay, Miss Reese. We are all free."

Not wanting to be disrespectful to her, I answered, "I understand we are free, but my meaning is that there are no signs in Los Angeles that read "White Only" or fountains that say "Colored."

"I understand what you're saying, Miss Reese. Thank you. You can sit down."

The classroom was silent, and I knew I had given them something to think about. The three o'clock bell rang and I wanted to run home. I was so tired of being stared at. *Why was I so different? So I was light-skinned. So what?*

Etta May and I were laughing about my first day in school and walking slowly when several girls approached us. One of the girls, with ten braids in her hair, came directly in front of us.

"Etta May, is this really your cousin?"

"Yeah. She is!" Etta May knew they wanted to make trouble and I knew there was going to be a fight. My first day at a new school and I would have to fight. Although I was frightened on the inside, I wasn't about to let them know.

Etta May explained, "She's from L.A., and they don't play there. So don't start nothin'."

I wasn't sure what she meant, but it made the girls think for a minute. "So, what's that mean, Etta May?" I quietly asked. The girl had a serious attitude problem and I knew she was looking for a fight.

"It means you stabbed a man. You's tough."

My heart stopped. *How did she know? I had not told her. She made it sound like it was something to be proud of but I was not proud of what had happened.*

"Tell her to stay away from our guys!" one girl yelled, as though I knew what she was talking about.

"She don' want your man!" Etta May was doing all the talking for me, while I stood there ready to fight. But my cousin was not going to let that happen, not that day, anyway.

The first girl said, "We don't want her here!" and held her mouth tight. If looks could kill, I would have been dead in a flat second.

"She not messing with you. Get out of here!" Etta May flung back and I could tell she was getting angry, and now she was ready to fight.

The girls could see we were not backing down and then one of the meanest looking girls I had ever seen said, "You ain't nothin' but a Yella' Nigger, and we don't like Yella' Niggers, so you better stay out of our way." Then she and her friends turned and walked away.

I exhaled in relief but my ears rang with the term, "Yellow Nigger." The words hurt so much I wanted to cry, but not in front of Etta May.

"Come on." said Etta May as she touched my arm. I jumped.

The last time I had been called a Yellow Nigger it had been by the man I had stabbed. Not only did he call me bitch throughout the ordeal he said "You a Yellow Nigga, huh,!" His words were imbedded into my mind and

I shivered at the memory. Again I had been called a Yellow Nigger, and I didn't like it. I hated being there. I hated being in Mississippi.

There was no conversation on my part as we walked home. Etta May kept telling me not to be upset and that they were jealous because the boys would like me. But I didn't want anyone to be jealous. I just wanted to be liked for me. I didn't understand why the color of ones skin was such a big issue in the south or why color between colored folks also was a problem. I remembered that Mother had told me once, that the Whites would not accept me once they found out I was Black, and the Blacks wouldn't want me because I looked White.

So, where does a person like me belong? The thoughts in my head said loudly, *You belong dead. That's where there is peace.*

Each day at school was a hassle. Some days I had no choice but to fight to defend myself. I pleaded with Mother to take me back to Los Angeles, but she was not ready to go. Many days I skipped school and hung out in the Embalming Room with Mr. Lary, the new Embalmer.

18

MR. LARY LOOKED AS IF HE HAD ALREADY BEEN embalmed and had a personality that was as dry as his looks. He was a single man, about forty- years old and after spending time watching him work, I knew why he didn't have either a wife or girlfriend. Every day Mr. Lary would go to work and keep to himself but he actually seemed to enjoy my keeping him company, watching him embalm. Sometimes I would tell him different things, and he was amazed that I knew so much. Sometimes I helped Mr. Lary with the hair and make-up when there were too many bodies for him to handle.

Aunt Norma Lee thought Mr. Lary was doing a great job and said, "He sure keeps that Embalmin' Room in order and the make-up on the bodies really makes them look natural—peaceful like." She had no idea it was my helping Mr. Lary that did it.

I told Mr. Lary jokes that Mr. Holmes and I had laughed about, until tears fell from our eyes. He would tell me great stories of how in the old days they kept the bodies from stinking. It used to be that friends prepared the deceased for burial. They would bathe and dress the body and then lay it on an ironing board, with a quarter placed on each eye, to keep the lids closed. Sometimes a saucer containing salt was placed on the chest to absorb or prevent undesirable odors, and the body would remain on the ironing board until placed in a coffin.

He also told me there had been many superstitions surrounding death in those days. How salt was also considered a deterrent for evil spirits, and the water and other items used for bathing the body could not be removed from the house before the burial, or bad luck would befall the family.

I found out that Mr. Lary had been embalming for over ten years and actually enjoyed his work. With a twinkle in his eye he once told me, "My customers never complain."

We listened to each other and I learned from him, and he learned from me. All the little bits of advice I had learned from Ima I passed on to him. When he told me I was his friend and that he was now a better embalmer because of it, I was more than pleased.

It may seem strange, but I actually looked forward to spending time with Mr. Lary. He didn't care about where I had come from, or where I was going, or what color my skin was. He really cared about his work, and I was comfortable and at ease with him.

It was hard to get Mr. Lary to show any facial expressions, so I spent time thinking of things to do to make him laugh, but it was work. One Monday morning I went into the Embalming Room before Mr. Lary arrived for work, climbed on one of the slabs and pulled a sheet over my body and head. The sheet had some blood on it, but it was not near my face. I lay very still, listening for him to come in. Breathing as slowly and shallowly as possible so the sheet would not move, I waited patiently.

Soon I heard the door open, and I could hear Mr. Lary clearing his throat. I did not move. I could hear him near the sink and the water was running as he washed his hands. Clearing his throat again, he began to hum. I had never heard him do that before. Then I could tell he was standing near the slab that I was lying on and so, waiting for the right moment, I moved the sheet a little. Nothing happened. I thought he might not have seen it. Next, I could hear him putting the tools on the table next to the slab, but I could not contain myself any longer and I quickly sat up with the sheet still over my head. Suddenly, there was a crashing sound as the table and tools hit the floor and the next thing I heard was someone bursting through the door, knocking it off its hinges. I was stunned and pulled the sheet from my head and found I was alone in the Embalming Room.. It had been a joke, but Mr. Lary had run out before he knew it was me. Then I was faced with a dilemma, *Should I tell him what I had done or pretend I knew nothing had happened?* I didn't wait to decide but got out of there in a hurry.

* * *

It seemed as if Fall would never end. I had missed a lot of school, but it really didn't matter to Mother. When aunt Norma Lee found out that I was ditching school, she called for me to come to her prayer closet. It truly was a closet, with a dim light, a chair, three candles, and a huge picture of Jesus. She only lit the candles when she went in to pray.

"Come in Darlin'," she said.

I thought, *Please don't close the door.*

"Lil Mary, you know I love you. You know your Mother has problems, but you know I love her. God knows how much I love her. Big Mary always was a rebel. Our Daddy and Momma couldn't control her. When she was in school, she was rolling rosebuds and smoking them and drinkin' whatever she got her hands on. I promised our Daddy that I would look after her, but Lil Mary, you know your Momma gonna do what she wants. She's a real handful," she said, shaking her head in agreement with herself. "I tried talking to her about you, and you missin' school. I know you hang around the Embalming Room with Mr. Lary, but that's no place for a child."

I stood there in her closet, feeling sad that I had hurt her because I really loved her, and wished she had been my Mother.

"I asked Mary if you could stay with us and go to school here. I would take care of you, but Mary got upset sayin' I was tryin' to steal her child."

My mind was racing. As much as I loved aunt Norma Lee, I did not want to live in Mississippi. The last three months had seemed like an eternity. If it had not been for Mr. Lary, I would have gone crazy. I rarely had seen Mother except at dinnertime, and she had turned them into unhappy meals. The kids loved her but hurried to eat and go to their rooms to avoid the nightly arguments. My cousins and I had fun, but there was a difference between us and I never felt as if I truly belonged. I was happy to know Mother would not leave me.

"Aunt Norma Lee, what's going on? Is Mother going home?"

"Yes, and she's mad at me 'cause I tell her she needs to stop drinking and bein' so mean. Lil Mary, I heard about the things that happened to you."

I dropped my head in shame. Would she think I was a terrible person? That was how Etta May knew. Tom had to be the one that told them. "Aunt Norma Lee. It wasn't my fault. I didn't want him to kill me."

She stood up and put her arms around me and I buried my face on her shoulder and began to cry. She held me, not saying a word. The silence was deafening.

"I'm so sorry," I said.

"Darlin', you didn't do anything wrong. The Lord knows you better than you know yourself."

"Then, why isn't He there for me?"

"Don't be angry with God," she said.

"But I *am* angry."

"Lil Mary, God loves you."

"No! He doesn't! I don't believe that! He hates me, and I don't care! I can take care of myself. I don't need God!" Through the tears I knew that I was wrong, but it was the first time I could voice what was in my heart.

"Sit down, Lil Mary, now you listen to me, and listen good. God loves you. Never forget that. He knows everythin'…."

I cut her off. "Does he know about the photographer, about the dog 'Mute' and the man that tried to kill me?" I sobbed. Mute didn't do anything wrong, but he was beat to death for nothing. This was the first time I had said these things to anyone, except to the dead people.

"Little Mary, it breaks my heart to know what you have gone through. But God has a plan for you."

"Why can't I just lay down and die? I pray at night that I won't wake up in the morning. That's what I pray for, aunt Norma Lee." My heart was throbbing with pain.

"Oh, baby. You are loved, and I love you. Don't give up on life so early. There are wonderful people in this world, and there are bad people. You have had your share of trouble, but you have a light in you can't nobody put out. Things will get better, but don't go given up on God, 'cause he won't ever give up on you." I looked her in the eye, and I still wanted to die.

"Can I go now?" My heart could not take anymore and I wanted to be alone. She loved me, but she could not take away my pain.

"I'm prayin' for you, Lil Mary, every day. I love you and God loves you."

"Yeah, Yeah," I mumbled. I left feeling sorry for myself. I did not want to hurt my aunt, but she didn't understand what my life had been like, and she didn't have to live with Mother.

19

WHEN I LEFT AUNT NORMA LEE'S PRAYER CLOSEST, I headed for the Funeral Home. At least there I knew I could talk to one of the bodies and pretend I was going to be okay. The breeze felt cool on my face and I looked up at the sky, but I only saw gray. Uncle Bud was sitting on the porch, as usual, so I wiped my face not wanting him to know I had been crying.

"Hi, Lil Mary. I hear you guys goin' back to California."

"I haven't heard that," I said.

"Big Mary and Tom was in here earlier and said next week they goin' home."

"Is that a fact?" I replied.

I was actually relieved because I didn't want to go back to that school anyway, and I hated it that there were no places to go where I didn't see signs that read, "White Only." I hated that. Even when we went to a movie, we could only sit in the balcony. Stores downtown were off-limits and the one time I did go with my cousins, White kids in a car passing by hit me in the back with rotten eggs. The horrible smell stayed in my nostrils for days. Yes, I was happy to be leaving Mississippi.

When I walked into the Funeral Home, I went directly to the Viewing Room. The room was dimly lit and I immediately felt a sense of peace. There were no lace curtains like the Viewing Room at Hubert and Reese Mortuary, but the walls were a light pink and the caskets were always pretty.

In the Viewing Room were two bodies; two women, one in her eighties and the other no more than fifty. Standing between the two caskets, I started by saying, "I'm going home.

But you two ladies are already at home. You have no more sorrow.

107

You're at peace. I wish that I were with you. I envy you. I don't expect you to understand, but one day I'll be at peace, too." It was so wonderful to be able to say whatever I wanted and I would not get an argument from them. "I hate myself," I continued. "All this time here I have not really stopped thinking about Daniel. He is married, with a baby on the way. I loved him so much and thought he loved me. Why can't I forget him? Why hasn't Ilona come to get me to live with her like she promised? She now has a new baby girl and I'm sure she has forgotten all about me."

I reached over and touched the younger lady on the hand. She was so still; so empty looking. "I feel as empty as you look," I said, I stared at her as if it were the first time that I had seen a dead person. She was just a shell of a body, full of embalming fluid. "What am I going back to? That is my worry. I have as many fears of returning to Los Angeles as I did of coming here to Mississippi. I know I will have no one there who will love me, and I will be on my own because Mother is all about Mother, and I know she wants to get rid of me. You see, I am the last child at home and I know she can't wait to see me gone. I'm just too young to go anywhere."

When you snoop around listening to other people's conversations, you hear things you don't want to hear. Still resting my hand on the lady, I said, "I overheard my Mother telling Tom she'd be so happy when I left home. Where can I go at fourteen? I'm still in school, and Daniel has a wife." Tears ran down my face and dripped onto the satin comforter of the casket. "Oh, I'm sorry. I don't want to stain your resting place," I said as I gently wiped the damp spot on the satin that overhung the casket. I left the Viewing Room without saying good-bye, not sure of what would be next.

I found myself in the Embalming Room, not knowing that was where I was headed. I had just walked there. Feeling very low, I looked around at the walls, the slabs, and the instruments used to embalm or do an autopsy. I thought, *Do I want to be a mortician?* Grandfather had been so respected and loved by all. His dreams and values had been handed down to his children and these values placed heavy emphasis on the belief in God, honesty, integrity, truthfulness, and hard work.

His motto hung in the Preparation Room and was still enforced. It read, "***This body is dear and sacred to the family. Treat it always as if the family were present.***" I wrote it down to take with me so that I could put it in the Embalming Room at Hubert and Reese Mortuary. Now I was proud to know of my heritage.

The great J. T. Stone was my grandfather and that made me somebody special. I still had a lot to learn, but I had learned a lot in three months.

With not too much time left, I was determined that I would spend the next few days asking uncle Bud to tell me all the stories of grandfather that he knew, especially how grandfather had become a Mortician, then a Preacher.

20

THE NEXT MORNING I KNEW I WOULD FIND UNCLE BUD in his favorite spot, the front porch of the Funeral Home. With time running out, I was anxious to make sure I heard the rest of the story he had begun the other day. Uncle Bud was a good storyteller and it was a sure way to take my mind off of Daniel. I did not want to think about Daniel and his new wife. The thought of them together made me sick. Now my hopes and dreams were all gone and I felt my escape from Mother and her drunken friends also seemed hopeless. I had nowhere to go. I had no one to make my life bearable. The thought of death stayed on my mind and I thought of killing myself, but I was afraid of pain. So, I began planning that one day I would do it, without pain.

The traffic out front was slow as usual, and a little bit of a breeze caused the willow trees to sway slightly. The smell of Fall was still in the air and I could see uncle Bud was napping. It seemed to me that if he wasn't talking, then he was sleeping. Not wanting to startle him, I quietly walked up the few steps and touched his arm gently and asked, "Uncle Bud, are you asleep?"

"No girl. I just restin' my eyes."

"What's going on? Any funerals today?" I asked.

"Nah, business is slow this week. Nobody dyin'," he said, with a grin on his face. It was a natural comment for him to make, and it was as natural as saying, "Pass me the butter."

"Uncle Bud, tell me more about grandfather."

"Lil Mary, ain't your Momma tole you all this?"

"No. Mother doesn't have much time for me. She and Tom are always fighting and drinking."

"That's sad. You grandfather would not like that at all. He'd be on her like white-on-rice."

"I wish he were here," I sighed. My heart felt sad and the thought of someone caring what Mother did was simply amazing to me.

The receptionist who answered the phones for the Funeral Home opened the door onto the porch. She seemed surprised to see me.

"Lil Mary, I didn't know you were out here. You want some lemonade?"

"Oh, yes, please." They had the best lemonade in the world. Everything they made or cooked was the best in the world to me. She didn't ask uncle Bud if he wanted any. I thought that was strange, but in a few minutes she returned with two glasses full of ice and lemonade.

"Here, old man," she said as she handed him a glass and quickly went back inside.

"She in love with me," he said with self-assurance written on his face, holding the lemonade with one hand and pushing his teeth with the other hand.

I smiled at him, knowing this was an ongoing thing with the two of them. She was young enough to be his daughter, but she put a spark in his eye and that made him happy.

"You know, Little Mary, I'm just an old man now, but in my day I was somethin'."

"You somethin' now," I said, trying to be polite.

"Your granddaddy, now he was somethin'. He was a good man."

I was alert because I knew a story was coming and sat and waited patiently as uncle Bud drank his lemonade slowly, a little sip at a time. I had finished mine in two swallows.

"Where did I leave off, child?"

"You left off at grandfather being reared by Mr. and Mrs. Morris. They were rearing him as a White child."

"Oh, yeah. They really loved their daughter, but they worshiped their son.

J. T.'s birth was kept a secret. No one knew about the servant girl. She was his Nanny and that was that. They spoiled him, gave him everythin' he wanted and more. Sent him to an all-White school. Then he went off to college and had the best education money could buy. His whole world was White. J. T. was to be graduated at the top of his class, with honors and stuff. He was so smart.

"While still away at school, he had received a letter from his Mother, Mrs. Morris, tellin' him that his Nanny was dyin'.

Mrs. Morris knew how close he was to his Nanny and J. T. had kept in contact by writin' her often and lettin' her know how he was doin'. Although she could not read, someone read his letters to her and she cherished J. T.'s letters and kept them tied up under her pillow.

"The news saddened J. T. so that he just had to see his Nanny before she died. There was a strange connection between him and his Nanny. He just hadn't known how connected they were. His arrival home was welcomed, but grief filled the big house. Everyone loved Nanny. She was part of the house, a big part, and no one wanted to lose her.

"J. T. went in the front door and headed directly for Nanny's bedroom, which was off the kitchen. Entering the room, the smell of death was in the air and tears filled his eyes. His love for Nanny was deep and it was hard for him to imagine not having her around. The room was dim as he slowly came through the door. Several friends were standing around the room and her very close friend Jama, was sitting next to the bed holdin' her hand.

As J. T. walked towards her bed, Jamal moved aside for him to get close. Quietly, he sat down and picked up Nanna's frail hand. He had always called her Nanna. She had been rather sick for a long while but when J. T. left for college, it seemed her will to live went with him.

"J. T. leaned over and kissed Nanna on the forehead and said, 'Nanna. I'm here.

It's J. T. Nanna, it's me. Please open your eyes. Don't leave me, Nanna,' he whispered as he rubbed her hand with all the love in his heart. The room was quiet except for the sobs of those standing around. Then Nanna's chest began to move and her breathin' more rapid. Slowly her eyelids twitched and with all her strength, she opened her eyes to see her J. T.

"Jamal and the others were shocked to see her respondin' to J. T. Their smiles lifted the smell of death. They shook their heads with a constant humming and praising to the Lord. Whispers around the room were saying that it was amazin' the love these two shared.

"'Nanna is cheating death. Yes, she is y'all.' Jamal could not refrain from praisin' the Lord loudly. His tears were now tears of joy.

"In a weak and feeble voice, Nanna said, 'Please everyone leave the room. Everyone but J. T.' When J. T. and Nanna were alone, and thinking every breath would be her last, she could no longer keep the dark secret. 'I'm your Mother,' she tearfully explained. Then she told him that the Morris brothers had taken turns with her, and that he was half Negro and half White. In those days in the South if you had one-eighth Negro blood, you were Negro. She told him why they called him J. T. and even though he had never met Tom Morris, she said he could be his son.

She explained how the secret had been kept—her life had literally depended on it. Her love for him as his Nanny was the only way she could be with him. She told him not to hate the Morris's, that they had loved him, and given him a life that she never could.

"Now J. T.'s life had been turned upside down. In a few minutes his life had been changed, and he had to deal with the fact that he was now another person that he did not know—a Negro. Oh, he was upset somethin' terrible. He went crazy. He cursed his parents with all the fury of hell. How could they have done this? He had been living a life of lies. They had taught him to treat Negroes with dignity, and to be fair at all times to all men. But they had lied to him all of his life. They had threatened to kill his real Mother if she told the truth. J. T. was outraged at what he was hearing; his face went pale as he sat holding her hand with tears running down his face. The Morris's had taught him how to be a good person but there was nothing that had prepared him for this. She had to watch him grow up as a White- man's son, when he was her child. Now J. T. understood why he had felt a special bond with her all those years. His heart had told him at an early age there was somethin' special between them.

"J. T. made plans to move because he knew he wanted to get as far away from South Carolina as possible. He wanted to make a new start where no one knew of the Morris's or their Plantation. His plan was to take Nanna away and take care of her till she died. He knew that she did not have many years left, and he wanted to make it up to her. In his mind this was the right thing to do. He would not leave her behind.

"The Morris's were devastated, but knew that they had to let him go. J. T. was not stupid and accepted a large amount of his inheritance the Morris's gave him to start a new life. J. T. Stone left South Carolina with Nanna, and never looked back."

"Uncle Bud." I had to stop and ask a question. "Did he forgive the Morris's?"

"They say he did, but I don't know. Mrs. Morris died within a year of him leaving."

"What about Mr. Morris?" I asked.

"He died shortly after her. He drank himself to death, and nobody ever heard from Tom. It seems as if he had just disappeared off the face of the earth."

I felt bad for my grandfather. That had been a life-changing event and in the 1800's, it had to have been very hard to change from being a White man to a Black man. As I listened I felt close to a grandfather I would never meet, but happy knowing his blood flowed down to me. I believed he had done the right thing. He had accepted his new life and the responsibility of his Mother, and took care of her. I sat there feeling very proud to be the grandchild of J. T. Stone, a man of power and integrity.

Uncle Bud continued with the story, and I was in my grandfather's world once more. Grandfather had ventured into many things, like a hotel business, and a grocery business. His experience in the community helped him realize his passion for his people.

He went to Chicago, where he received his Degree in the Science of Embalming. He then went to Mississippi and purchased his basic equipment for opening an Undertaking Business in the year 1898.

During that era, the preparation and burial services involved the purchase of a wood coffin from a general store, and a member of the family would transport the coffin by wagon to the home. Grandfather knew of the past health hazards and the difficulty he would face in getting people to change. But he persisted in helping the Negro community understand the necessity of the funeral profession, and the care of the burial of the dead.

"Lil Mary," uncle Bud said. "I could go on for days talking about your grandfather but I think that's enough for today. We can talk more tomorrow."

"Thanks, uncle Bud. I learned a lot. You made me feel as if I knew him. You made him real to me."

"Well, he was somethin'. You just remember, you come from good stock." With his smile, I knew it was time to leave. It was time for uncle Bud to take a nap. His memory was good and I wanted to get all of the information about my past before he died. I left feeling full of adoration for my grandfather, wishing I could have known him.

21

AS I NEARED THE EMBALMING ROOM, I SAW MR. LARY enter. I wondered if he knew that it had been me under the sheet. I decided that if he didn't say anything, neither would I.

"Hi, Mr. Lary. How you are you doing today?" I asked trying to sound cheerful.

"Just fine, girl. How y'all doin'?"

"I'm just fine. Is it okay if I hang around?"

"Sure. I only got one body in there. Not sure you should see it though."

"Why not?" My curiosity had always gotten me into trouble, and today wouldn't be any different.

"This one messed up bad. You shouldn't see him like that."

I didn't understand why he would not want me in there, so I moved quickly to get through the door before Mr. Lary had a chance to keep me out. Glancing over I saw that the body on the slab was covered with a bloody sheet, and the blood had dried making the sheet completely red.

"Come on, Little Mary. You don't need to see this one."

"Mr. Lary, I'm a big girl, been working in the Funeral Home all my life. I've seen stuff you've never seen."

"Okay, but you ain't ever seen a man lynched and castrated, have you?"

"No." I didn't know what castrated mean't and even though I knew Mr. Lary truly did not want me to see this, I did not intend to let him off. A little cocky, I thought I could handle anything in an Embalming Room. When he pulled the bloodied sheet down, I gasped in shock. The horror of what I saw caused the lemonade to come up and out in just a split second. Even though I had quickly covered my mouth with both hands, it was too late. The contents of my stomach forced its way past my closed lips and down onto the floor. Quickly Mr. Lary rushed over to the sink and grabbed as many towels as he could.

"Little Mary. You okay? Come on, girl. I told you. You don't listen. I told you that you shouldn't see this one."

My heart was racing, my knees felt weak, and I gratefully leaned on Mr. Lary as he walked me outside.

"Mr. Lary, what happened? What happened to that poor man?" I asked even though I was shaking my head, trying hard not to cry. My whole body trembled with fear, fear of the unknown. I had the worst taste in my mouth and the towels were wet and smelled of a sour stomach.

"I told you, he had been lynched and castrated, but you just had to see for yourself."

Mr. Lary's tone was angry because he knew this was a hard way for a man to die. He had wanted to spare me the reality of what life for a Black man was like in the South. We sat for awhile on the bench outside the Embalming Room door with Mr. Lary rubbing my arm.

"You okay child? I'm sorry you had to see that, but life is hard here. They don't do stuff like that in California, do they? That's why your daddy took y'all away from here."

Trying to compose myself, I had this picture in my mind that was the most horrible thing I had ever seen. "Mr. Lary, what happened? Why would anyone do that to a man?" I was filled with pity for the poor dead man. What had he done to deserve such a horrible death like that?

"I don't know who or why it was done. Could have been he looked at a White girl or somethin'. Some of these folks don't need a good reason, just a reason." These were words of sorrow from Mr. Lary's heart, as he looked down. "Little Mary, the White man has so much hatred for the Black people. We ain't slaves no more, but we are still in slavery. One way or another, they gonna keep us down."

I could feel Mr. Lary's pain and wondered to myself why he still lived there. I guess this was the only home he had ever had, and to move away was never an option for him.

"Little Mary, you better go to the house and wash yourself, girl. You a mess."

"I'm sorry if I made you angry, Mr. Lary. Please forgive me."

"I'm not angry with you. You just seeing too much for a child your age." His voice was Fatherly, a trait I had not noticed before. I realized he was not a man of expression, but a man with a big heart.

When I entered the house it was empty and I was glad because I hadn't wanted anyone to see me, or smell me. I rushed to the room, took off my clothes and ran the bath, hurrying to get the smell of my stomach out of my nostrils. The sight of that dead man flashed before me constantly and I couldn't think of anything else. I could not fathom that someone could hate so much they would mutilate a human being that way. I cried silently, knowing that I had looked hate in the face. I had been told to fear the White man, and now I knew why.

Los Angeles was going to be a welcome sight for me. I wanted to go home in the worst way. At least there, the White people didn't lynch or castrate men. Only three more days left before we would be going home.

My Mother helped out with some of the funerals, and I rode with her and saw how things were done so much differently there as compared with the Hubert and Reese Mortuary. The cemeteries in Mississippi did not have blankets of flowers everywhere, and no big headstones. There were crosses on some, markers on others, and every five or six graves had some dead flowers lying around. There was no sense of peace there, and to me it looked depressing and glum. The grass was tall, and the weeds that were trying to take over had been untouched.

I hated walking over the graves with thousands of gnats buzzing around, going up my dress and nose, and I having to pretend they weren't there. In Mississippi, the funerals were also long and I was used to that, but not to the bugs. I decided that from then on I would bring my fan with me so I could either swat the bugs away, or smash them. I also knew that if I did that, my Mother would give me the evil eye because I would be acting "inappropriately."

22

O N SATURDAY MORNING WHEN MOTHER CAME TO WAKE me up, I was surprised to see her in such a good mood.

"Come on. Get up," she said, with a smile and softness in her voice.

I was suspicious and asked, "Is something wrong?"

"No. I want you to go somewhere with me. It's a surprise," and she left the room with a smile on her face.

As I got out of bed I had an uncomfortable feeling because that was not my usual Mother, and decided that something must be wrong. When we met in the kitchen for breakfast she was happy and playful, even with Tom. Knowing that we would be leaving for California in a few days seemed to have changed everyone's attitude, especially mine.

"Where are we going, Mother?" My curiosity was gnawing at me.

"Are you ready?" Mother asked.

"Yes," I replied.

"Then let's go."

I followed her out to the car and off we went—just the two of us as Tom had not been invited, and that made me happy. She drove as if on a mission and I sat quietly, hoping she would not be taking me to another photographer. With her, I never knew what to expect, and when we were alone my fears were always present.

Looking out of the car window, I watched the willow trees as we passed. I saw them blowing slightly, their strong trunks holding them with a deep-rooted strength. Mississippi had huge trees, but the only one I could call by name was the willow tree. Maybe that's why I liked them the best.

I could feel the history in this place and idly wondered how many Black men or women had hung from their branches. After seeing that poor man who had been killed, I felt a fear I could not explain, even to myself. If only those trees could talk!

The neighborhood homes were small and not pampered like most of the Homes I'd seen in California. Here, the people that I had seen were mostly poor, but rich in their love for one another and for life itself. There were no beautiful lawns, or red swings in the front yards for children to play on, just old tires hanging from a rope on a large tree, or little wooden wagons that were put together with rope and rusty nails. I saw kids throwing horseshoes at a pipe in the ground. They played and laughed as though they did not have a worry in the world.

As we drove along, we saw many people sitting on their front porches. I had learned that the front porch was the main hangout for both the young and old. The old folk would sit in rockers and shell peas, telling stories of the past. The young folk would sit on the steps, throwing rocks or pitching dimes against a board. Whoever was the closest would win.

For a moment, I envied their happiness and wished I had their life, but only for a moment. I hated Mississippi because there you were not free! You were not liked if you were a person of Color, and I wanted to go home!

The car slowed down almost to a complete stop and I asked, "Mother, where are we?" I saw a field directly ahead of me.

Mother said, "Come on. Get out."

She was acting strange, but I didn't feel as if I were in a harmful situation. We walked into the field and the grass was up to my waist, but I soon knew we were in a graveyard.

"Come on," she ordered.

"What are you looking for, Mother? I'll help you."

She became frantic. "I can't find them!"

She was turning all around, looking in all directions, and I could see she was confused. "I haven't been here in so long. Why hasn't anyone taken better care of my parents' graves?" She inhaled with such frustration in her voice. "I can't find them," she kept repeating to herself.

She was hurting and I didn't know how to comfort her so I said, "I'll find them for you. Don't worry. We'll find them!"

I was determined to find the graves of J. T. Stone and Nellie Stone and would not stop until my mission was finished. Moving through the tall grass, praying that there were no snakes, or big bugs to jump out and bite me, I knew I had to find those graves. Mother seemed unable to look. She just stood there with tears in her eyes and a look of defeat on her face. My heart melted for her.

"Please, don't cry, Mother. We have time. We'll find them. Just give me an idea where they might be. What direction should I go?"

I was thankful that it was early in the day because I may not be afraid of the dead, but I sure didn't want to become lost in that miserable graveyard at night. I had to wonder why no one for years had tended the graves, or if maybe the graves had been forgotten if there were no living relatives. However, that wasn't true, Mother was alive, and her parents were somewhere out there, but where?

I stumbled over grave markers that were very old, and I bent down and pushed the dead grass off the markers as I searched one grave to the next in the hopes of finding J. T. Stone's marker. Many were so old I could barely read the names and was surprised to find that most of them were dated in the late 1700's and 1800's. There was no order in which they had been buried; no straight rows, and actually most of the graves were unmarked—just big rocks with old vases or large cans that might have been used to hold flowers. I found some small crosses that lay on the top of graves; some were broken, some still intact. Maybe at one time they had stood tall. Now they had been forgotten.

As I looked for his grave, I wondered, *How could this have happen to such a great man who had been loved and respected by so many people? He had helped so many, and here he lay in a graveyard with grass so tall it came up to my waist, with no headstone standing tall with the dignity he had represented. Obviously, there had been no visitors to show their respect through the years, not even his children. How quickly do we forget the ones that came before us?*

I searched and I searched and an hour passed, and I was still searching. By then, I was sure I had searched that same area before when all of a sudden I saw something to my right that glinted in the bright sun. I saw a grave that was completely covered with grass and weeds, except I could see the letter "J" from where I was standing and the edge of the stone marker. I was sure I had searched that spot before, and puzzled at how I could have not seen it sooner. When I ran to it I started pushing and pulling the grass off with renewed vigor. My hands were filthy, but I knew I would not quit until I had found my Mother's parents' graves.

With excitement in my heart, I yelled, "I found it! I found it!"

The sun was hot, and I was sweating something awful when Mother walked over to where I was standing. I got down on my knees again and frantically pushed and pulled the weeds off the entire grave.

"This is it!" I was so excited that I had found her Father's grave.

She began to weep, tears running down her face and I sat there on the ground, at the foot of J. T. Stone's grave, wondering what to do next. This was a person I did not know. I read the headstone:

In Loving Memory of
J. T. Stone
1872 - 1938

Since my grandfather had been so important, I wondered if my grandfather had known President Roosevelt. He was certainly old enough to be in a history book.

My Mother's feelings were written on her face. She was mourning and I saw the love she had for her Father was sincere. I felt sorry for her and wanted to reach up and hold her, but I didn't. I sat there on the ground with my head down. For the first time, I could feel her pain and realized that she did have feelings, but it wasn't often that she expressed them for someone other than herself. It was a revelation to me: Mary Reese had a heart!

It had caught me off-guard to see her mourn, and I had to break the silence and so asked, "Mother, are you okay?"

There was no answer. She just held her head down, in deep thought. I knew she was going down memory lane and grieving her loss.

"Where would grandmother be?" I asked. I didn't know what to say to make her feel better, but I thought that maybe I could find the other grave.

"She's to the right of him," she answered, as she wiped the tears from her eyes. "Her grave should be just a couple of feet apart from his."

Turning on my knees, I moved a few feet to another unattended spot. I pushed and pulled the impossible weeds and junk until I could read the marker:

Beloved Mother
Nellie Stone
1880 - 1938

"Here it is, Mother!" I excitedly cried and then realized my excitement was not appropriate for that moment. This was a time to reflect on the past. I calmed my thoughts, while holding my head down to show my respect.

My silence was appreciated. I watched my Mother get down on her knees and softly say how much she loved them and missed them. She touched the marker and rubbed her hand along the letters, J. T. Stone. "I'm so sorry Father for not living up to your standards…" She continued apologizing and weeping for not being the daughter they thought she should be. It sounded like she might be having guilty feelings about her past, even though I didn't know what her past was like. But I did know how mean she could be in the present.

After minutes of quietness, I touched her hand and placed mine in hers. The thought in my mind was, *Please, Mother, don't squeeze!* My heart ached for her. I loved her so much, and did not want to see her hurt. I cleaned the markers the best that I could so at least they were visible for anyone to read.

23

I THOUGHT THE RIDE BACK TO MY AUNT'S HOME WOULD BE tense, but not at all. Mother began telling me her life story and I quietly sat in awe. Never before had she talked about her life in Mississippi or her family...at least that I was aware.

"My Father was a great man," she said, still glassy-eyed, trying not to cry. "I worshiped him, but he could never be pleased. He was so strict. You could not do anything; not even my Mother had a word in the house. Ours was a love/hate relationship. Although I admired him, I hated his controlling ways..."

She told me how she had started smoking at the age of seven. She really had rolled rose buds and smoked them just like aunt Norma Lee had said.

"I started drinking when I was thirteen and when my Father found out, he whipped me and put me on punishment. But I only sneaked out again and again." With anger in her voice she said, "He thought he could *control* me, but he couldn't. He hated my standing up to him, so he sent me to a convent, but it didn't last long before they expelled me," she laughed as if she was proud of that.

"I walked into my classroom, and a bottle of whisky fell out of my pocket, and broke right there in the aisle. The smell went through the room like a whirlwind." She laughed at herself. "The nuns were furious, pulling me by the ear and immediately taking me to the Principal's Office. All the while they were dragging me, they kept saying, "Satan is in you, girl.

"Little Mary, I'm glad you're not like me. I know I gave my Father the blues. I embarrassed him every chance I got. I plain enjoyed pissing him off."

That shocked me, but I didn't say a word. I wanted to hear more and she seemed willing to let all or some come out. I was hearing things about my Mother and hoping it would help me understand her, and maybe, just maybe, we could be closer.

She stopped talking and began moving her head back and forth as though she were going into a trance, or having a spiritual moment. I dared not say a word and break her spell or concentration.

Then she continued, "When I was your age," now she was bragging, "I had already had sex and I loved boys. I smoked, drank, and did whatever I wanted. My Father told me I was his favorite child, but I knew he loved my brother more than his God. After Nathan was murdered, my Father blamed himself for not sending him money, and he turned against everyone. It turned out his daughters didn't mean shit to him! I tried to get close to him, but he pushed me away. I believe he grieved for Nathan till the day he died. My Mother grieved also because she not only lost a son, but a husband, too. Did you know she died seven days after Father?"

"No, I didn't," I answered even though I really did. I just didn't want her to stop talking so I asked, "How did he die, Mother? How old was he?"

"Father was sixty-six, and Mother was fifty-eight. He was eight years older than she."

"That was young," I said.

"I believe he grieved himself to death, and my Mother couldn't live without him. Grief can kill you, you know!" She was so serious. "Father..." (She always referred to him as Father, never Daddy. I had called my Dad, "Dad" or "Daddy." To me "Father" had seemed so proper and austere, but I guess in the old days the proper way was the correct way.) "Father took ill with pneumonia, and my Mother stayed by his bedside day and night. Then she took ill and died seven days later. We buried them a few days apart." She sounded a little shaky, but she was still in control of the conversation. "We were devastated, but my sisters and I fought like cats and dogs over the estate. That's when I met your Dad, Willie, and I didn't know which direction to go. I was so hurt. I wanted to make up to my parents for being so rebellious, but it was too late. I had two children and no husband. I didn't know what to do. Your Father came along, and he had loved my Father as if it had been his own Father. Willie was a big comfort to me. Shortly after my parents had passed, he asked me to marry him."

This was a brain shock. My mind struggled. *What two children? Oh, yeah. J. T. my brother, and Lenore, my sister, had a different Father.*

I remember that Mother had often told them that Willie was not their real Father. She had enjoyed hurting them and she knew that it also hurt Dad. Dad had adopted my older sister and brother and given them the Reese name. Actually, he was the only Father they had ever known, and I never thought of them as my half-brother and half-sister. To me, they were my whole brother and sister.

Mother seemed comfortable talking with me, but I could not help but keep my mind on guard—a habit for self-preservation. I sat quietly, hoping she would know that I loved her and I was there for her. I felt the loneliness of her past and wished there was something she could do to go back and make things right with her Father, but I knew that wasn't possible.

"I didn't want to leave Mississippi, but it was your Dad who insisted we move to California. He said you kids would have a better life, but what about me? I loved Mississippi. I had friends and people who loved me. I had the best of both worlds. I had money, looks and was well-known and respected in the community. Why would I want to leave Mississippi?"

I could feel her anger coming to the surface and she went on. "If your Dad even looked at me, I became pregnant. I didn't want all those children, but he did.

My heart sank to my stomach; even though I'd heard it before, it hurt each time as if I were hearing it for the first time. Her voice sounded sad even though she nonchalantly blurted out words that pierced my heart. She was not ashamed of her feelings. It did not faze her that she was hurting me. In my mind, I remembered when she had said she hadn't wanted me and if she could have gotten rid of me, she would have. That's what I was hearing her say again, and she was not ashamed to let me know that I was not in her plans. Actually she made it clear that I was in her way.

The moment of closeness I felt at the cemetery faded. My mood dropped and my head stayed down, and I just looked at the floor of the car the rest of the ride back. Mother continued to talk as if she was talking to an audience, but she was really alone in the car. She did not care if I was listening or not.

"Did you know that your Dad had an affair with my sister, right under my nose? I could never forgive him for that, but I needed him. My sisters and I were always at each other's throats. We fought all the time. I didn't want all you kids. You were my last, and after you were born I insisted the doctor fix me, and had him tie my tubes so that there would be no more babies. I had never wanted kids!"

Yeah. Yeah. You didn't want us, but you had us, so stop telling me, I thought. I wasn't listening with the interest I'd had before. My sense of well-being was bruised, and it was a good thing my Mother could not read my mind.

"After you were born, things got so bad here. We were always in fear of the Klu Klux Klan. I thought maybe your Dad was right, so I agreed to move but my heart was still in Mississippi, not in California. I tried, Little Mary." She looked my way, and I continued to stare at the floor. "I tried to make it work, but your Dad and I had nothing in common. He wouldn't let me go out, didn't want me to drink. That's something I wasn't giving up for him or anyone."

Was I supposed to feel sorry for her now, after she'd told me she didn't want me?

"Then I met Mr. Hubert, and he fell in love with me, so one thing led to another."

I felt angry toward her. *Why does she remind me that she never wanted me? Why tell me? I don't want to hear it any more!* At this point, my fears of being like her welled up in my throat and as I sat in that car, right then and there, I promised myself to never be like her.

My Mother had opened up to me and talked with me and told me things as if we were friends, not Mother and daughter. She was sharing her thoughts and desires, also her personal relationship with Mr. Hubert. I wondered, *What was a Klu Klux Klan? What sister did Dad have an affair with?* I was too interested to interrupt and I listened and nodded with understanding, even though I didn't understand her at all.

With bitterness forming in my gut, I wondered, *Why she drank so much and fooled around with all the men that came and went in our lives?* My understanding would never be clear, but I listened and hoped she would hear herself and think about how many people she had hurt.

"Oh, well, Mr. Hubert's another long story…there are so many memories here. I feel like I have gone back into the past. I was really something special in my day," she stated. Smiling for the first time all day, almost shouting with excitement she said, "Little Mary," she continued, with pride in her voice, "my Father was a friend of Booker T. Washington, at Southern University."

"Gosh. He must have been older than dirt," I said aloud. *Oops! I hope that doesn't anger her.* They seemed so old, and now my Mother seemed old to me. I thought about Booker T. Washington. I'd heard his name before but couldn't remember where. I knew he wasn't a President.

Mother read my thoughts and continued, "Your grandfather was a friend to Booker T. Washington. There was a speech that Mr. Washington gave before the National Educational Association, in Madison, Wisconsin, way back in 1884. He spoke on racial harmony and Black progress. It was something to remember! I can't quote the whole speech, but I remember the gist of it.

"He said, 'Whatever benefits the Black man, benefits the White man. Educate the Black man, mentally and industrially, and there will be no doubt of his prosperity.' I wish I could quote the whole thing for you but let me tell you this, he made a big difference for the Black race."

She knew her history and it made me wonder why she had not encouraged me to go to school. It sounded so interesting, and I wanted to learn more about Black History. The mood had changed again and our car became a classroom—just the two of us. She educated me on Black History, and I loved every moment of it. I soaked up all that I could and savored every minute. I knew it was temporary, but I was thankful for this day, even if she reminded me that she didn't want kids. That was how I wished our relationship could be all the time.

Finding my grandparents' graves were the best part of my trip to Mississippi. I not only found their graves, but I found a Mother deep inside Mary Reese.

24

W HEN WE PULLED INTO THE DRIVEWAY OF THE FUNERAL home, I saw uncle Bud sitting in his favorite spot on the front porch, and my cousins sitting on the steps near him. Immediately I knew he was telling one of his stories, and was disappointed to be missing it. But at the same time, my heart and mind were full of thoughts of Los Angeles, and the pull it had on my heart was a pretty strong tug. Now that Mother had stated we would be returning, I finally admitted to myself that that was where I preferred to be, and my thoughts of leaving Mississippi occupied my mind and made me truly happy. After all, this was not my home and only *used* to be my Mother's. I belonged in Los Angeles, where there were no signs to direct me to a "Colored Restroom or, "Coloreds, go to the back of the bus." No, I'd had more than my fill of the South, and was both anxious and glad we would be leaving.

It was hard to hide my true feelings, and I did not want my cousins or aunt to know how excited I was to leave. Actually, I had mixed feelings because they had taught me about family life and that it was possible for a number of relatives to sit down together and talk about things, without having a knock-down-drag-out fight. They showed and shared a lot of love and it was there I came to the realization my Mother had somehow missed getting her share, and so was unable to show or pass it on to her own children.

That day as the sun was setting, my cousins and I sat out on the porch of the big house, playing with the neighborhood kids, pitching dimes against the wall, and I was winning. Soon, sure enough, we heard aunt Norma Lee call, "Y'all come eat. Wash your hands and don't be runnin' through the house. Y'all hear me?" Aunt Norma Lee cooked meals that would make you want to **"hit your Momma!"**

While there, I'm sure I gained a few pounds and that was good because

I definitely needed them. The added weight helped me fill out my size-one jeans and emphasized my slender, budding curves. I was delighted to find I was finally developing into a shapelier young girl.

There were only two more days before we would be leaving, and then there would be no more soul food. The meals I would definitely miss because when we returned I would have to fend for myself again. Even though they were sisters, Mother and aunt Norma Lee were nothing alike in many areas—but especially when it came to cooking. Mainly Mother only cooked if she was in the mood—and that was not very often.

On the last day, my cousins and I found all kinds of things to do. One thing we did was go downtown to a movie theater where Coloreds had to sit in the balcony. That wasn't so bad because I actually preferred it up there, except for the stares and the distance White people kept from us, as though we were lepers.

Cousin Etta May said, "They stare at you, Little Mary, 'cause you look like one of them." She was laughing and the other kids began to laugh also.

My face burned with anger and my blood seemed to boil because I hated for people to laugh at me. Since being in the South, I had learned to hate the Whites and resented being told I looked like them. "Etta May, just shut up. I'm Colored just like you, so shut up!" I all but shouted.

"Don't get all upset, girl. You can't help it," she calmly replied.

Giving her a look that let her know I was getting pissed and to leave me alone, I said in a huff, "Let's go." As we walked home, she and I didn't talk but the other kids joked and played around while keeping their distance from us.

The anger I felt over my cousin's statement caused me to shut out the world as we all walked home. In that state I was very confused because I didn't know who I was, or where I was going. All I could think about was that I wanted to hide some place where I could kill myself. I hated how I looked and hated everyone around me.

In my own world, I walked quickly and as soon as I got back went directly to the front of the Mortuary, anxious to get to the Viewing Room. My thoughts were going something like this: *Who can I talk to today? Who really cares what I feel or what I do? Actually, there's nobody! But I have always been able to vent my feelings to the dead people because with them I never have to worry or fear I'll be told I don't fit in.*

There was uncle Bud sitting in his chair, head down and sleeping as usual, but I managed to slip by him unnoticed. Upon entering the Front Office, I saw Mr. Prestly who had also worked for my grandfather. To me he looked as dead as any of the dead people I had seen.

"Hey, Little Mary. Where you goin'?" he asked with a big smile.

"Just walking around," I vaguely replied, as I didn't want to talk to him. *Just get out of my way, old man,* I thought.

"What's up with you, little girl? You look upset," he insisted.

"I'm okay, just walking around," I responded as I kept walking right past him in order to avoid any more conversation.

The halls were dark in the Mortuary and that caused me to often wonder why they didn't turn on some lights in the place. It was then I had decided: *If I ever go into the Funeral Business, it will be a brightly-lit place. After all, the corpses are dead so the lights won't hurt their eyes.*

Anger seemed to be running rampant through me and I didn't know why I. Yet, I felt angry enough to hit someone. Evidently, my visit to Mississippi had taught me to be tough, to fight if needed, and to fight for life, because the living were out to kill you. Also, I learned something important that I hadn't felt or known prior to our trip to the South, and that was: White people are your enemy and never, ever, trust a White person!

When I walked into the Viewing Room I automatically looked for a light switch. But what stopped me was I knew if I turned on a light, someone would probably come and I would get into trouble. Plus, I really didn't want anyone to know I was in there, as I wanted to be alone.

The dim lighting did calm my spirit and I felt myself begin to relax. I walked over to dark gray, almost black casket, with a silver comforter flowing over the sides. Just the torso of the body was exposed and a heavy lace comforter lay on top of the casket, with each pleat perfectly folded. Flowers had been placed around the stand and a large flower blanket lay on top, covering the bottom half of the casket. The floral smell in the room was almost overwhelming and as I drank in the atmosphere, my mood changed from angry to calm, and the calmness ran through my veins as if I'd taken a Valium. For me, I had come to the right place for help.

There lay Mrs. Hattie Johnson in her casket, looking as if she were just sleeping and with not a care in the world. "Hello, Mrs. Johnson. Can I call you, Hattie? Thanks. I wish I could be with you. I'm leaving tomorrow for Los Angeles, and even though I can't wait to go, I'm afraid..." Suddenly tears began to flow like the gates of a dam had opened. With the sleeve of my shirt, I wiped my nose and tried not to cry anymore. I wanted to hug Mrs. Johnson, but I didn't want to mess up her make-up, or clothes, so I settled for a gentle touch on her crossed hands.

"Hattie, I'm afraid to go home and afraid to stay. There's a bad man in Los Angeles that wants to kill me. I stabbed him with his own knife. I didn't kill him, Hattie, but he was going to kill me, and that was the only way to get away from him. I know you can't answer me, but I wish you could. I'm tough, and I can fight, so I can protect myself. Yeah. I'm not afraid of him.

I beat him once and I can get away from him again."

The Viewing Room was quiet except when I heard myself talking, so I whispered lower. "Hattie, did you ever hurt anyone? Did you have kids? Do you love your kids? Oh, Hattie, what should I do? I wish I were dead like you." I rubbed Hattie's hand, feeling the dryness of her skin. That was the only hand I could trust. It was the only hand I had to hold. There was no pain in holding her hand.

"Hattie, where's your family? Do they miss you? Do you think I'd be missed? I don't think anyone would really miss me. Even the boy I fell in love with left me. If we had had sex, I'd be the one pregnant, and he'd be marrying me instead of someone else." I stared into Hattie Johnson's face, hoping for movement, a twitch or a sign of breath in her chest, anything to not feel so alone.

Mr. Prestly was coming down the hall. He walked so silently that I didn't hear his footsteps, but I could smell him and hear his breathing.

"Well, Hattie, I have to go. Thanks for listening. One day I'll meet you again," I softly whispered my adieus.

"Little Mary, you in there?" Mr. Prestly's shaky voice gently called.

"Yeah, it's me. I'm in the Viewing Room."

"Girl, what you doin' hangin' around dead folks all the time? I see you ain't got nowhere to go. Dead folks ain't got nothin' to give you."

"I don't want nothing from them, either," I answered, with a defensive attitude. How dare he talk about my friends! I believed I had many friends, even though they came and then they were buried, but I remembered each one. It was comforting to me to think they knew my deepest thoughts and me. Also, even though they couldn't talk, they still loved me in spite of everything.

"Folks start thinkin' you crazy, girl, standin' around talkin' to dead folks. You too pretty, too young, hangin' around this place. Everythin' ain't what it seems about livin', not dyin'," he said.

"I don't like the living," I answered as I burst uncontrollably into tears and felt my stomach begin to ache.

Inside I was dying, so afraid of what was next—going home with Mother and Tom, neither of whom could care less about me. Telling Mr. Prestly my business was not what I intended, it all just came tumbling out and once I started shaking he grabbed my arm and said, "Come on, girl. Let's go to the Front Office." I was so glad no one else was in the Funeral Home. "Should I call Mr. Lary? I know you talk to him a lot."

"No, I'm okay. Just sad I'm leaving."

"Little Mary, life is about makin' choices. Sometime folks make the wrong ones. Your Mom Mary, she spoiled all her life. She drinks too much, and it controls her. She a good lady, just drink too much for her own good. You still young. You got a long life, just don't mess with that liquor. It don't mix in your blood."

I thought to myself, *Mary, straighten up. Don't let anyone see you fall apart like this again. You're tough. Remember that.* But out loud I said, "Mr. Prestly. I'm sorry that you saw me crying. I don't cry often. I guess I'm just full and had to let it go. Please don't tell anyone you saw me crying!"

"Girl, ain't nothin' to be ashamed of. Go on now. This between us, okay?" he kindly reassured me.

"Okay, and thanks for being there," I mumbled feeling both relieved and not quite so tough.

25

UNCLE BUD WAS STILL IN HIS FAVORITE SPOT, BUT HIS NAP was over. When I opened the screen door his head popped around in surprise. "Hey, Little Mary, what you up to?" he asked with his usual big smile.

"Nothing. On my way back to the big house."

"Well, sit with me a few minutes. Big Mary ready to go home?" he asked. I was sure glad he hadn't seen me crying like a baby.

"I guess so," I answered.

"What about you?"

"Yeah, I like it here, but I'm more used to Los Angeles," I explained.

"Well, I always wanted to leave Mississippi," he said with sadness, as if it meant going halfway across the world.

"Why didn't you?" I was curious.

"Uncle Bud too old. I belong here. In this home, I seen so many changes. I hope to live to see the day all "Colored" signs go down and when our folks can come and go wherever they want. I want to see kids, Black and White, being friends, goin' to school together."

"Uncle Bud, in Los Angeles, they do," I quietly assured him.

"I heard that, but I wanna' see it here, in my home, in my lifetime." The tears in his eyes told a story of their own.

Then he asked, "Did your Momma ever tell you what caused your Daddy to move y'all away so fast?"

"No...just that he wanted a better life for us."

"Well, let me tell you this story."

I knew to get good and comfortable because I was going to be there awhile. Boy, one thing I would surely miss were uncle Bud's stories, because I had discovered he was really my only key to the past. The history of the

Stone family lay heavily on his heart. I had truly learned to love this old man.

"Your Dad used to work here at the Funeral Home after your grandfather died," he began. "Your Mom and sisters fought all the time and with no man around to run things, your Dad stepped in. JT and your sister were too young to do anythin', but JT liked runnin' around with Big Willie. Your brother, Little Willie, well, he was just too little, and Ilona was helping out with the kids, and you Little Mary, was like a china doll, so White and cute, small as a button. Carried you around on a pillow, they did, you pretty little thing."

It was nice to hear nice things about me as a baby and I was surprised to hear myself blurt out, "Did Mother love me then?"

"Oh, girl, your Mother loves you now."

"No, uncle Bud. She has said over and over that she never wanted us. She said if she could have gotten rid of us she would have."

He seemed shocked and asked, "Your Momma told you that? I can't believe Big Mary would tell y'all somethin' like that."

"Well, she tells us that a lot," I assured him with my head quickly nodding up and down for emphasis.

"I know she loved livin' here and your Dad made her move, so I guess she never forgave him for that. The last straw that made Big Willie say 'No more,' was one night when he had a call, and JT, your brother, begged to go with him. Your Dad had a bad feelin' and didn't want to take him but your Mother got mad, accusin' Big Willie of not lovin' JT, so your Dad gave in. The call was across town.

"Back then when Coloreds were killed or died, the Funeral Home went to get the body on the spot wherever they had died. The police were parked on the side of the road when your dad and JT, who was no more than ten years old at the time, pulled up. Big Willie told JT to stay in the hearse, but JT's curiosity evidently got the better of him and he sneaked around the back of the hearse and listened to every word the White policeman was sayin'.

"Down off the side of the road, in a somewhat wooded area, he could see policemen walkin' around and talking to Big Willie, like he was a boy. JT was gettin' angry to hear how mean they talked to his Dad, and wondering why his Dad didn't talk back. Trying to get closer, he slipped on a rock and fell, and the noise was loud in that secluded area.

"'What you doin', boy?' the White policeman yelled. 'Git over here. What you doin' out here?' Your Dad grabbed JT and pushed him behind him, away from the police officer.

"There was a lot of activity goin' on down below, and JT had only wanted to see what was happenin'. Your Dad took JT by the arm intendin' to walk him back to the hearse to make him wait, but the White officer said, 'Let the little Nigger stay. He needs to see what happens when you boys get out of line.' Then the policeman grabbed JT by the neck and shoulder, leadin' him to the spot where there was a body hangin' from a tree covered with Black tar with feathers stuck to the man's lifeless body. His eyes were bulgin' in a state of agony. Blood covered his teeth and run down his chin, and his naked body was stripped of any dignity.

"JT screamed in fear, burying his face in Big Willie's stomach as the White officer looked and laughed, like he was watchin' a comedy. Big Willie started for the hearse, tryin' to protect JT from seein' anymore, but the White officer had no mercy on the fact that he was a child. He insisted he watch his Father cut down the dead man, and put 'im in the hearse.

"'You Niggers make me sick,' the officer said with disgust in his voice. He had a big red face and fat belly that hung over his belt, and he spit out tobacco juice as he talked and chewed at the same time. His teeth were yellow and brown from the tobacco stains. He felt proud of himself for makin' your Father and brother do this. But your Father had enough sense not to react, 'cause this cop was out to get any Black man. Just to say he killed a Nigger was a notch on his belt.

"That was the day your Dad said, 'Enough is enough.'"

My heart was in my mouth and I managed to say, "What an awful thing for JT to see. He never told me anything about what happened."

"Well, I don't think it's something that he would want to talk about, let alone remember."

"Uncle Bud, I love you," I said impulsively.

"Thanks, Little Mary. I love you too! Now, you keep your head up all the time. You a pretty girl and there's a light in your eyes, tells me you goin' to be somebody big one day."

"Uncle Bud, I'm scared all the time." I knew that again I was telling my business, but I was hoping he could tell me something to make things better.

"Life is full of surprises, Little Mary. Always do what is right and God will take care of you."

I had a smirk on my face as I replied, "Yeah, not so far He hasn't."

"Don't talk like that, girl. Don't play with God!"

"Well, God doesn't care nothing about me, or you! God's not real, uncle Bud. I've prayed to Him many times to help, but he doesn't hear me. I don't think my prayers go any further than the ceiling!"

"Little Mary, you missin' the point. God answers prayers of those who believe."

"Yeah, well I don't believe and you can pray, but it hasn't helped you any...has it?"

"You got serious heart problem, little girl. God put that spark in your eyes, and He hasn't given up on you, so don't you go givin' up on Him."

"Uncle Bud, if God is so good, why do you see folks sweeping their porches early in the morning thinking somebody put a spell on them? Why does God let people put evil spells on other people?"

"You have to understand. There's good and evil in this world, and you can choose which side. I choose good. What do you choose?"

"I'm not evil. Am I?" I fearfully asked.

"No, no. Not with that spark in your eyes. No. You are good, but it's 'cause God is good, and He loves you even if you don't love yourself."

"I gotta go, uncle Bud. Thanks for talking with me, and please don't tell Mother anything we talked about," I pleaded.

"I'm keepin' you in my prayers, Little Mary," he promised. I just thought to myself, *Yeah, that's just what I need. But I know his prayers for me won't reach the ceiling either.*

I stood up and walked over to uncle Bud and gently sat on his lap, put my arms around his neck, and held on hoping his goodness would rub off on me. "I love you," I said, with all the heartfelt emotion of love I possessed. My heart hurt because the sadness of leaving a man like uncle Bud was terribly hard. Upon returning to Los Angeles, there would not be anyone to replace him.

26

LEAVING UNCLE BUD AND WALKING TOWARD THE BIG house, my eyes roamed over every corner, every window, the porch, the roof with it's chimney, and the yard—taking a picture for my mental memories. Most houses there looked like shotgun houses, with a long open breezeway and small rooms on either side, but not this one. It looked like a mansion to me. I knew I would miss it…but I was going home. The ride with Tom and Mother, I knew, would be miserable, but I told myself I would survive it. Planning to sleep the whole trip home would be my way to escape.

That evening we all sat around the dinner table—Mother, Tom, aunt Norma Lee, Etta May, and Little Sister. The table was crowded with all my favorite foods, yams, greens, ham, chicken, rice, red beans, monkey bread, and potato salad. Aunt Norma Lee outdid herself and to me it was a feast fit for a king. I knew I probably wouldn't get to eat like this again until Christmas. *Maybe Mother will cook then,* I thought.

Daybreak came all too quickly and by 5:00 a.m. we were loading up the car. Aunt Norma Lee and all my cousins also got up early to say their good-byes. Care packages had been prepared: ham sandwiches, watermelon, fruit, chips, srawberry Kool-Aid in big jelly jars, and peppermint candy. It was going to be a picnic in the car.

When I left, I knew I would always be grateful for my months spent with my extended family in Mississippi. Even though I would always remember that trip, I also would be eternally thankful my Dad had taken us away from there.

My Mother had tears in her eyes—she really would miss her sister. Aunt Norma Lee and Mother had been the closest in her family, but most of all Mother loved being in Mississippi, as that was still home for her.

There on the porch of the Mortuary, I saw uncle Bud, and couldn't believe he was up so early. I had already said my good-byes to him but he stood, while holding on to his rocking chair with one hand raised, to wave us good-bye. When he touched his eyes as if wiping tears, my throat had a lump in it and I yelled out, "I love you, uncle Bud!" I knew it would be too much of a walk for uncle Bud to come over to the car because he walked as slow as he talked. So I quickly jumped out of the car and ran over to the Funeral Home and up the porch stairs, two at a time. Uncle Bud let go of the chair with open arms for me and I fairly flew into that haven of love, peace, and comfort. He hugged me with such compassion and warmth that I could feel his strength passing right through me.

I could not fight back the tears. My heart ached for a man that I had come to know and love even though I had only known him a short time. Though he really was not my uncle, I could not have loved him more and he was the grandfather I'd never had. The wisdom and family history he had shared with me were priceless. It was too bad that my sister Ilona could not have met him, as I knew she would also have been crazy about him. There were still so many stories he had yet to tell, but I had to leave them behind.

The front door of the Funeral Home opened, and Mr. Lary called to me, "Did you think I was goin' to miss saying good-bye?"

I turned around and jumped up into his arms. My reaction shocked him a bit probably because he was not a man to show his feelings. "Oh, Mr. Lary. Thank you for everything," I enthused as tears were going at full speed down my face and as dry as his personality was, his face was also wet with his own tears.

"I'll miss you, Little Mary. You somethin' special, and don't you forget it."

I kissed him on the cheek and put my arms tightly around his neck. "Thank you for being my friend," I whispered in his ear.

Running back to the car, I knew I could not look back at him and uncle Bud. My heart was breaking into a thousand pieces. The pain of leaving them reminded me of losing Ilona. The hurt and pain of not seeing her was more than I could bear. I felt as though I would explode with all the emotions rolling inside of me.

Uncle Bud had told me the J.T. Stone family history was something I could be proud of, and that I should learn from their mistakes. I had hoped to understand my Mother better, but she was a puzzle and some of the pieces were missing. One thing I had determined was that I did not want to be like her. So I made a promise to myself, that morning: *I would never drink for fear a Mary Reese might be hidden inside me. I would never take the chance that even one drink might release the demon.*

Something else I determined was that uncle Bud was someone after whom I would pattern myself—only I would talk faster. He radiated love, the old-time Southern love for family and friends. I knew leaving him would be a void in my life. Selfishly, I wanted to have uncle Bud come live with us but instinctively knew if that happened, Mother would destroy him. Mother's drinking could change her personality within minutes and you never knew what she would do, or whom she would hurt. Then I laughed to myself remembering she had a rule, "There was to be no drinking before noon." She had actually said, "If you drank before noon, you were an alcoholic."

Tom was rushing us to get a move on so we could leave. Mainly, I believed, because we had a long drive ahead of us plus the plain and simple truth that he had had enough of the South. Good-byes took over an hour before we actually got on the road, with all the hugging and kissing of each other many times over, accompanied by lots of promises of, "I'll see you again, soon!"

When the car was finally moving and we had waved until we could no longer see our precious family, I leaned back in the seat and got comfortable for the long drive. That is when it finally hit me…that sinking feeling of, *What is next? What awaits me at home?* Then I mulled over the lessons and information I had learned from my loving family there in Mississippi.

Mr. Lary and uncle Bud had both told me secrets of the Funeral Home and things about what some gravediggers do. Evidently, some gravediggers would go back to the grave after a funeral, in the evening. "That's when most people do bad things, in the dark," uncle Bud had told me. They would dig up the casket and take any jewelry, or even gold from the dead person's teeth, because it was their opinion that whatever was placed in the casket, rightfully belonged to them. Also, there were stories that some gravediggers had even stripped the clothes off of a corpse, and then had put the body back in the casket, naked.

I mulled what I knew and what I had been told about gravediggers in my mind for a while. *Gravediggers have no shame. How could they get the gold out of a corpse's teeth? Most of the time the mouths are sewn together.* Uncle Bud had said, *"The gravediggers don't care about knocking the dead's teeth out, or pulling them out with pliers. Couldn't hurt a dead man," he had said. That sure sounds cruel to me. How could someone defile a dead person? What makes people do things like that? Uncle Bud had also said, "Men will do anything for money, and the heart is wicked." I don't always understand, but I know if uncle bud said it, it had to be right.*

I know that uncle Bud always talked to the families of the deceased and tried to convince them not to put anything of any value in the casket. He had told me, "Their grief makes it hard for them to say good-bye so they want to put something of themselves in the casket…a sending-off gesture. When people are grieving over a lost one, they don't think good. Your job is to show them the way. You have a light in you, Little Mary, and they'll pay attention to what you say.

"*The dead are like an empty house, nobody home. They gone up yonder,*" *he had said with his feeble hands gesturing up toward the sky,* "*or gone to hell. Only God knows. You tell them with love, Little Mary. You got a lot of love waiting to come out.*"

Uncle Bud was a piece of work. I could sit and listen to him for hours, and still want more. I'd like to believe he knows what he is talking about…God…and heaven. But I know that that is something only old folks believe in.

Sitting there in the car with my head in my hands, unable to hide my feelings, I thought about how wise uncle Bud was, and hoped just a little of his wisdom had rubbed off onto me. It was hard for me to believe like him, when there were men like Reverend Miles who only believed because it was their job and he got paid a lot of money. Having seen so much wickedness, it was hard for me to believe there were many good men.

My thoughts kept running rampant as I daydreamed of all that had happened in the last couple of months: *Had I changed? Yes. I was wiser for being there. I had memories now of the South, where I had been born, and what my family looked like. Some had dark skin and some were as light as me. I'm thankful to see I'm not so different after all.*

Tom drove rather slowly so as not to have a run-in with the law there in the South, and I looked out and noticed the beautiful willow trees as we drove through the many poor neighborhoods. There were kids outside playing, even though it was very early in the morning. *What could they be so happy about,* I thought? Women were sweeping their porches, making sure there hadn't been any saltpeter sprinkled on their porches in the middle of the night because they thought if they walked in it, a spell would have been placed by someone out to hurt them. You may wonder what spell. It was a voodoo spell that could cause them all kinds of trouble. In the past Mother had told me of some of the spells she had put on people, and I always thought she was joking until we had gone to the South and I saw how seriously the people reacted.

Mother began laughing and said, "Look at them out there, sweeping away."

"Why do they do that? Honestly, you guys take this stuff too seriously," Tom said trying to act as if it was no big deal. But Mother just went on and on about how she knew things that she could do to him. I could tell the conversation was shaking him up because he began to drive faster.

"I'll teach you when you're older, Little Mary," she said, turning to look at me in the backseat.

When she said that, I felt the presence of something evil just from the sound of her words. "That's okay. I don't want to know. It's evil, and it scares me!" I adamantly resisted.

"Oh, girl, if you know what you're doing, there's nothing to be afraid of."

"Well, thanks, but no thanks. I don't want to know. They don't do stuff like that in Los Angeles," I said, with relief in my voice.

With an evil laugh, Mother said, "You'd be surprised what people do in Los Angeles. You'd be surprised what people do all over the world."

Tom was getting angry. This was a subject he didn't enjoy talking about and he told Mother, "Shut up!" I was glad to hear him say that to her as I didn't want to hear anymore. It was wrong, it was evil, and I knew it.

But Mother enjoyed irritating Tom and with a grin on her face and laughing under her breath she said, "I'll put a spell on you, fool."

I could tell it was going to be a long, miserable ride. We had hardly been on the way but a few miles and already the bickering had started. Placing my head on the seat, I closed my eyes with the intention of sleeping away most of the next three days.

It seem that Mother and Tom argued constantly. "You're driving too slow. You're driving too fast," and on and on. But I had the ability to block it all out of my mind and before I knew it, we were pulling up in front of our big, beautiful house. I was so excited and pleased, I wanted to kiss the ground. Back in Los Angeles, the home of the free where there were no signs to remind us how much the Whites hated all Blacks. The air seemed fresher and the sky bluer and the homes prettier and bigger. Also, the traffic on the streets moved more rapidly and people seemed to walk faster. I was home and the joy on my face was evident for all to see as I jumped out of the car and ran to the front door. All I wanted was to have my own space again.

Mother and Tom yelled to me, "You better come help get all this stuff. Hurry up now!"

27

AFTER HAVING UNPACKED, CLEANED AND ORGANIZED my room, I flopped on the bed, thinking it was good to be home, but where was Ilona? Where was Daniel? I was in my room, and I was alone. Now I had nothing but time on my hands in which to think of what to do next. Since the Hubert and Reese Mortuary was off-limits, I missed the Embalming Room and the talks with the dead people, Mr. Holmes and Ima. Basically, I didn't have anyone to talk to and it struck me that without the Funeral Home, I had nothing.

Mother and Tom were in her bedroom and their voices could be heard clear down the hall, all the way to my room, even with both our doors closed. I sat on the floor with my back and head leaning against the door listening to everything they were yelling.

"I'm selling this house, and that's that, you son-of-a-bitch! You don't tell me what I can and can't do!" Mother was really loud and Tom yelled back at her just as loud. I could visualize them getting into each other's faces, and hoped the situation would not end with them coming to blows.

Then I was surprised to hear Tom standing up for my well-being when he said, "What about school for Little Mary? She just got back. Why change her again?"

Had I missed something? When did he start to care? I was rather puzzled.

"I'm moving to the East Side. Reverend Lindsey and I are going to be partners, and start the J.T. Stone Funeral Home. My Father's name will live on forever!" she verbally threw in Tom's face.

"I ain't going!" Tom said more firmly, "I ain't leaving my daughter and I ain't taking her over to live on the East Side."

"Well, keep your poor ass here, but you got to get the hell out of my house!" Mother shot back. She knew Tom needed her and loved her, and that his bluff was not working. My heart sank to its lowest. I had hoped to see some of my old friends, but now it sounded like I was going to be moved to the East Side, and had no idea what to expect. My heart felt fear again - *the bad man that wanted to kill me.*

The doorbell rang and rang, but the argument between Mother and Tom did not stop. So I went to the door and hoped I wouldn't see a policeman when I peeked through the curtain. Instead it was Lenore standing there, and very impatient, that it had taken me so long to answer the door.

"Our first night home and already a fight is in progress," I told her as I opened the door.

Lenore pushed me aside and ran up the stairs, four at a time, and as she threw open the door to Mother's bedroom shouted, "Shut up, you guys! You can be heard a block away. Somebody's going to call the cops on you again!"

"I don't give a shit!" was Mother's unrepentant reply.

"What's going on?" Lenore asked.

"We're moving to the East Side," declared Mother.

"Why?"

"Reverend Lindsey and I are planning to open a new Funeral Home and name it after my Father—The J.T. Stone Funeral Home."

Lenore was as shocked as I was and asked, "What about school for Little Mary?"

"Oh, she can go to school over there. You know, they *do* have schools all over L.A." She raised her beer and said, "This is to the East Side."

Lenore touched my shoulder and said, "Come on. You should go to bed. It's after midnight."

"What are you doing here so late? Why aren't you home?" curiously, I asked.

"I just wanted to come see you guys. You've been gone a long time."

Lenore wasn't fooling me because I had overheard Mother and her ,and knew she was having marital problems. But what seemed crazy to me was why she'd come to Mother for advice.

Then Tom interrupted and began yelling at Mother again, "You know that Reverend Lindsey ain't nothin' but a crook! All those 'suppose to be Preachers' are nothing but crooks!"

Now Tom had really done it! He had really got under Mother's skin because she stood up for her friends, and even I knew they always came first in her book. Quick as a flash she turned on Tom like black on coal, shouting "You son-of-a-bitch! Who the fuck do you think you are? They are ten times the man you are!"

Not to be outdone Tom came back fast with a snarl, "How do you know?" You fucking them too?"

My heart began beating faster because I knew they were really going to fight now. It had really gotten out of hand. Lenore had also sized up the situation and swiftly ran over to Tom and as she literally pulled him out of the room, she tried to calm him down. All the while, Mother kept up a stead flow of screaming obscenities.

I went to my room, closed the door, and lay on the bed where I placed the pillow over my head and cried myself to sleep—a lost little girl.

* * *

When Mother decides to do something she doesn't let the grass grow under her feet, and it wasn't long before we were moving to the East Side. There were so many movers, the big house was emptied out in one day. A lot of our things were put into storage or given away because we were moved into an apartment above the new Funeral Home, where we would live until we moved into our new house. I had not seen the new house, but my opinion didn't matter. Mother would show it to me when she got good and ready.

Soon, the new Funeral Home had a grand opening and I was enrolled in Edison Junior High. The transition was just what I expected—hard. Even though I had made friends rather quickly, because I lived above a Funeral Home my friends did not want to come visit me.

Mother purchased three brand new, 1958 Cadillacs, lavender and purple, plus a hearse. After all, money was no object because she was rich. Once again all her "friends" became freeloaders, but she didn't care. They were people with whom she could party.

* * *

It was my day to work the Front Office, which meant light filing and answering the phones, when I overheard Mother talking to Reverend Lindsey. She was saying she would take him to see the new house.

My ears perked up at the New and I interrupted, "Mother. I'd like to go and see it, too."

"All right, come on. Get Mr. Blakley to come up front for awhile."

Immediately, I buzzed Mr. Blakley in the Embalming Room and he answered as if he were pissed about something. I couldn't imagine him sitting out front and greeting anyone let alone answering the phones, but that wasn't my problem. He would just have to handle it for a short time, as I really was anxious to see our new house.

"Yes? This is Blakley here!" he all but snarled.

"Mr. Blakley, Mrs. Reese would like you to come up front for a half hour or so," I sweetly explained.

"I'm in the middle of an embalming. Tell her I can't right now."

I knew you didn't tell Mother "No," and from the look on my face, Mother evidently realized I was not getting anywhere with Mr. Blakley.

"Give me the damn phone!" she shouted. She grabbed the phone with such force it bounced off my ear. "Mr. Blakley, I need you to come up front and tend to the Front Office for me."

Her tone was more of a command and he knew she would take no excuses. In a more user-friendly voice he replied, "I'll be right there, Mrs. Reese."

Mr. Blakley was nothing like Mr. Holmes, and had even less of a personality than Mr. Lary in Mississippi. He was short, had a hard face that looked dead, and needed a haircut in the worst way. Many times I had wondered if most embalmers looked or acted like as if they were one of their dead clients, and if the dead rubbed off on them? Oh, how I missed Mr. Holmes; he had been the greatest embalmer I had ever met. The lavender and purple cars were a hit in the Inner City, and people passing by would slow down just to look and admire them all. It was no accident the cars and Funeral Home were perfectly coordinated. The Funeral Home was white trimmed in purple, with large lettering on the front in purple, that almost screamed at you: **J.T. Stone Mortuary**. Lavender and purple was also the theme that adorned the walls inside every room.

When we arrived at our "new" house, it was located on the corner of 60th and Compton Boulevard. Mother seemed as proud of it as if it were a mansion. But it wasn't. It was just a small frame house, with a small porch, two bedrooms, one bathroom, and a little yard in front. Compared to our other house, it was quite a letdown for me. Then I looked on the bright side, it would be better than living above the Funeral Home, so I didn't complain.

When we parked in the driveway and I got out, I thought, *I don't like this.* What I saw was a small house with a one-car garage in the back. Also, I noticed the back yard was quite large and even though the grass needed mowing, I thought it was nice. A huge tree stood off to the side, almost in the neighbor's yard, but it was definitely our tree. I looked at the tree and realized I had no desire to climb it. A few years earlier I would have been eager to find my own limb on which to sit.

Looking at the yard I thought, *So many things have changed; so many things I thought about or wanted seemed to have disappeared as though they were only vapors. I no longer dream. I have lost hope of being happy. Daniel had been my great hope and now he was dead to me…a married man with a child. All my fears seem to surface along with the sunrises and I feel as though I'm in a prison with no way out. Why is it the days always seem too short and the nights so long?*

Touring the house only took a few minutes and soon we were on our way back to the Funeral Home. When I walked in the door Mr. Blakley had an attitude, but behind me was Mrs. Reese and he smiled at her.

"Thanks, Mr. Blakley. Little Mary can sit here now." Mother knew he didn't like to be up front and with his looks and attitude, he really did need to stay in the Embalming Room.

I sat at the Front Desk while Mr. Lindsay and Mother went upstairs, laughing and talking. The phones seemed to ring constantly and for the rest of the day I took messages.

Word had quickly spread around Los Angeles, that Mrs. Reese had opened another Funeral Home. She still had clout, business was good, the Embalming Room was full, and the phones rang day and night.

28

EVEN THOUGH MOTHER WAS QUITE BUSY WITH HER NEW funeral home, she always seemed to be able to make time to go out and have fun. Through the new friends she had made since being back from Mississippi, she became acquainted with a newly discovered comedian by the name, Redd Foxx. At the time he was performing at a club called Strip City. Personally, I thought he was a nasty man because he told dirty jokes and made fun of people. It seemed if he wasn't cursing, he wasn't talking. But for some unknown reason, Mother thought he was great and insisted I go with her to see his show one Saturday evening. I didn't want to go but she insisted and told me, "It will be good for you to see what nightlife is all about. After all, you are fourteen going on fifteen.

That evening Lenore came over as she was going with us, and she made up my face. When she finished, I could have easily passed for eighteen. I felt very insecure but she promised to look out for me.

Riding in our limousine gave my thoughts time to race around and I could not relax, as I didn't want to be there. Mother kept encouraging Lenore to drink more and I was quite surprised, and acted it, when she offered me a cigarette. She just looked meaningfully at me and said, "I know you have been smoking ever since Mississippi."

She was right, and here I had thought I was so slick, keeping it hidden. Well, now I could smoke freely. Next, she offered me a drink of vodka and since I had been found out about the smoking, I was too intimidated to refuse and stick to my promise about not ever drinking. Slowly I took a tiny sip just as the car hit a bump. That caused me to choke and I spilled some of the drink on my good dress. It tasted terrible.

"Careful," Mother kidded playfully. Don't worry, you'll get used to it.

Next time take it with orange juice, and it won't taste so bad."

I really didn't like it, but felt caught about the smoking, and that I was now obliged to act like I belonged with them.

The limo came to a stop and the chauffeur got out and came around and opened the door for us. Mother believed in going first class and was always a big tipper, and this was no exception—especially as the chauffeur was a tall, dark, and handsome young man. As he reached for my hand to help me out of the car he whispered to me, "Don't drink too much. You don't need it."

With a smile and a nod of my head I gestured an affirmative as if to say, "Thank you for the advice." I have to admit driving up in a limo like a VIP and all the attention it entailed, made me feel important. Since this was my first time at such an event, I was amazed when stepping out of the car to see so many people, all dressed up, fit to kill. The women wore the latest in high fashion with spiked heels, and enough make-up they looked like they were in a stage production. The line to get in was rather long, but a gentleman at the door saw us and walked over to personally greet Mother and treated her as if she were a celebrity. Being in her element, she acted the role, strutting ahead of the crowd that had been standing in line for hours before the doors opened.

Lenore and I stayed close as we followed Mother through a door covered with bright lights of yellow and red with a neon sign flashing, "Strip City." Inside, big balls made of faceted, cut mirrors, hung from the ceiling, sparkling like stars in the galaxy. As we pushed our way through the crowd my blood was racing; I was becoming even more uncomfortable. We were seated directly in front of the stage at a very small round table. It was so small with the four of us squeezed around it—our knees couldn't help but touch. The gentleman who had escorted us to our table sat down next to me. I was really uncomfortable then and afraid to look at him, but I could feel his eyes on me as though he were checking me out.

I hated that feeling—like a rabbit caught in a trap and I kept looking for an exit sign, but all I saw were basically naked women, topless, with just little tassels hanging from their nipples. Some were also bottomless—wearing strings that could barely be seen. It amazed me at how free these women acted. They had no shame as they walked around, waiting on tables and serving drinks. Naked! I felt they were nasty and did not want to drink or touch anything they touched. When I looked over at Mother, she was having a good time laughing and talking with the gentleman who had walked in with us. Then I realized Lenore had been drinking enough that she was kind of out of it by then.

Actually the club was not very big but with such a large crowd, people were standing everywhere with no space to move. Then I decided I was happy to be sitting. In checking out the men in the room it seemed all were well-dressed and very friendly, but the crowd's laughter and chatter was so deafening you could hardly hear what the person next to you was saying. People had to shout when they talked.

I didn't talk, but just watched in shock and wanted to run away but didn't because the last time had I run, I had almost been killed. So, I decided to sit this out, but vowed I would never come back with them again. I did not like being there and instinctively knew in my heart I should stay away from that place.

Then flashing lights came on and moved all around the club, the brightness hitting me in the eyes and for a few seconds blinding me. The music suddenly became louder, and a tall, skinny man, came on stage with a microphone.

"Ladies and gentlemen..." he paused, "well, I mean there might be some ladies out there!"

To me what he said was an insult but Mother and everyone else laughed. He continued in that same vein, making crude jokes about all the pretty women walking around with their tits hanging out. Fortunately, he talked for a short time and then introduced, "The Comedian of the Century, the one and only, Redd Foxx!" Then he passed off the microphone as if it were a baton in a relay race.

Mr. Foxx ran out on the stage with his arms open, ready to entertain his adoring audience. What a shock it was for me when he opened his mouth. The words that came out were so vulgar; I think I actually went numb. He talked as if he lived in the gutter; they were so filthy and crude. A short man, with red hair and sloppy mannerisms, a nasty mouth on a handsome face that seemed incongruous. When he walked around the stage it was like he owned both it and the audience. They thought he was hilarious and had tears in their eyes from laughing so hard. The intense applause seemed to encourage him to get even nastier.

I was sitting with my head down, biding my time and hoping he would hurry up and finish, when I heard him say, "I want you to meet a lady that is an extraordinary woman. She is a Southern gal from Mississippi, and is soul personified."

Immediately I thought, *Oh, no, I hope he doesn't call us on stage!* But he did.

"This is Mrs. Reese, who is the *real body* at the J.T. Stone Mortuary!" Redd stood there and looked my Mother up and down. "You one fine mortician, lady. I'd die just to get with you." Then he gestured for her to come on stage, with his hand reaching out to help Mother up the stairs.

Mother shocked me by looking back and hissing, "Come on you two!"

155

Lenore and I were hesitant, but Redd was not going to let us off the hook so easily.

"Come on up here, you fine things. Mrs. Reese, your whole family is fine. Ain't they?" While the crowd laughed and clapped, I stood holding my hands not knowing what to do and fervently wishing I wasn't there. "Mrs. Reese is one good-looking woman. Don't you think so?" he asked the crowd, which then applauded and laughed, clapping their hands as if we had done something worthy of applause. "These are her two daughters. Ain't they fine too?" Redd was grinning and making gestures of a sexual nature, only I wasn't sure what they meant. I was even more embarrassed and desperately wanted the ground to open up and swallow me that very instant. Instead, I just held my head down. Redd wouldn't leave well enough alone and reached over and lifted my face as he said, "Ain't this a fine something…but she jail bait. We have to wait for her."

Mother ate up all the attention. She hugged Redd while reaching for the microphone. Now that she was on a stage, it was her party. Looking at Redd, she smiled and then laughed. "I got my eye on you," she said with a wily smirk. "Don't forget. I got my eye on you!" Then she looked out into the crowd, and said, "I got my eye on all of you. Someday you all gonna come my way, and I'm waitin'." The crowd became hysterical. Her "dead" humor had been a great smash. Now, if possible, I was even more embarrassed and didn't know what to do. So, I mentally blocked out everything and after that I no longer heard a word being said.

That night seemed interminable and I thought it would never end. After Redd Foxx had finished his show, the strippers came on stage and took *everything* off. My eyes were as big as dollars as the dancers were definitely better endowed than the waitresses. They danced around a pole while tossing their breasts around and the tassels going in circles. I was amazed how they twirled their tits. When the lights were turned down, the tassels glowed in the dark. I could not believe my eyes. What talent. What a show. All the red lights around the stage gave me the feeling of being naughty.

The men were going crazy over the dancers, putting money into their g-strings and grabbing at their breasts. I was in awe as I had never imagined, let alone seen anything like that before. Looking around at the audience, I saw men and women kissing and rubbing on each other right there in the club for all to see, and obviously didn't care who saw them. I tried not to stare, but I really couldn't help myself as stuff was going on all around me.

As I sat there, unable to move, a man leaned over in my face. "Hey, baby. I got something for you," he leered, rubbing his hand near his private parts. He smelled awful with sour alcohol reeking from his mouth.

Startled and frightened, I jumped and then I heard a voice say, "She's with me. Fuck off!" The handsome chauffeur had come to my rescue. "You okay?" he asked.

"Yes. Thanks for getting him away from me."

I couldn't see the chauffeur's face very well because it was quite dark in the room, but his voice I would have recognized anywhere. It was strong and yet soft at the same time. "You shouldn't be here," he said.

"My Mother wants me to be exposed to the night life," I answered in a shaky voice.

"Bull shit! You're too young, and she shouldn't have brought you here." *Who did he think he was, getting into my business,* I wondered.

Then he admonished, "Don't drink anything they give you…not even water."

"Why?" I asked.

"Just don't! Sometimes, they put stuff in the drinks. Please, don't drink anything. Okay?"

He then left me sitting there, and I realized Mother had not even noticed that I had been inappropriately accosted. The noise and music were deafening and I knew in my heart this was a, "Den of Iniquity" and a very dangerous place for anyone to be—let alone a fourteen-year old. I was thankful the young man had warned me about drinking anything and being now afraid, I didn't touch a drop the rest of the night.

My recollection of how we got out of the main room is hazy but I do remember finding myself in the upstairs of the Club. Lenore was sitting on a stool at the bar, while I was sitting in a chair across the room trying not to be noticed. Soon the party from downstairs gravitated upstairs and it seemed as if at least half of the crowd from the Club was up there. The showgirls, still not dressed, pranced around rubbing on the men, smiling in their faces, sitting on their laps, and talking loud.

I even saw one of the showgirls walk over to Lenore who was sitting alone and singing, not too loudly but off key, "Whatever Lola Wants, Lola Gets." Actually, she always sang off key. The showgirl put her arm around Lenore and kissed her on the neck and I thought someone had shot a gun. Lenore jumped up screaming and as she violently shoved the showgirl away from her yelled, "Are you crazy, bitch? I don't fuck no women. Do I look like a freak to you?"

Lenore would not stop and when the showgirl pushed Lenore out of her face, Lenore hit the girl so hard blood spurted from her mouth. Suddenly people were there holding onto Lenore and the showgirl.

Mother just sat at a table with Redd and some other comedians and seemed unmoved and uncaring as to what was going on. So I ran over to her and anxiously said, "Mother, Lenore is in trouble!"

"She's okay. She can handle herself."

"But Mother, that girl is going to hurt her! She's talking about killing her!"

I couldn't get a positive response out of Mother so I ran back through all the commotion over to Lenore and while pulling on her arm begged, "Let's get out of here. Come on Lenore. Let's go!"

"That bitch was coming on to me!" Her words were slurred and she was unable to stand up straight.

The showgirl continued to curse and threatens to kill Lenore even while two guys restrained her, and I thought, *Don't let go of her, please.*

"Please, let's go Lenore," I pleaded again and tried to pull her in the direction of the door.

Then again, to my surprise, our chauffeur came to the rescue. He took Lenore by the waist and as she leaned on him, we made our way down the stairs, out the back of the Club and to where the limo was waiting.

"Thank you again," I said.

"You're a cool girl, just not ready for this life," he told me.

"What about Mother? She's still in there. Should I go get her?"

"No. I better go. That bitch said she was getting a knife, planning to cut Lenore. You might get in her way. I'll go get Mrs. Reese."

"Hurry! I hear sirens coming. I think somebody must have called the police."

"Be back in a jiff," he called as he ran back into the Club. Minutes later, he was walking out with Mother.

Since she had definitely been drinking she had an attitude and accused, "Lenore, why'd you mess with that showgirl?" But Lenore was too wasted to respond.

I sat back in the limo with my arm around Lenore and had to listen to Mother complain all the way home. By the time I finally reached my bedroom, the clock said 3:00 a.m. It had been a dreadfully long night!

Before I went to sleep though, I did some thinking about the events of the night. I realized I had learned another lesson in life: Nightlife was not for me! I had learned where I did not belong and where I would never go again. Also, I realized I was nothing like my Mother. Maybe I looked a lot like her, but I did not act like her, nor did I ever want to be like her. She was a wonderful businesswoman, respected by everyone, but no one knew who she really was. Maybe I was stuck living with her, but my plan was to grow up and get as far away from her as I could.

Then I remembered a story my Father had told me years before about an old man walking in the desert and enjoying the sun. The old man came upon a rattlesnake that had been badly hurt and the snake was close to death. He felt sorry for the snake, picked him up, wrapped him in his shirt and took him home. For many days and nights he sat up with the snake, putting salve on his wounds. Slowly the snake began to heal, and the old man and the snake became friends. They slept together. They ate together. He walked around with the snake wrapped around his neck and did not fear the snake because after all, he had saved the snake's life. One hot evening, the old man and the snake were sleeping. Suddenly, the old man woke with a sharp bite to his neck. Shocked and stunned out of a deep sleep, he looked over at the snake. The rattle on the tail of the snake was still shaking. The old man had tears in his eyes because he knew the bite would be fatal.

"Why? Why did you bite me, snake? I took you in when you were hurt. I nurtured you back to good health. I loved you as a friend."

The snake slithered around the bed, raising his head, his tongue flipping in and out. "Why are you surprised, old man? You knew I was a snake when you took me in."

My Father was a wise man. He left my Mother because of her lifestyle, but I had no choice; I had to live with her. That night, I determined never to be like her and if necessary, to fight to be as different as possible.

29

COMING DOWN FROM THE UPSTAIRS APARTMENT TO
the Funeral Home proper, I ran into Lenore who whispered, "I spent time
with Ilona!" Immediately my ears and face perked up and I quickly looked
around because Mother would be angry if she knew.

Lenore took me by the shoulder and gently led me into the Viewing
Room where the lights were dim, with only two bodies ready for viewing.
Leaning toward my ear, Lenore said, "Ilona wants to see you, but I don't
know how to get you over there without Mother finding out." My heart
jumped for joy, as I had missed Ilona so much. "She wanted to know if you
got the birthday gift she left at the front door?"

"Lenore, Mother said if I call or talk to Ilona or Dad, she'd never forgive
me for betraying her. I never got a gift or anything—and it had been almost
four years."

"Be cool. Don't say anything. I'll figure a way to take you to see her, but
if Mother finds out, I'll deny being involved."

"Okay." Now my heart had something to be happy about. I had hopes.
I'd see Ilona.

Lenore came over that evening and told Mother she wanted me to go
with her to see her mother-in-law. Mother had a lot of company, the phones
were quiet downstairs and the party upstairs had just begun. So I was able to
leave without her questioning us. I didn't like the feeling of being sneaky, but
knew it was the only way I would be able to see Ilona.

The drive over to Dad's seemed to take only a few minutes—probably
because I was so excited, anxious and happy all at the same time. I loved
Ilona more than words could say and on that drive, decided, *I wanted to be
just like her. She is kind, pretty, and always fun to be around. Sees the good in*

people—even in Mother.

I thought, *Hate is a terrible thing because it eats you from the inside out. It can even change a person's facial expressions. It ages you, causes you to be sick. Mother hates Dad and Ilona in the worst way. I don't think I'll ever understand that. I only want to get as far away as possible. Maybe death will be my only way of escape.*

Many years prior, I had taught myself to tune people out so as to be in my own private world. In that world I'd imagine how I would kill myself. At times I think I constantly thought about how I would do it. I remember spending many nights lying in my bed, planning how to do it—visualizing the ceiling being the floor and the floor the ceiling. That way, the door would be hard for anyone to climb over and come into my room. I craved to know the peace of the dead as they slept with no fears, and no one could hurt them any more. One idea was I would shoot myself, but had to rule that out as we didn't own a gun…at least I was unaware of one. Another plan was to stab myself, but I hate pain and it had to be painless. An overdose of pills sounded good, until I remembered a lady that had killed herself with an overdose of pills. When they had brought her body to the Mortuary, she really stunk.

Lenore's voice finally got through to me just as her car pulled into the driveway. I hadn't been here since the night I had run away from all the fighting, and this time I saw things differently because I paid attention to details. There was a big front yard and on either side was a large window. From the driveway I could see the two small houses in the back where Ilona and Willie Jr. lived.

Ilona screamed, "Little Mary! Little Mary!" as she jumped over the steps, running full speed to the car. In my haste I fought with the car handle, as it would not open fast enough. My insides were shaking with more excitement than my heart could handle. Finally, the door opened and I ran full bore and jumped into her arms, tears flowing. We clung to each other like we were stuck with glue.

My eyes were so full of tears, I could not see anything but her shoulder. Then my brother gently touched me and said, "Hey, sis. How are you?"

Moving back a little, I looked at him and smiled, so happy to see him. Willie Jr. and I had hardly spent any time together, so closeness had not had much chance to grow. But I loved him and felt his love for me. It was then I understood that he also had been another of Mother's victims.

Dad was standing on the porch with a huge smile and I kept hugging Ilona as we walked toward him. That beautiful smile told me all I needed to know…I was loved.

Lenore gently reminded us we only had a little bit of time as we entered our Dad's house. Ilona had cooked cornbread and spaghetti with strawberry Kool-Aid to drink. They were all my favorites and we fell in love all over again. It was a wonderful feeling—to know there was a real place where I knew and felt I belonged. I would only have a short time there and I would have to keep the joy and excitement locked in my heart. Sharing this with Mother would never be an option.

When Dad started saying bad things about Mother, Ilona stopped him. She knew I didn't want to waste my precious time with them hearing about why they hated each other. Instead we hurriedly tried to get caught up on each other's lives. The hour passed quickly and much too soon Lenore and I were headed back to the Mortuary. On the drive back, I allowed myself to cry, silently, getting it out of my system so as not to make Mother suspicious. Lenore had been wonderful to me. She knew the hell I was living in, but she too had her hands tied. Things would always be Mother's way.

When we arrived, the main Funeral Home lights were out, but the upstairs was lit up like a nightclub. We could hear the laughter and music before we even had opened the car doors. Our strategy was I would go to the Viewing Room and talk with whoever was there while Lenore went upstairs to show her face so Mother would not question how long we had been gone.

Dim lighting lit the way through the Front Office, down the hall and past the Chapel. The darkness of the Mortuary never frightened me, it was only when I was outside or in my bedroom that it bothered me. To me, the darkness in the Funeral Home meant peace. Mr. Holmes had told me, "Remember. It's not the dead that will hurt you."

Momentarily, I stood in the doorway of the Viewing Room while I reached my hand behind the curtain and turned on the light. Two beautiful caskets were revealed—one a steel gray and the other light blue with one woman and one man, on separate sides of the room. Then, in the middle of the room facing me, I noticed a smaller, wooden casket where there lay a little boy, about five or six-years old. Immediately I walked over to the little casket and gazed down at the small hands that had been gently placed one on top of the other. I touched his hand and gently rubbed it, wondering how and why he had died. My heart ached for him as I stared at the lifeless little body, so still, so peaceful, free from harm. He looked dressed for church, in a navy blue suit with a light-blue bow tie. His skin was dark bronze and his black hair was curly, with a part on the left side.

What a short little life he had. Why did he have to die? Tears fell from my eyes down to the light- blue satin cover that draped gently from the casket.

Then I became aware of all the flowers filling the Viewing Room and the strong lavender fragrance. I couldn't help it and said out loud, "Don't they know? A dead nose can't smell a rose? I'm sorry little fellow," I whispered to him. "You're okay now." I turned my back on him because looking at him made my heart hurt too much—feeling jealous because he was free and I was in a prison in my own soul.

When I turned back to look at him again, feeling his loneliness I asked, "Why are you here, alone? Where is your Mother? Why have they left you here in the dark?" I wanted to hold him and comfort him, so I said, "I'll stay with you. I'll stay here with you." Taking his small hand I held onto it. Because it was cold and hard, I wanted to warm it. He was a child, and his parents had left him alone. I told him I knew what it was like to be alone, about the bad man that wanted to kill me, and that one day I would meet him again, because one day I would get up the nerve to kill myself.

The clock did not stand still, and I was unaware that an hour had passed. Mr. Blakley had heard me and had been standing outside the Viewing Room, listening to me. "Child, come on out of there. Folks gonna think you crazy talking to dead folks!"

"I know. I think I am crazy," I said, as I headed out of the room, "but I don't care." Mr. Blakley was not as open and friendly as Mr. Holmes, or Mr. Lary and it would be a full-time job for me to win him over.

When I left the little boy it was with a heavy heart. I decided I would work his funeral, because I wanted to see his parents. I wanted to light into them—give them a piece of my mind for leaving him all alone but, of course, I could not do that as I was a mortician like my Mother and so, would act accordingly.

Going upstairs to the apartment I found the living room full of people. Among them were a few gravediggers I had met at one of the cemeteries, and Reverend Miles and his lover David. Everyone was drinking, laughing, and loudly talking.

I didn't say a word to anyone but headed directly to my room. Before I had taken more than a few steps Mother yelled out, "Can't you speak?"

"Yeah. Hello. Good-night."

I closed the door and pulled a stool up under the handle to secure it, hoping it would keep the drunks from finding their way into my room. Since the unnaturally loud noise kept me from falling asleep, as I lay there my thoughts were about the little boy and how much I wanted to be with him.

Suddenly my reverie was interrupted when someone shook the doorknob to my bedroom. I sat up and froze, watching the stool move until it fell over and the door was forcibly opened and there stood one of the gravediggers.

"What...what do you want?" I yelled, letting him know I didn't want him to come in. But he came in anyway and sat down on the side of my bed, putting his hand possessively on my leg.

"Little Mary, you're so pretty," he crooned in a drunken voice. He was an ugly, older man—at least thirty-five or forty.

"You have to get out of here! Now!" I yelled.

His hand pressed down harder on my leg as he asked, "Why don't you like me? I'm a nice guy."

I hated the smell of alcohol and begged, "Please, leave me alone and go back to the party."

"Okay, but I'll be back. I'm not going to hurt you. I like you a lot," he promised.

That whole night I was afraid to go to sleep for fear of being caught-off-guard by him, or another of his drinking cronies.

30

SUNDAY MORNINGS WERE USUALLY PRETTY QUIET AROUND
the Funeral Home mainly because Mother usually partied until the early
hours. Also, since she didn't go to church, she allowed herself to sleep until
at least Noon. No one was allowed to disturb her for any reason, other than
someone dying. She reasoned we were in church and heard Preachers preach
every other day of the week.

"Sunday is my day off," Mother would say. "I work six days and if God
rested on the seventh day, so will I."

Sitting at the kitchen table waiting for Mother to wake up that particular
Sunday, I began wondering how I compared to my Mother and decided I
handled people with the same charisma that she did, but...she was the Queen
of the Funeral Business; I could never forget that. For years I had watched
her work—she was incredible to watch. When Mrs. Reese directed a funeral,
it was first class all the way. People stood in line to shake her hand with
gratitude for the service she'd given them. I decided I wanted to be just like
her, just working on funerals, I mean.

* * *

The next day Monday, there were three funerals scheduled and everyone
seemed to be on edge. It kept the staff on their toes as they hurried around,
making sure the programs with the obituaries were in the right places for the
right funerals, and that there were enough fans in the pews. The new fans
now read: J.T. Stone Funeral Home, with a single picture of Mrs. Reese in
the middle.

The funeral service for the little boy was scheduled first and I knew it would be hard because I felt I really had connected with the young child. When I saw the parents getting out of the family car, grieving uncontrollably, I felt ashamed for wanting to yell at them the night before for leaving him. I had wrongly judged them for not loving the little boy but watching them grieving, I could actually feel their pain. They had loved him and I had had no right to judge their feelings. I wept like a family member, running to the restroom so as not to be seen because that was not "professional."

The service started on time with a full Chapel and the grieving Mother's cries could be heard above the Preacher's voice. I strained to hear what the Preacher was saying, hoping he would tell how the little boy had died. The Father, also very emotional, rocked back and forth, holding onto the Mother, keeping her in her seat.

At the end of the service, while the hymn "Jesus Loves Me" was being softly sung, Mother walked the Father up first to say good-bye. He leaned over the casket, taking his last look at his precious son and his sobs sounded like thunder in my heart. Mother then walked over and stood next to the child's Mother, waiting for her to compose herself enough to stand. Jan stood directly behind her with smelling salts, fanning the woman gently, hoping she would not faint. Mother gently touched her arm and the Mother finally stood, trembling. Jan and Mother put their arms around her waist and slowly moved her toward the casket. The sobs and moans from the pews could be heard above the singing and the organ music. I watched his Mother fall on the casket, trying to pull her child out. His little body came half out; his legs and feet staying in the bottom half of the casket.

"My baby! My baby!" she cried out in agony. My heart was pounding. I tried to stay composed but my feelings were getting away from me. Quickly I moved toward them, catching the end of the casket and trying to stabilize it before the stand gave way. Mr. Blakley, Jan, and Mother, were holding on to the child's Mother and trying to pry her hands from the little navy suit. In the tussle, his little blue-bow tie had come off and flowers had been knocked over with wreaths thrown as far as the third pews.

The instant reaction of Mother was astounding. "Stop!" she commanded. "He's gone! Look at me!" She was stern but very compassionate, holding the Mother by the waist. Mr. Blakley, Jan, and I, put the child back into his casket, picked up the flowers, and organized things as quickly as possible. Mother calmly walked the little boy's Mother back to the front pew, all the while talking soothingly to her as she fanned and passed the smelling salts by her nose. There was not a dry eye in the place.

Mother and I rode from the cemetery together, but neither of us wanted to talk. With all the emotions expended in the Chapel and at the gravesite, neither of us knew how much more we could take. I kept thinking about the little boy in the wooden casket. It was still a mystery to me as to how he had died, but at that point, I no longer wanted to know—he was gone.

As you can imagine, the rest of the day was hectic for all of us. Fortunately, the second funeral was a closed casket. Closed-casket funerals usually ran well. People would cry, but they could contain their feelings without a lot of screaming or fainting when looking upon the deceased.

The third funeral was held at a church on the other side of town, and the Preacher preached for an hour on what a wonderful woman Sister Harris had been. That hour gave me time to sit and rest while I watched Mrs. Reese do her thing. Now, I had a better understanding as to why she was usually so tired after a funeral. The constant feelings and heart that is put into showing the family you care, is hard, emotional work.

At last, the time had come to open the casket for the final viewing when the family was to walk up and kiss or say their final good-byes. Mother was the one to open the casket, and she moved with the grace of Ginger Rogers, putting aside the wreath of flowers draped across the top of the casket, unlocking the latch to lift the top for the torso to be viewed, pulling out the satin cover and draping it over the side.

Suddenly the top of the casket slammed down. Mother stood there for a moment with her back to the people. I wondered what was going on. She then walked to the center of the church and waited.

Calmly, Mother turned to the mourners and said, "I have to apologize. The latch has broken, and it is impossible to open it at this time. With your indulgence, this is going to stay closed for the rest of the service." She reached and pulled the flowers back, draping them over the casket. I couldn't imagine what was wrong, other than the latch had broken.

As we drove to the cemetery, Mother looked at me, and said, "Child. We got the wrong body! We got Mr. Packard. Not Mrs. Harris!"

"Oh, my goodness!" I gasped. "What are we gonna do?"

"Nothing. We're gonna bury him for now. Later we'll switch them."

I just sat there in amazement. This had been one of the most stressful days I had experienced. The gravediggers would have to switch the caskets during the night.

31

AFTER WE MOVED FROM ABOVE THE FUNERAL HOME to our house, Tom's daughter Ethel came to live with us, which meant I had to share my bedroom. Surprisingly, we became friends and even though we were quite different, learned to love each other as if we were whole sisters instead of stepsisters.

Mother made over Ethel constantly. Always saying what a wonderful girl she was, and more or less ignored me as usual. Since Ethel didn't like being in the Funeral Home, I had the advantage of being able to get away from everyone by going over there.

Tom and Mother got into really nasty fights at least twice a week—the rest of the week was part-time. Ethel learned quickly not to get in their way because during one of their knock-down-drag-outs, she got hit on the head with a plate. After that she stayed out of the way in the room with me.

Sometimes I'd play tricks on Ethel and she'd fall for them every time. On the rare days she would come to the Funeral Home, I'd hide behind the door of the Embalming Room when there were a couple of bodies on the slabs. Ethel would be calling me, but I wouldn't answer. I would wait patiently until she came through the door, then jump out directly in front of her face yelling, "Boo!" She'd turn and run, screaming and I would laugh until tears ran down my cheeks. Of course, later Mother would put me on punishment, but Ethel always forgave me, while Mother stayed angry with me for days.

Ethel and I were a year apart in school, so I became the cool, big sister because I had had so many fights that I had earned respect in the Inner City. I had no trouble with the boys liking me, but my very fair complexion made kids question if I were Black or White. I tried to do whatever it took to look Black and to dress Black, even putting on five pairs of panties, trying to make my butt bigger. I had small bones, small legs and no butt. Ethel was tall and skinny and shapely compared to me.

We were both good students and with her patient help my grades improved and I was back to being an "A" student. During our spare time we liked to go roller-skating. We were cute and knew it; all the boys liked us. junior high was a breeze and we were in control. I tried to stay away from home as much as possible, so for me, school became another form of escape. There I could be "cool" and was given the attention I so craved.

Being the daughter of Mrs. Reese had its rewards. Mainly my classmates thought we were rich and that went a long way in helping us easily make friends.

The J.T. Stone Mortuary's reputation quickly grew. Mother was on the radio every Sunday, and the newspapers ran articles about her. Fans had been distributed to all the Black churches, so her face was recognized everywhere we went. Business was good…real good.

* * *

Before each funeral I would go and check out the Viewing Room, look at the bodies, and say my good-byes. Mr. Blakley began to warm up to me, as I'd sit quietly with him while he did his embalming. At first I thought he looked at me with an upside-down smile, like a frown. But I soon realized that was just the way he had been born. With a dry voice, he'd often say, "You know, Little Mary, I believe you could make a dead person talk." Coming from him, that was a great compliment.

The first time a body passed gas while we were together in the Embalming Room, I looked at him with a big question mark on my face and asked, "Did you do that?" I would wear a silly look with a frown. I knew it was the corpse, but it made him laugh. In time, our friendship grew and I learned I could confide in him, and he in me.

Mr. Blakley would tell me stories about gravediggers and Preachers for which he had absolutely no respect. Sometimes he would say, "The things I've seen done would make you sick, Little Mary."

A few days after the little boy's funeral I told him, "Mr. Blakley, a lot of the things I've seen make me sick, too." I dropped my head for a moment, thinking about the little boy. "In all my experiences, the little boy the other day was the hardest one I worked."

Mr. Blakley said, "Let me tell you about one I did a few years ago. I had to embalm a little girl, two-years old and that nearly broke my heart." He shook his head, retrieving the memories. "That poor little girl. When I picked up her body from the morgue I physically got sick. They got some

172

sick SOB's out there!"

His face hardened and I just had to ask, "What? Mr. Blakley, what happened?"

"I hate thinking about it, girl. If she'd been my grandchild, I'd have killed her Momma, probably her Daddy, too, since he let it happen."

"Come on, Mr. Blakley. You gotta tell me. You got my curiosity up."

"Drunks and fools shouldn't have kids. They should pass a law, or put saltpeter in their water. Stop 'um from making babies, that's what they should do."

That was the second time I'd heard something about saltpeter. "What is saltpeter, Mr. Blakley?" I was afraid to ask Mother, because she said people were sweeping it off their front porches in Mississippi. I figured it had something to do with voodoo and that scared me.

"Little Mary, I ain't the one to tell you about this kind of stuff. Ask your Momma."

"Come on, Mr. Blakley. I tell you all kinds of things. You're my friend. Please tell me. I won't tell anyone about our talks. I want to hear about the little girl…I'm not leaving till you tell me." I climbed up onto the stool next to the slab with the body he was working on and with my hands resting in my lap said, "I'm ready."

Giving a reluctant smile he said, "I told you, you something else, girl." I knew he was giving in. "Saltpeter is what they give men in the military. They put it in their food, and it kills their nature."

"What nature are you talking about, Mr. Blakley?"

"Their sex drive. The saltpeter supposes to kill their sex drive!" He was almost shouting. I could tell he was really embarrassed—now I was, too.

"Why do they do that?"

"Cause, ain't a bunch of women in the military, you know. Don't want men going crazy."

"Oh. So if men don't get sex they go crazy?"

"Little Mary. I can't talk about this with you no more. Ask your Momma."

"Don't get angry with me, Mr. Blakley. I don't understand men very much. I just want to understand. Daniel got someone else pregnant, cause I didn't give him sex. So is it my fault I lost him?"

"Daniel was dumb and you were too young," he replied. He loved you but he's a young man, and the need to have sex drives a man to go with women they may not love. That's what happened with him."

That was a painful subject as I had loved Daniel with all my heart and lost him. Just then the Everly Brother's song, "Dream, Dream, Dream", came on the radio, playing softly. I had not even noticed the radio had been on. The song made my heart ache as I remembered Daniel, and that I dreamt about him often. *He had promised to save me from all of Mother's drunken friends and from her wrath by taking me away. We had planned to have a home and kids. But that dream is now dead—all gone because Daniel couldn't wait for me and had to have sex with someone else.*

I sat there and lost my desire to talk and sadness filled my eyes. Mr. Blakley said, "Hey. Snap out of it! Don't think about him no more. You're a pretty girl. You'll fall in love again, again, and again. You'll be breaking hearts. You'd break my heart if I was younger."

"I'm sorry. I guess you don't want to be in on my pity party, huh?"

"No way. Pity is for fools, and don't you forget it!

"There's an amusement park in Long Beach, and they got a roller coaster—a big sucker. The thing goes up real slow, and then it comes down real fast, folks screaming with excitement. But when they get to the bottom, the excitement only lasts a little while. Then it stops. The thrill is gone. So they have to go up again, just for the thrill. Little girl, that's what life is all about—ups and downs. The ups and downs keep the excitement in our lives, otherwise we'd be dead, just like this man here on the slab. No more ups for him, or downs. No more living; death is final; no more chances. He can't make his wrongs rights. It's over for him. Do you understand what I'm saying?"

Mr. Blakley was making strong points, and I was paying attention. "Little Mary, if you ride a bike, and fall off, you get back on. You don't throw the bike away and walk, do you?"

"No. I know what you mean," I nodded in agreement.

"I hope so girl. You gotta always remember if you get knocked down, get up, dust yourself off, and start again. You don't let anyone keep you down! Remember, you're stronger than you think, and God don't give you no more than you can handle."

"Mr. Blakley, thanks. I do understand. I'll make my life count. But I can't wait to finish school and move away because I hate all the parties and Mother's friends. There are some nights I have to fight them off. Even though I lock my door and put a chair under the knob, they still get it unlocked. I don't know what to do."

"I know, child. I know." Mr. Blakley walked over to me, his arms stretched out. He gave me a hug, patting me on my back. That wasn't his usual nature. "You better go on home. It's getting late."

"But you said you'd tell me about the little girl."

How about I tell you tomorrow. I'm finished in here and I want to go home. I'm tired of looking at dead folks. You brighten up this Embalming Room. You know that?"

"Not today, I don't."

"Yes, you do. You got a big heart, Little Mary. You're special, child. I can see it in your eyes."

"Thanks, Mr. Blakley. I think you're special, too."

* * *

The walk home could take as long as five minutes but I was in no hurry. The new house did not compare to the big house on the West Side. To me, all the homes in the Inner City looked alike—small frame homes with yards not very well manicured. Often I saw undernourished and obviously abused dogs running loose, and that always made my heart ache.

That day I walked home rather slowly as I thought over the lessons on life I had heard from Mr. Blakley. *I just realized he is much wiser and nicer than he looks. Isn't it interesting as I look back over my short years, I see the Embalming Room has been the real classroom in my life. Why is it I feel alive when I am in the presence of dead bodies but feel dead when in the presence of the living? I do not belong here.*

The more I thought about it, the more I was convinced death was the only way for me to ever find peace.

32

WHEN LOU PULLED INTO OUR DRIVEWAY THAT NIGHT, I ran and put my prettiest blouse on and combed my hair the way he once had complimented. Then I stole a few drops of Chanel Perfume from Mother's room before running to sit in the front room as though I hadn't noticed he had arrived.

Lou Rawls was one of the nicest friends my Mother had. The thought of killing myself was on hold for awhile because I so looked forward to being with him. I'd sit on the piano stool with him while he sang songs that made my heart melt. His deep voice caused me to tremble with excitement; my heart beat like thunder as I wondered from whence came that magnificent voice? I'd sit in awe listening, not wanting him to stop.

For awhile, Lou became a regular at our house and I greatly anticipated his visits. I think I could have listened to him talk or sing all night long. During that point in time, was the only period when I truly enjoyed my Mother's parties. My crush on him was never detected because I was good at keeping things to myself. Whenever I saw Lou I felt silly, like the schoolgirl that I was. I had wanted him to notice me, but since I was still a teenager and he was a young man, our relationship was truly only a friendship. I'll never forget those hours when we sat on the piano bench and just talked.

When Lou sang, we just quietly hummed. His voice made even Mother sit quietly. It was really something how he could control a room and we would applaud him with the praise of a king. The outstanding thing he taught me was the meaning of never giving up on anything.

"Never react. Always stay cool," his words would echo in my ears. "That way, you're the one in control." He once said, "Little Mary, I know things are not easy for you. I've seen what goes on and I wish I could help you. Finish school and if you want things to change in your life, you have to be willing to change first."

I guess Lou had seen my Mother go off on me several times for no known reason, and I assumed that was his reason for some of our talks. Whenever he touched my hand, my knees would shake.

"Think about what you want to be when you grow up. You can do or be anything you want. It's up to you."

His voice had been so deep and strong I wanted to lean on his chest and say, "Take me away, please!" But I could never let him know that he was my dream man.

There was only one Lou Rawls. He was talented, handsome, strong, and most of all, he was a gentleman. He was in a class of his own. I had learned to hate every man that came through our front door, but Lou was a good man and when he was around, I didn't think about dying so much.

Another evening, as Lou and I sat on the piano bench, I said, "Lou, one day you're going to be a big hit. Your songs will be all over the world. I know people will love you. You'll get big bucks and then you'll forget all about me."

"With fans like you, I'll be okay," he had answered.

"Will you remember me when you become a big star?" I felt so stupid for asking such a dumb question, but in my heart I knew he wouldn't be around much longer. Mother would run him off, just like she did everyone else.

"I'll never forget you, Little Mary," he said with a hug and a twinkle in his eye. I believed him. I smiled all evening; nothing could ruin that night. I believed in my heart that I had Lou for a friend for the rest of my life, and secretly hoped when I was grown he would look at me differently.

Many times just the memory of the tone of his voice, or his smile of assurance, are what kept me going. I knew I would be grown in a few years and I had determined to live my life differently than my Mother's. I believed Lou knew that I loved him, in my teenage way, but that was the problem—I was just a young teenager, the property of my Mother; she owned me, but not my soul.

* * *

The people who came over on a regular basis became "family." Anyone and everyone who had any talent would take their turn performing for us. I loved aunt Robbie, who really wasn't my aunt, but Billy Preston's Mother. She sang like an angel, and Billy would play the piano or the organ and he was only my age. His talent was truly a gift from above.

Mother was quick to remind me on many occasions, "Little Mary, I don't think you got a gift from above. If you did, your talent is hidden so deep I don't think it will ever be found."

Aunt Robbie worked for Mother at the Funeral Home where she sang for the funerals. I always thought her voice was as beautiful as Mahalia Jackson's. Many times I wished she was my real aunt and that my Mother was more like her. She also made sure Billy didn't miss any of his music lessons and he practiced, practiced, and practiced some more. There were days I wanted to spend time with Billy, but he had to practice. So, I'd sit on his porch waiting until I could not sit anymore.

* * *

The house was almost always full of people. There were the gravediggers, Lenore, JT, Reverend Lindsey, a few musicians, and Tom. It was fun for awhile, when Lou was there but as soon as he left, I would go to bed.

JT had not been around much for a number of years as he had been in the Service. But once he was discharged, he was in and out of our lives quite frequently, even though he had recently gotten married. In fact, for a short time he worked at the Funeral Home.

Once he was back in our lives on a regular basis, things changed because he was her favorite son; he knew it and took advantage of her feelings. He was the one person who was not afraid of her and felt free to say or cuss, whatever he felt to her. Surprisingly, JT did not like Mother's friends and there were many loud fights between them, as he felt free to voice his displeasure and dislike.

Even though he was such a prima donna, Mother favored and catered to him. In fact, I stayed out of his way as much as possible because Mother used him to dole out her sick type of punishment to her hapless victims, and that definitely included me. Whoever it was that had angered or displeased her, she would either make up a story or grossly distort the truth in her complaint to JT. He would then find the poor victim and cuss them out. To be cussed out by JT was a terrible experience! All Mother had to do was tattle to him and he became judge, jury, and executioner—like her personal avenging angel—and she loved it!

Gradually, Lenore began staying more and more at our house day and night because she loved all the company Mother had. Though she really could not carry a tune, she kept trying to sing along with people. She had never had any training and had such a loud voice she could not be ignored—especially when her drinking erased any sense of logic. Then she would dance and sing until you needed a drink in order to tolerate her noise.

179

On the other hand, JT had a great voice and Mother was inordinately proud of him. JT was Mother's "Jesus." It seemed she worshiped him, and everyone knew it. Every chance she got she'd rub Lenore's face in it by saying, "JT is so wonderful and talented."

I'd watch as each night started out with everyone singing, drinking and having fun. No matter how much fun people were having, Lenore and JT would get into big arguments, because she would not let him sing without her singing along in her off-key voice. This would get him so upset that they soon would be cursing and screaming at each other, while Mother just sat back and laughed. Sometimes Tom would get in the middle of the argument and then Mother would curse him out for attacking JT. She made sure everyone new that JT was her son and no one said "No" to him.

When the arguments would start, a few people with good sense would leave. There were a few times when Lou was there when these arguments arose and he always left at the first sign of a fight. But most parties were fun and it seemed to me as if we were one big family. It wasn't until after 11:00 p.m. that personalities made their metamorphosis. The slow, continuous alcohol consumption during the evening finally caught up with them and they became drunks out of control.

I had a few aunts and uncles of no blood relation that I respected for who they were. Aunt Robbie, for example, was a classy lady. She'd leave early, kiss me on the forehead, and say, "Don't drink," and with a smile, she'd leave. My heart always wanted to leave with anyone who showed they cared. But I was the daughter of Mrs. Reese, and no one wanted to confront her on her behavior.

* * *

Reverend Lindsey was a tall, dark-skinned, charismatic man, in his mid-forties. He looked just like what a Baptist Preacher should look like. His church was in South Central Los Angeles, with a thousand or more followers. He worked as Mother's partner on the funerals. Mother trusted him, but he was plotting behind her back.

Mr. Jones, another partner, was a short, stumpy man. He had worked in Mississippi, and knew the J.T. Stone family very well.

Business was at its highest peak and they all were making a lot of money. Reverend Lindsey and Mr. Jones knew Mrs. Reese had a weakness for liquor, and they used that to their advantage. Personally, I think they were jealous of her but they kissed up to her, drank her liquor, and ate her food. She is the one who made the Funeral Home what it was, and they rode along for a free ride.

Mother's reputation spread and she was well recognized throughout the Los Angeles area. In fact, she received the "Mother of the Year" award from Governor Brown. During the ceremony, I sat there watching her graciously accept it and felt both proud of her and at the same time wondering if anyone knew, really knew, what she was like as a Mother. Boy, did she have the public fooled! It always amazed me how much the people of the Inner City respected and looked up to her accomplishments.

That evening, I lay in bed looking at the ceiling; the noise in the front room was loud. I had a chair at the door and wished the ceiling were the floor and the floor the ceiling. For some reason I thought if the room was upside down, then maybe I'd feel safe. So wanting to fall asleep, I thought about the little boy we had buried recently, and about the story Mr. Blakley was going to share with me about a little two-year-old girl. Then my thoughts skipped to picturing myself lying in a casket. That I had never done but I would, and I thought I'd try it out before I died. After that, pleasant thoughts about Lou came into my mind and how he gave me hope. I wasn't sure what kind of hope, but knew he could always lift my heart whenever I saw him, and that was a good thing. Whenever he was around, I didn't see all the craziness in the house. I only saw him.

33

MOTHER HAD AN ACCOUNT WITH THE LIQUOR STORE around the corner and on Fridays I would be sent to pay the weekly bill. Once, out of pure curiosity, I opened the envelope to see the amount of the check. To my shock it read $255.00, and that was for only one week! I gasped, because I didn't earn that much in a month.

The nightly parties were where all that liquor disappeared. Each night a different group would come over. Sometimes the parties would get so loud the neighbors would call the police. When a black and white police car pulled up, there was no panic anymore. They knew Mother on a first name basis and if their shift was over, they would come in, get a drink, and have a good time with everyone else.

Each evening, I would sit near the window to see if Lou would drive up. Mother said that he had started his career singing in clubs, and that he was traveling. I missed him, but I could not let my feelings be known. Gradually, I stopped looking for him.

Sam Cooke also came by a few times, and then we heard he had been killed in a sleazy motel. The parties went on and on. People came and went, some nice, some outright mean.

* * *

Lenore hardly spent any time with her husband; she was spending it all with Mother. Mother always liked to remind Lenore that she and JT had the same Father, a man they never remembered knowing or meeting. This was to separate them from Ilona, Willie Jr. and me.

Them having the same Father was an issue I never did understand because

Lenore and JT had a love/hate relationship—more hate than love I believed. It seemed every time they were in the same room they argued, always fighting for Mother's attention, fighting to entertain her friends.

Ethel and I tried to stay out of their way, but some evenings we had no choice but to try and break up a fight between Tom and Mother, or Lenore and JT. Each night was a struggle for us to stay out of the way of a fight. Lenore would get a knife out of the kitchen, threaten to kill herself, and then Tom would wrestle to take it away from her. Then Lenore would run out of the house and down the street with several people trying to catch her. I would not run after her as I'd had my share of running the streets of Los Angeles. Running down a dark street was something I would never do again—I hated the night. While everyone was yelling and screaming and chasing after her, I would see Mother sitting at the kitchen table with her Jack Daniels in her hand, and a grin on her face. For some reason she enjoyed watching her two oldest fight. Why? I never understood.

* * *

After Ethel and I graduated from junior high, Tom sent Ethel away and I was alone again. Mother and Tom spent most of their time destroying each other. I stayed in my room, and when I could hear things breaking, I'd put my hands to my ears and pull the covers over my head.

One, evening, I woke to hear shouting and screaming. Mother came into my room "Get up. We're leaving."

"It's three o'clock in the morning. Where are we going?"

"Just get up! We're getting the hell out of here!"

She continued to scream and curse and I prayed, "Please, not over to my Dad's again."

I dressed fast in a pair of jeans and a shirt. Since I didn't know what to pack and for how long, I just took a bag with my cosmetics as Mother kept yelling for me to hurry, while Tom was calling her names and threatening to kill her. As quickly as I could I moved to get out of the house and into the car. I could see him standing in the doorway with tears in his eyes, and white foam at the corners of his mouth. His anger terrified me.

"Where are we going?" I asked when she started the car, put it in reverse and stepped on the gas, backing so fast out of the driveway she ran off the curb. My head jerked and my hands trembled. I didn't know what to expect.

"We're going to a hotel," she said after she calmed herself down a bit.

"Why?"

"None of your damn business!" she spat at me.

"Okay." This was not the time to ask questions so I just sat with tears in my eyes, tired of all the fights, tired of being afraid of the dark, not knowing where I was going or what to expect. Wondering: *How would I protect myself if I had to? Would I be able to sleep? Would I ever finish school? Mother lives her life without any concern for what other people think or feel. I am only in her way. Hasn't she said over and over "I do what I want." Then she'd sing a few words of the Frank Sinatra song, "I Did it My Way."*

We drove for a long time that night and I had no idea where we were going. I kept trying to identify my surroundings in order to know just where we were in case I had to run. But I already knew I would never run again.

Soon, I realized I had not been on this side of town before and then I saw a big sign that read, "BEVERLY HILLS." Mother turned the car, and slowly pulled up in front of the Beverly Hilton Hotel. A man in a black suit, white shirt, black bow tie and top hat, walked over and reached to open my door. My first reaction was I jumped, and then hit the lock thinking he was out to get me.

"Unlock the door. He's just the doorman," she said calmly, not amused at my stupidity.

I got out of the car and followed her lead. The entrance to the hotel was like nothing I had ever seen. It was glamorous, with huge chandeliers and flower arrangements that were larger than any I'd ever seen at a funeral. There in front of us was a long desk with several people standing behind it.

"Welcome to the Beverly Hilton," one of the people said with a smile.

Mother gestured as she said, "Thank you. I'd like a room. No, I'd like a suite for my daughter and me."

"Do you have reservations?"

"No. But I need a place, tonight."

The clerk was pleasant and told Mother, "I have a suite on the twelfth floor. Will that be to your satisfaction?"

"That's perfect. How much?" Mother replied.

"That's $125.00 a night."

"That's fine," Mother said as she filled out and signed the necessary papers, never flinching. Money was no object to her.

The elevator ride was exciting to me, and the suite was like a palace. Exhausted, I looked at her and she just pointed to the smaller room. When I went in, I hit the bed like a rock and thought, *It's four-thirty in the morning. Good thing I didn't have school today.*

Someone knocking on the door woke me the next morning but it was not morning as it was noon. Mother yelled from her bed, "Get the door!"

As I left my room and entered the main room, I turned all around in one spot, looking at all the beautiful gold and white linen, lamps of enormous size trimmed in gold, a large sofa, and a desk with two chairs. My eyes were now able to take it all in because early that morning I had been so tired I had missed so much. *Boy, this sure is first class!*

I opened the door to find a waiter dressed in black and white outside the door. He must have seen my puzzled look because he said, "This is your Room Service; the lunch you ordered."

"I didn't order anything," I answered.

"I did!" Mother yelled from her bedroom. "Come get some money and hurry up and bring me my coffee."

"One moment," I said and opened Mother's purse as she tried to sit up in the bed.

"Take five dollars and give it to him." Mother ordered.

"That's more than five dollars worth of food out there."

"That's the tip. The food order will be on our bill."

"Oh. I knew that."

Taking the money I gave it to the waiter, who was nice enough to put the food tray on the table and open up a white napkin that held silverware. After he poured a cup of coffee, he took the money out of my hand as he said, "Thank you, Miss."

"Mother? Do you think he knows we're Black?" I asked because I felt weird. "Isn't this hotel for Whites only?" I had never been in or seen a hotel except only in the movies.

"In this hotel, green money is the color they respect," Mother answered. "They don't know what we are anyway." She needed the coffee because she had a full-blown hangover.

I asked, "How long are we staying? I don't have any clothes."

"Take some money, go downstairs and buy some clothes."

I really enjoyed our stay as I felt like a celebrity. She was right; people treated us like we were VIP's.

I soon learned not to ask questions about her and Tom. We stayed at the hotel for a few days and then went back to the real world—South Central Los Angeles; I had now been exposed to a first-class hotel because my Mother wanted to hurt Tom—punish him by hiding out. It had been great to be there and now I really knew there was a difference between the rich White world, and the Black world in which I lived. It was money that made the difference and I was sure that was the world in which I wanted to live. I liked being treated as if I was important and knowing the luxury of anything I wanted was at my fingertips. Now I had seen a new way of life …no fighting for three days, no evil men, and Mother was happy. That was where I wanted to stay.

That hotel experience brought some new thoughts to ponder: *If White people were so bad, why did they smile all the time? Staying at the hotel showed me that White people were happy people. White people didn't seem so bad when they thought you were one of them or if you had money. Since I never want to pretend to be White, I guess I'll just have to have the money.*

On the ride back to South Central I asked Mother, "Why were those White people so nice to us? The Whites in Mississippi let you know they don't like you."

"Whites will smile in your face, but they don't like you. Don't ever forget that," she warned.

"But they seemed so nice to me. Maybe some of them are nice," I said hopefully.

That stay in the hotel had been a wonderful experience for me and I had enjoyed the friendly faces, and the "Hello Miss" whenever I'd walk by. There I had been made to feel like I was a good person for no special reason. I sincerely thought they liked me—just because.

"If you're staying at the Beverly Hilton, they know you have money. That's what they like. They don't give a shit about you! With money, you can make anybody like you," she informed me.

"Well, I had a good time. Thanks for bringing me."

"Yeah, it was a good few days for both of us. Tom's probably gone crazy worrying about me."

"Why didn't you call him and let him know where we were?" I asked.

"I didn't want him to know."

"Mother? Why don't you love him?"

"That's not what's important."

"Then what is?" I asked.

"I don't know," she said with a shrug.

34

As USUAL TOM AND MOTHER MADE UP, AND WERE ALL lovey-dovey again. I felt they deserved each other. They fought like cats and dogs and evidently found some sort of perverse pleasure in it.

Evidently Mr. Blakley was happy to see me when we came back as he said, "Hey, Little Mary, where you been for the last three days? I thought you was sick or somethin'."

"Oh, Mother and Tom had another big fight so Mother and I left in the middle of the night, and went to a fancy hotel in Beverly Hills."

"Wow! You guys acting like big shots, huh?"

"Mr. Blakley, it was just like on TV with White people everywhere—nice people. I had a great time."

"I bet they didn't know you and Mrs. Reese were Colored."

"I don't know, and I don't care. I'm who I am. I know I'm Negro, and I'm not ashamed of it either. But no one ever asked. It was never a question," I replied.

"Mr. Blakley? Why do White people dislike us so much? I know our history of slavery and stuff, but that's over isn't it?"

"I think they think we're not smart, because they've kept us down for so long—not letting us learn how to read or write. If they can keep you ignorant, they can keep using you. We have come a long way. That's all I can say. That's why education is so important for us. It's our weapon because with education we can fight back. We get smart like them, then we can't be used." " I'll be smart," I said.

Changing the subject, he asked, "Have you heard everybody is ticked off at Mrs. Reese?"

"No. Why?"

"She took off with a Funeral Home car and Reverend Lindsey needed all the cars for the funerals. He was sure pissed and made everybody around here miserable, telling everybody, "When I run this place, things will be different.""

"Oh, no. Does Mother know?"

"Girl, your Mother knows, but she don't care. She's the boss, but she shouldn't of taken the car off like that, but that's your Momma. Little Mary, folks are whispering a lot. Sounds like the Reverend Lindsey and Mr. Jones be planning somethin'. I keep trying to hear what they sayin' but when they see me, they stop talkin'. Mrs. Reese needs to watch out. Something is not right, but I don't know what."

The thought of them being angry with Mother hurt me. I wanted to know more to tell her, but wondered if she would believe me. I decided no, she only believed what she wanted.

I decided that night I'd try to tell her about what Mr. Blakley had said, but I didn't want to get him in trouble for talking to me. But I needed to warn her especially since I had never really trusted Reverend Lindsey, or Mr. Jones. They had real attitude problems and seemed to frown and moan, just to say hello. Another thing that bothered me, they were close friends with Reverend Miles, who to me was the scum of the earth.

Mother was sitting at the kitchen table with her Budweiser and when I came in. I evidently startled her because she said, "What the shit? Don't sneak up on me!"

"I'm sorry. I didn't mean to," I automatically responded as I sat down next to her.

"Get me a beer before you sit down," she ordered. I was already sitting down, but I jumped up and got the beer and the opener, and opened it for her. I noticed there were already three empty cans sitting on the table and picked them up, and threw them into the trashcan. Since it was then only six o'clock in the evening, I had a feeling it would be a long night.

I began, "Mother, did you know Reverend Lindsey was mad at you for taking the Funeral Home car?"

She looked at me with an evil eye and asked, "What the hell are you talking about?"

"Well, I overheard somebody at the Funeral Home saying that Reverend Lindsey was really upset with you and if it was his Funeral Home, he'd run it better."

"You don't know what the hell your talking about! Don't start no shit with me!" she threatened, now angry with me. All I had wanted to do was let her know people were talking and planning something behind her back.

"I'm sorry. I just wanted to let you know…"

Before I could finish my sentence, she yelled at me, "Get me another beer, and get the hell out of here!"

So, I got the beer and got the hell out of there, but it was too late to go back to the Embalming Room because by then Mr. Blakley would have already gone home. So I sat in my room and thought of how I would kill myself and how old should I be when I did it. It was still light outside, so I thought I'd go back over to the Funeral Home and check out the caskets. I wanted to know what it would be like to lay in one, to actually know how it felt. When I walked through the entrance of the Funeral Home I saw Jan sitting at the Front Desk.

"What are you doing here, Little Mary?" she asked.

"I left something in the Embalming Room. I'll get it and leave out the back door. See you tomorrow," I glibly told her.

Since I knew no one but Jan and I were in the Funeral Home, I went straight to the Casket Room. The caskets were lined up around the walls with four caskets in the middle of the room. Carefully I looked and touched to decide which one would be the easiest to get into. I needed something to stand on, and I found a stool in the corner. Trying to be very quiet, I climbed up and slid myself into the top half of the casket, feet first. Not messing up the comforter was impossible. Then I lay my head gently on the pillow. I chose the casket I thought was the prettiest in the room. It was light silver, with dark gray metal handles and white satin interior. I placed my hands under my breasts and took a deep breath of relief. Finally, I was laid out.

The softness was unbelievable. A dead person had no idea of the comfort prepared for them. Next I closed my eyes, imagining what was next. *Where did their spirit go? Was there really a heaven and a hell?* With my eyes closed the darkness seemed unbearable, as being in the dark was not a place I liked. But still I lay there wondering what comes after the darkness. *Daylight? Would there be a light for me? When I died would I be in the dark, alone?* Suddenly I opened my eyes and realized death was final. *When I did kill myself, I would not see daylight again. Would I go to hell, if there really were a hell? I thought hell was here on earth.* Lying very still with only my eyes moving around, I focused on the top of the casket and thought, *If this closed on me I'd be locked inside and no one would know I was here.*

I was comfortable, and surprised at the cozy feeling and warmth of the casket surrounding my body. I lay there, hoping to get an answer to my questions about what happens after you die. Growing tired of lying there I sat up, and just at that moment Jan opened the door to turn off the light. She screamed at the top of her lungs and even though I shouted, "Jan! It's me! It's me!" as loud as I could, she just kept running down the hall. I heard the doors slamming as she went through them. Evidently she thought she had seen a real ghost. *Boy was I going to be in big trouble,* I thought.

Jan left in such a hurry she did not lock up the Funeral Home so I locked up and walked home, knowing I would catch hell tonight. I was sure Jan would have called either Mr. Jones or Reverend Lindsey, and by the time I got home, Mother would have heard. Therefore, I walked slowly, hoping someone would be there so I would not have to face Mother alone.

The front door of the house was wide open—waiting, and before my foot crossed the threshold Mother came out with the fury of hell on her face. "What the hell were you doing scaring Jan like that? You could have given her a heart attack!"

"I'm sorry. I was only playing." Her hands were around my neck.

"Playing! What kind of fool gets into a casket? Are you crazy?"

"I'm sorry. I'm really sorry. I'll call Jan and tell her."

Mother grabbed me by the arm and pushed me toward the hallway. "Go to your room, and stay away from the Funeral Home!" she ordered.

Tears filled my eyes. *I didn't mean to frighten Jan. I was not crazy. I just wanted to see what it felt like to lie in a casket. Did that make me crazy?*

35

FEELING ALONE AND REJECTED AGAIN, I CRIED MYSELF TO sleep. As usual, a crowd had gathered in the front room that night. A man on top of me, with his hand over my mouth awakened me. It was Eugene, one of Mother's friends from Reverend Lindsey's church. I struggled for a moment and he said, "Don't fight me, Little Mary. I love you. I've always loved you." He took his hand from my mouth and began kissing me on the lips and rubbing his body on me.

I could feel his manhood, and I held my breath a moment before I begged, "Eugene! Please stop! Don't! I don't want to!"

Eugene was strong, with big muscles and bad breath. My mind raced trying to figure out how could I reason with him and get him to stop. When he rubbed his hand over my breast I pulled his hand away, whispering, "Please, stop." I was waiting when I could catch him off-guard and push myself from under him and run.

I was trembling and Eugene kept saying, "Don't be afraid. I won't hurt you."

Reasoning wasn't working so I pushed him with all my strength but he just pushed back. He slapped my face and with the other hand held my wrist tight. "Don't fight me, Little Mary. I don't want to hurt you."

"Please! I'm begging you to stop!" I heard my voice as if it were coming from the ceiling of the room. "Stop!" I screamed and I flailed my arms and hitting him with all my might. Suddenly, the sound of the door slamming against the wall was the sound of help to my waiting ears.

A man burst through the door and grabbed Eugene by the back of his neck. "What the fuck are you doing?" he yelled at him as he pushed and shoved him out of the door. His fist hitting Eugene in the face actually made me jump.

I just sat in the bed trembling. My lip was swelling up and my cheekbone was throbbing where Eugene had struck me. Holding myself tightly, afraid to make a move, I rocked back and forth in the bed.

When my rescuer came back into the room, I finally burst into tears. Gently he sat on the side of the bed and taking my hand asked, "Are you okay, Little Mary? It's okay now. He won't be coming back here. I promise."

"Where's Mother?" I tearfully asked.

"Sleeping."

"A house full of people and she's sleeping?"

"She's got a busy day tomorrow, couple of funerals."

"Who are you?"

"Tommy. I'm a friend of Reverend Lindsey. We've met before."

"Sorry," I said. "I don't remember. How did you know I needed help?"

"I saw Eugene leave the room and just thought he'd gone to the bathroom. But he was gone so long I went to see if he was okay. I thought I heard a scream and then I heard you again, so there I was."

"Thanks for coming in when you did. I can't believe Eugene would do this to me. I thought he was gay!"

"He is!"

We looked at each other for a moment without saying a word. I had a feeling Tommy was gay, but I was afraid to ask.

"Are you going to tell Mrs. Reese what happened?" Tommy asked.

"Of course! But I won't wake her tonight. She gets real upset if you wake her when she has funerals in the morning.

"Tommy, who's in the living room?"

"Reverend Lindsey, Reverend Miles, Tom, May, and a couple of other people I don't know," he answered.

"So Tom had no idea what was going on back here?"

"You want me to get Tom for you?"

No. He wouldn't care, anyway. I'll talk with Mother in the morning."

"Little Mary, I'll stay till everybody leaves and I'll lock up. No one will bother you. I promise. All right?"

"Okay. Thanks."

I lay down and thought, *God, Eugene is supposed to be a Christian. Where were You? Why don't You let me close my eyes and never wake up again?* I cried silently, questioning why no one could love me for me. I had loved Daniel. I had fallen for Lou Rawls, but I was not enough of a woman for either of them. Yet men were coming into my room and forcing themselves on me. Loneliness filled my heart and I truly thought I would welcome death.

When I heard the laughter in the living room, it angered me. I wanted to scream and tell everyone to go home. After all, it was two-thirty in the morning and Tom and the others were talking much too loud. I couldn't understand why they didn't go home? Now it was anger not fear that kept me wide-awake. To myself I cursed all the people in the front room. I hated them and I knew when I woke I would have to clean up after them. Meanwhile, Mother slept; blissfully unaware of my near escape from rape.

My thoughts next centered on how I could learn to protect myself and also find a way to get away from that house. The next time someone came into my room, I wanted to be ready for them. In my drawer I had a switchblade that someone had lost at school. So I got up, retrieved it and decided to sleep with it opened under my pillow. But I couldn't go to sleep as my mind raced from one thought to another, planning what I'd do if I had another night like that night. *Next time hit him with my knee, right in his manhood,* I thought. *Oh, I wanted to hurt him. I want to hurt somebody. I'm tired of being afraid. I want to lie down without fear!*

The morning did not come quickly enough. When I did awake, Mother was getting dressed and I thought, *Get up and tell her what happened.* So I went into Mother's room. Her radio was on and she was standing at the mirror in the bathroom.

"Good morning, Mother."

"Good morning. I'm rushing. What do you want?"

"Mother, last night Eugene came into my room and tried to force himself on me."

Her flash of anger surprised me. "You're lying!" she snarled. I couldn't believe she was angry with *me*.

"No. It's the truth. Tommy came in and threw him out. You can ask him."

"Why would Eugene do that? He's gay."

"I know, but he did. He slapped me. Look, my lip is still swollen," I answered.

"Did you lead him on? Cause he likes boys."

"Why would I do that?"

"I don't believe you. You need to stop leading these guys on!"

My eyes filled with tears and my stomach ached with a hopeless pain. "Mother, I didn't lead him on. I haven't led anyone on. I was in my own bed, asleep, and he woke me when he got on top of me, holding his hand over my mouth."

"Girl, you're lying. Eugene wouldn't do that so get out of here and stay away from the Funeral Home. I haven't forgotten what you did to Jan."

"Mother, I'm sorry. I want you to believe me. I didn't lead him on," I sobbed.

"I don't believe you. Get out of here!"

I knew no matter how many times I said I was sorry or it wasn't my fault, Mother would always believe her friends before she would believe me. I was no longer a child. I worked and took care of the house. Only fifteen-years old, I felt at least twenty-five. Absolutely disheartened, I went to my room wishing I could disappear or die...but there was no escape. God would not let me die even though every night I prayed, "Now I lay me down to sleep - Lord, please take my life as I sleep." If only I had really believed in God how different things might have been.

Through the days and weeks after that, my anger and hate for Tom, JT, and for all the Preachers that came and went grew worse. In my mind I cursed them, wishing I had the nerve to put a voodoo spell on them, but afraid that the God I didn't believe in would get me. The only place safe was my mind.

I kept promising myself; *I will not be like my Mother and always be the opposite. If she does bad to someone, I'll do good.*

They cared for and encouraged me to be the best at whatever I set out to do. I spent hours with Mr. Blakley and the Embalming Room became my hiding place, my place of peace. Often I skipped school and Mother never knew. She lived in her own world—the world of Mrs. Reese.

36

I FOUND MR. BLAKLEY IN THE EMBALMING ROOM WITH only one body to embalm that day. My intention was to get him to tell me the story about the little, two-year old girl that had him so upset the other day.

Without any preamble I waltz in and said, "Mr. Blakley, tell me about that little girl."

"Oh, Little Mary. It's a terrible story!"

"I want to hear it. Come on! You promised."

"Girl, why you want to hear a bad story?"

"Cause it makes me realize things could be worse for me."

"Little Mary, your life's going to change. You're going to be a special lady one day."

"Yeah, yeah, I've heard that many times before but things just keep getting worse. I don't want to think about me. Just tell me the story, okay?"

Mr. Blakley sat down next to the body, and I pulled up a stool. "Well, I never really understood it all, but there was this couple over in East L.A. They had a little girl, cute little thing. I would have called her Ebony; her skin so dark and smooth, like a baby's bottom. I got a call one night to pick up a child's body from the morgue. Whenever I hear 'child,' I just shake with anger, but I went. When they showed me her little body, I just couldn't help it and I broke right down and cried. Her face was twisted and she was all swollen up like a balloon—it was pitiful."

As I listened, I began to wish I hadn't insisted on this story.

"Little Mary, people can be mean. The hate people carry round, and you don't know they are filled with demons."

"I know that Mr. Blakley. I've come across a few."

"Her parents were out-right crazy… That baby had been taken away from them more than once, but somehow they had got her back. The Father

197

loved the child, but the Mother was jealous. She didn't want him to love nobody but her. So every chance she got, she'd beat the little girl. Well, when the authorities found out they took the child again, and put the Mother in jail…a six months' sentence, or something like that."

"Good. Then she couldn't hurt her anymore, could she, Mr. Blakley?" I interjected.

"Not so," he answered. "They let the Father take the little girl home and somewhere in his sick mind, he decides to take the girl to see her Mother. Evidently the Mother had been let out on good behavior or something like that."

"Oh, Mr. Blakley! That's crazy."

"I know. So they take the little girl to a park, and she has to go to the restroom. The stupid SOB lets the Mother take her to the restroom ALONE! Later, the little girl kept complaining her stomach hurt, and on the drive home the Father looked in the back seat of the car and her bowels was coming out of her mouth. She died that evening. It was later discovered that the Mother had taken the child into the restroom, and beat her in the stomach so hard her bowels had ruptured."

Tears filled my eyes as I imagined the pain the little girl must have felt, and my stomach ached as if I had been hit too.

"But this is the real kicker—that son-of-a-bitch requested they let the Mother out of jail to come to the funeral. And can you believe they let her come? I wanted to kill that woman myself, and then hang the Father up by his toes. Life just doesn't make sense sometimes. But I cradled her little body and wept for her. She didn't deserve to die that way, and her parents didn't deserve to live."

"Mr. Blakley, you've seen a lot of awful things." We both had tears in our eyes, and I was proud to see Mr. Blakley was not ashamed to cry.

"Yeah, Little Mary, life's a bitch and then you die. I haven't figured it out yet, but one thing I do know. You are special, and remember my words. You have a heart of gold; don't let anyone change you. The light in your eyes says the Almighty has a plan for you."

"Well His plan is pretty bad so far," I said with a wet smile and a heavy heart.

I left with a sinking feeling. Why did I push for that story? It broke my heart and now has left me feeling so sad. I just don't understand people at all. It seems I mostly only hear about or know mean people. I'm glad I was not around for that funeral. I don't believe I could have contained myself when I saw that murdering Mother.

* * *

Life's lessons were tough, and seemed to be getting tougher for me. I now dreaded going home because of the haunting fears and thoughts of what might or could happen to me each night. There were times I wished I enjoyed drinking so I could "escape", but the taste and the feeling of not being in control was enough to keep me away from all alcohol. My biggest fear was that I just knew the day would come when Mother would find a way to fix me up with one of her gravedigger friends, or a church member.

Isn't it strange, the only place I felt safe and at peace was in the Embalming Room—not in my own house, which was not, in the true definition of the word, a home. Also, that I felt I didn't have any true friends—except for the dead people to whom I talked almost daily. I do have to admit; of the living, I did trust Mr. Blakley and my friend Faye.

Faye hasn't been mention before, but she was the beautician who came by daily to do the hair and make-up on the bodies at the new Funeral Home. She was a full-time beautician who did this at our Mortuary in order to earn extra money. Sometimes I waited for her to come and then watched her perform her expertise. There were times when she would let me help her by painting the nails on the bodies, and other times when we just chatted while I kept her company. Those were special times for me. I remember how we would laugh when a body passed gas or made a sighing noise as they exhausted their last breath. As I have said before, I loved being around dead people. Maybe I felt they were finally at peace, and I desperately wanted what they had.

37

ALL LOS ANGELS WAS IN A BIG STIR AND THE NEWS spread like wildfire when it was announced that Daddy Grace had died. The reason? You see, Daddy Grace had promised his followers that when he died, he would be resurrected on the third day, just like Christ. He had been a well known, high-profile Preacher in the Black Community, and owned a hotel that he dedicated to the homeless in the Inner City. Also, he had been known for all his charitable work with the poor. His appearance too, had been as flamboyant as his preaching style. A huge, charismatic man, he had worn his gray hair long - his skin was dark brown, and he always had long fingernails that were painted red, white, and blue. It seems everything that man did was in the extreme.

Many times during his church services, he had told his congregation to open their purses or their wallets, and give everything to the church as Christ had given it to them. And they did! So it is no wonder Daddy Grace had become rich from all those donations and had lived in a mansion, while his followers remained poor. Nevertheless, the Black Community had loved him. Also, he had a very popular radio program, and held many healing meetings all over the area. He had been as visible as he had been big, and considered himself a prophet to the Black Community.

Thus, it was a great honor when the Funeral Home received a phone call that Daddy Grace had passed and the leaders of his church wanted the J.T. Stone Funeral Home to prepare the body for showing. After the public viewing, his body was to be shipped to North Carolina, where he was to be buried. This was a great opportunity for the J.T. Stone Funeral Home, as it would give us all the advertisement and clout we needed to be the best Funeral Home in Los Angeles. We had been told that his casket would arrive early Monday morning—a special glass casket had been ordered so that his body could be viewed from head to foot.

I never met Daddy Grace, but I had heard him on the radio many times. Listening to him with his charisma touched me a few times, but not enough to open my purse.

Rumors that he would be resurrected murmured throughout the Funeral Home. His followers kept reminding everyone listening on his radio program that he would raise up on the third day. Naturally everyone and anyone talked about his untimely death, and his presumptuous boast that he would be resurrected.

The phones seemed to ring non-stop, so we corralled Lenore into coming in and helping with answering the phone. We had been instructed to tell all callers that Daddy Grace would be shipped to North Carolina, but after a while Lenore became so frustrated Mother had to take her off the phones and have someone else take the calls. People were calling before the body had even arrived at the Mortuary because they had heard via the radio the announcement of his death, and that he would be at the J.T. Stone Mortuary for viewing. Everyone was excited, waiting to see the body.

The body of Daddy Grace was delivered from the morgue around 8:30 a.m., on a Monday morning. By then people had already begun camping outside the Funeral Home, waiting to see him for the last time and also hoping to see him rise from the dead as he had predicted. Traffic slowed to a crawl with an untold number of cars slowly passing the Funeral Home; the passengers staring as if they were trying to see through the walls.

Tuesday arrived and still the special casket had not arrived. Nothing was running, as it had been planned. Daddy Grace lay on a slab while his followers were all around the Funeral Home wanting to view his body. The mourners grieved out loud, wailing their love for him and getting angrier as time passed. Their reasoning was, they wanted to see their "Messiah," and we wouldn't let them. Part of the problem was that he was too large to fit into any of the standard caskets in our Showroom.

Mother was getting nowhere on the phone as she screamed and cursed the casket company. After slamming down the phone, Mother came over to me at the Front Desk, stress showing on her face. Her calmness, which normally warmed people and relaxed their mood was not with her today. "Little Mary, I want you to go outside and try to calm the people down. Tell them to come back tomorrow. The body will be viewed between 4:00 p.m. and 8:00 p.m."

"No way," I said, terrified at the thought.

"Go on," she demanded. "Just stand at the door and tell them. Ask them to pass it on, and then you come right back in."

I went to the door and thank goodness, JT was right behind me. He had a strong voice that could be heard over a crowd. "Get out of the way, girl. I'll tell them." Boy, was I relieved.

Mr. Blakley embalmed Daddy Grace and put some make-up on his face. Someone from Daddy Grace's home brought red, white, and blue polish for his nails. So Faye polished the nails, fanned them till they dried, and then brushed his hair, trying to fix it the way he wore it in a photo given to us.

I admit, I wanted to see this man everyone seemed to revere, but when I looked at Daddy Grace's body I said under my breath, "You don't look like you're going to rise from here…not today or tomorrow."

Even after JT had made the announcement about the viewing being scheduled for the next day, the crowd outside became louder and more insistent. They wanted to see Daddy Grace now! We were viewed as the bad guys, because we wouldn't open the doors. What they didn't know was that behind those doors, Daddy Grace was still resting on a slab because the special casket had not yet arrived.

We all prayed that casket would arrive soon but by that Tuesday evening, there still was no casket. Panic seemed to have filled every room when a call finally came. We were told the casket would be there by Noon on Wednesday, the next day.

Noon came and still no casket. Sweat ran down Mr. Blakley's face and JT called the casket company, threatening to sue them for everything they had. Mother, trying to keep everyone calm, suggested that we just squeeze him into a standard casket. We laughed, but we knew it was not a funny matter. The people outside would not be put off another day; after all, it was the third day.

At 2:00 p.m. I heard voices in the back of the Funeral Home and someone saying, "It's about damn time!" The casket had finally arrived, and since we had announced on Tuesday that the viewing would be at 4:00 p.m. on Wednesday, we had less than two hours to prepare.

Getting Daddy Grace in the all-glass casket, putting him in the Chapel, arranging the flowers and roping off the section was chaotic, but we all worked together with Mother leading us. "Put this here. That over there," she directed as usual. Several of our strongest men struggled to get that body into the casket and in the process broke one of Daddy Grace's fingernails. Mother started screaming, "Find the goddamn nail!" Everyone dropped to the floor and crawled all around the Embalming Room and down the hall, hoping to find it because his nails must be visible. After all, they were a big part of who he was.

"Maybe it's in the casket," I said.

Sure enough, Faye shoved her hand down inside the casket, and when she pulled her hand out, there was the broken nail. It was her job to put it back and she did with a little bit of invisible tape. I ran around lighting candles and straightening the ropes, making sure there would be enough distance between the crowd and the casket. Mother showed everyone where to stand and how to control the crowd in an orderly way. My place was at the head of the casket, behind the ropes.

"Make sure no one comes across this rope. Do you understand?" her voice commanding and harsh. You bet I understood.

By 3:30 p.m. the crowd was pushing and banging on the front doors and I was rather nervous, as I had never experienced anything like this before. When JT unlocked the front Chapel doors at exactly 4:00 p.m., the crowd, crying and whispering, "He's gone, I can't believe he's gone," surged forward, moving en masse toward the casket.

Dutifully, I stood at the front of the casket while Mother was at the foot, and Mr. Blakley, Faye and Lenore, assisted some of the other helpers with the crowd. They led the line out slowly, trying to keep them moving so that others would get their chance to see Daddy Grace. To me it seemed there must have been at least a thousand people lined up for blocks and blocks. I had known he was popular, but I had no idea so many people loved him.

Those four hours seemed like a day and when I saw the clock said 7:55 p.m., I was thinking it was almost over. The doors would close at eight. Mother was always prompt about time, so 8:00 p.m. meant 8:00 p.m. But the crowd was still coming in, some whispering, "This is the third day. You think Daddy will rise?" Others cried, and some reached out their hands toward the casket, knowing they could not touch but felt the power, they said. The line still seemed endless to me.

Suddenly, every light in the Funeral Home went out. Total darkness! The gasping and screaming from the crowd echoed through the Chapel. I fell to the floor and hid under the casket, hoping it wouldn't fall on me. You couldn't see anything, it was so dark. All I heard was the thunderous screaming of people as they ran and trampled over each other. Then, as suddenly as the lights went off, they came back on. What seemed like forever was probably less than a minute, but an extremely long wait.

I looked out over the ropes as I stood to my feet and saw the Chapel was empty! The crowd had run out of the Funeral Home, knocking over pews and the Chapel doors right off their hinges. It was the third day, and his followers had wanted to see Daddy Grace rise, but instead they ran. When I turned around to the head of the casket and saw Daddy Grace was still there, I knew he wasn't going to rise—ever. After all, I had seen him embalmed.

Naturally Mother fussed and accused all of us of having something to do with the lights. But no one ever took responsibility. So Mother said, "Maybe Daddy Grace did rise; we just didn't see it."

Daddy Grace was finally shipped out and things went back to what we liked to think of as "normal." However, I did notice JT spent the next few days walking around with a rather pleased smile on his face.

38

WHEN MOTHER AND REVEREND LINDSEY, WITH Mr. Jones always in the middle, began to have problems, the Funeral Home ceased to be a fun or safe refuge for me. They argued daily and I could feel the tension mounting.

That was when Mother's drinking started earlier and earlier in the day; however, she made herself wait until noon since she had let everyone know for years, "If you drink before noon you are an alcoholic." Her anger escalated into bursts of rage, lashing out at anyone near. She didn't want to believe all the rumors about Revered Lindsey and Mr. Jones trying to take over the Funeral Home, but I think in her heart she knew they were true.

Her parties at home continued, and I continued to find more creative ways to secure my bedroom door. To me it was strange that with all their fighting, the Reverend Lindsey and Mr. Jones still came over and had drinks with her on regular basis—smiling to her face and yet plotting behind her back.

By then Mother and Tom were fighting on a nightly basis, and I seemed to spend all my time in my room. After being hit a few times with plates and glasses flying across the room, I had said to hell with them and now no longer ran in to try and break up their fights. I'd lie very still on my bed, listening to the sound of glass breaking as it hit the walls and the voices of Mother's guests, yelling over the music, telling Mother and Tom to stop. I was in a war zone hiding behind a flimsy door, trying to stay safe, with thoughts of dying still a big part of my thoughts. Many times I wondered, Why was I such a coward? I know how to get the peace I long for...but I'm just a big coward!

The noise from the front was always irritating and I hated the nights. My room was square and for some reason, when I looked at the ceiling I always thought that if I could turn it upside down, I'd have some protection because then anyone trying to come in would have to climb over the top of the door. Isn't it silly, what thoughts kids get into their heads when they are desperate for love and security? When I thought this type of thought, my next conclusion was that I must have been going crazy.

Nights were always long, so long for me and with no one to talk to; it was then I achingly missed my special-sister Ilona. Lenore had told me Ilona had a baby girl and I desperately wanted to see her little girl, but knew that would take a miracle. One worry I had was now that she had her baby, I had been replaced in her life and would never be part of any happiness she had.

I'm not sure if I had no control of my thoughts—or if I was so lonely my thoughts were really all that I had that were truly, privately mine, and they were safe from everyone. Yet, there were times when it almost hurt me physically to think. That was when I wanted to blank everything out and sleep without being afraid. But instead, I was tormented with images of the past and afraid of what the future held for me.

A dark cloud hung over our house. The fights between Mother and Tom worsened, and our house always seemed to be full of strangers coming and going, all hours of the day and night. There were the usual gravediggers, preachers, churchgoers and musicians—all of them talking loudly and lying about how great they were. Mother would be angry with me if I didn't speak to her friends or sit with them for awhile, so I had to force myself to sit with them, sipping a coke and smoking like I was one of them. I was there in body only as my mind was somewhere else. Like a good little hostess, I served their Jack Daniels or vodka, and emptied the overflowing-ashtrays. Not being an entertainer like JT or sociable like Lenore, I was relegated to the level of "the servant."

It got to be the evening would not be complete until Mother and Tom got into it. They made every subject that was raised a debate. If Tom said it was night, Mother would automatically take the opposite view and say it was day. If Tom said it was blue, Mother, said it was black. Sometimes I'd just stare at my Mother and watch her go into action and think, I look so much like her, and that really scared me. Would I one day act like her too?

I was living with two different people. There was Mrs. Reese of the J.T. Stone Funeral Home who was respected by the community and who demanded respect in the business world, then at home there was Mother who did not resemble Mrs. Reese at all. As far as I was concerned, Mother had not earned any respect, at least not from me. But I feared her, and I feared the God I did not know. So many times when Mother wanted to pull me in line if she thought I didn't give her enough kudos or whatever, she would remind me the Bible said, "Honor thy Mother and Father so that your days would be long…" Of all the Commandments, that one is imprinted on my mind because I heard it so much. I told myself there was no way I would become anything like my Mother, but patterning myself after Mrs. Reese might not be too bad an idea.

When JT and Lenore came over, I'd watch how JT and Mother loved each other. Even though they fought sometimes, there was a special bond between them—like invisible glue that kept them stuck together. I would watch their interactions with envy and wonder, thinking once more, "Why am I so uncomfortable? I just don't fit in anywhere." For some unexplainable reason, Mother loved JT, her eldest and barely tolerated me, her youngest. Many, many times she loved to say, "Lenore, Ilona, Willie Jr. and Little Mary were all mistakes because if their Father's even looked at me, I got pregnant."

Once I asked, "Mother, you didn't want us to be born?"

Then I wished I had never asked when she looked me straight in the eye, and said, "No. I tried many times to miscarry by bouncing down the stairs and taking castor oil, but everyone of you guys hung on."

To her this was funny, but I never laughed because the words cut like a knife into my heart. She laughed and then continued, "But I did have you." After that the subject would be closed and left alone.

I'd visualize myself as a tiny baby in the womb, holding on for dear life while she did things to try and abort me. My tears were not visible but I died on the inside. I never wanted to give her the satisfaction of knowing how deeply she hurt me, so I kept the pain inside. This attitude helped me cope through those dark times.

Evidently a child who is rejected tries to do things for the rejecter in a desperate bid for their approval and acceptance. Ilona, when she had still been at home, did that and I found I followed her example. Therefore, I found myself doing my best to take care of Mother. I tried to take care of her every need as best as I could. Every morning I got up early and fixed her coffee and toast, and cleaned the house. But you already know, my catering to her every whim was never enough—she was ungrateful and always expected and wanted more.

As her child, I loved her and wanted her to love me back, just like she loved JT. They had a little routine going and I don't know how many times she would say, "That's my son," and JT would parrot back, "That's my Mother." And that says it all. The rest of us were just in her way and only useful to serve her. Mother never cleaned or cooked unless the mood hit her—which meant there were weeks and weeks without meals, and I had to just fend for myself.

As you probably have surmised, Mother had a cruel and mean streak and often played games with her children's feelings, pitting us against one another. She would secretly pull us aside to talk about another and telling one that the other was talking bad about us, just to stir up trouble at every chance she could.

Since she made no attempt to hide her love for JT, I was full of bitterness towards him and it was quite obvious. Whenever he came over I'd leave the room, trying to avoid an argument with him, or having to observe Mother's outlandish attentions towards him. One of her favorite things was to tell him I did or didn't do something, knowing full well he would get angry with me and cuss me out. And when JT cussed you out, you knew you had been really told off in no uncertain terms.

* * *

Lenore was determined to bring Ilona and her little baby girl over to the house and pleaded with Mother to be nice to Ilona. Finally, Mother agreed. A few days later Ilona came by with her three-month old little girl, Tracie. Oh, she was beautiful, with brown-satin skin, light-brown eyes, and a head full of dark curls. I sat on the sofa holding her for the first time with joy and love in my heart, unaware that rage was building in Mother because no one was paying any attention to her—all the attention was centered on baby Tracie. So enthralled with the precious little bundle, none of us had noticed how much Mother had been drinking, or when her mood made a drastic change.

Out of the corner of my eye, I saw Mother get up from her chair and before any of us knew what she intended, she literally lurched toward me and suddenly began screaming as she suddenly tried to grab for the baby, "I'll kill that little bitch!" Over and over she kept screaming like a possessed demon, grabbing for the baby and pulling on the little blanket. You can imagine the total chaos that erupted. Ilona jumped up from the sofa and tried pulling Mother from the back, while Lenore tried to pry Mother's hands off the baby's blanket. As for me, I was holding on to my precious little niece for dear life. Typical of a person who is demented and out of control, Mother's grip was strong and a fierce fire of hatred burned in her eyes. Everyone was screaming, yelling and pulling or pushing at the same time. It was a nightmare out of some horror movie.

I remember screaming in anger and incredulity, "What's wrong with you, Moth…"

Before I could finish my question, quick as a snake Mother, had turned on Ilona and was hitting and threatening to kill her. At the top of her voice she yelled, "I hate you and your fucking baby!"

Finally we prevailed when Lenore was able to hold Mother enough so that Ilona and I were able to run out the front door with the baby. I was still holding the baby and Ilona raced to unlock the car door and put little Tracie inside. In our urgency to get away from the traumatic scene, we had no time for words to pass between us, and just like that Ilona jumped into her car and sped off and we never got a chance to say good-bye.

Watching her drive away, I stood there in the driveway and cried like a tiny baby and felt so ashamed of what Mother had just pulled. Then I tried to figure out what had happened and why Mother had suddenly acted that way. It puzzled me that she could hate Ilona so much and for what reason? The only reason I could come up with was that maybe Ilona was a constant reminder of Mother's intense hatred for our Father.

Then the thought came to me: If tomorrow I asked Mother about what had just happened this night, she would absolutely deny it ever happened and turn the tables on me and accuse me of making it up or something. There is no way I can ever deal straight with my Mother...she's crazy!

After Ilona and little Tracie left, Lenore and I were totally, physically and emotionally drained. Poor Lenore felt so bad since it had been her idea, and she had been the one that arranged for them to come over. She had so hoped Mother would be happy and delighted to see her grandchild. But the evening had been a disaster—just like most evenings at the Reese home.

It broke my heart to realize that Ilona would never come back again, and I could not blame her one bit. Then the realization dawned, and I knew for a certainty I would not see my sister Ilona again until I was grown. Life just was not fair.

I was so depressed; I wanted to give up and all I thought about was dying. Taking some of Mother's sleeping pills with her vodka, and go to sleep for good. But...there was this nagging little voice in my head that said, "If you do that, you might miss out on something good tomorrow." Something good has to happen, I thought. Bad stuff can't happen forever. Can it?

39

ETHEL, MY STEPSISTER, CAME BACK TO STAY WITH US FOR a short time. Having a sister at home sure took some of the pressure off me. That was because when Ethel was there, Mother didn't push her friends off on me as often. But I knew it wouldn't last because sooner or later Mother would run her away just like she did everyone else good in my life.

We both loved to skate and skated at a skating rink called, The Savoy. It was at that rink we had our best times because while we were skating and showing off, we didn't have to think about what was going on at home. Mother would always have someone take us and pick us up. "I don't trust you," she'd say to us and that was another thing I never understood.

There I was, sixteen, and she didn't "trust me," but I sure was mature enough to entertain her friends and later fight them off when they'd come uninvited into my bedroom. Telling Mother about her friends had become a waste of time, because she would always call me a liar and say I was the one that encouraged them to make their advances. Basically, I didn't have any time to get into any trouble on my own.

It didn't take me long to realize skating was one way I could escape. I was cool and the boys liked me. The girls, well to them I was a "High Yellow Nigger." That almost became a nickname for me because the girls felt the boys only liked me because I looked so White.

I was gifted with rhythm and skated rings around most of the other girls. It was another world at the skating rink—one where I was a star. The music touched my soul as I skated and fanaticized that one day I'd be a real star. As I moved my body to the music, almost sexual, I could see and feel eyes following me. Kids whispered to one another, "She looks White, but she Colored, and she can skate her butt off. She's good!" That was one area where I was proud of myself—I was somebody and could hold my head up with pride. I was cool, and I knew it! Up until the time I had begun skating, my Color had been an issue to most of the Black kids; but the more I skated, the more they began to see me as Black. So you can see how skating helped bring it all together for me. There finally was a place I fit in and was admired for my talent. For me, skating almost seemed to make life worth living.

Mother usually had Earl, a neighbor across the street from our home, pick Ethel and me up when we were through skating, and on the ride home we would laugh and talk about the guys with whom we had skated.

One night in particular I remember. "You guys must have had a lot of fun," Earl said.

"It was great. We skated all night. For every record they played, we had a guy to skate with." Ethel had sounded so proper we all laughed.

"That's good."

"Earl? Who's at our house?" I was happy, and I guess I knew that would change as soon as I walked through our front door. My expectations of home were always right. It would be a house full of peachers, choir directors, some musicians, and JT and Lenore, who constantly fought for Mother's attention. They would all drink until the liquor was gone and then argue some more before the evening would end.

"Bunch of folks. I think Lou Rawls came in as I was leaving," Earl informed.

Trying not to show my excitement, I fumbled around in my purse for a lipstick as I said, "It will be good to see him."

"Yeah, Little Mary. I know you got the hot's for him."

My face flushed because I had never thought of my feelings for him as "having the hots for Lou." All I knew was that he made me feel important and pretty. He was a nice guy, with a wonderful voice that made me melt when he sang. I did not want Earl to know he was right, so I tried very hard not to react to his comment.

As the car pulled into the driveway, I saw a police car and my heart stopped. "Oh, no, Earl. What's going on?"

"I don't know." Just then another police car pulled up and he told us, "You two stay in the car. I'll go see what I can find out."

Ethel and I looked at each other and then slumped down in the seat and lowered our heads. The pain of what might be going on was something we could not change, but it hurt just the same.

Pretty soon Earl came back to the car and said, "Come on."

"Is my Mother okay?" I asked, while at the same time Ethel asked, "Is my Dad okay?"

Earl was so kind and understanding. He knew there was always something going on at the Reese house. "Come on girls! They had a little fight, and one of the neighbors across the street called the police. Nobody hurt, just hurt feelings flying around in there"

"Is Lou in there?" I wanted to know.

"No. Evidently he left when they started arguing. That's what the fight was about. Lou is going to be on the Merv Griffin Show and wants your Mom to go as his guest. I guess he didn't invite Tom."

Sadness was written on my face as I realized he hadn't invited me either. Even though I knew he thought of me as just a kid, it hurt just the same. I was just a kid, I thought, who wanted to grow up in the worst way; grow up and get the hell away from this house. Ethel and I quietly went to our room, not speaking to anyone.

That night I thought how things might have been if Daniel had not gotten another girl pregnant. Also, I mentally toyed with the make-believe images of how life might have been if Mother and Dad hadn't divorced and if Mother loved all of us like she loved JT. "What ifs" are always the biggest questions for which I probably would never have any answers.

When the time came, Mother did go to the Merv Griffin show and while in the audience, Lou introduced her as, "A woman who is like a Mother to me." This was on national television and Mother was so proud she bragged for weeks until we were all sick of hearing about it—especially Tom. Even though he knew she rubbed it in to hurt him, it worked because she took great pleasure in doing it. She'd talk about Lou so much, Tom was jealous even though Lou was young enough to be her son.

Lou soon stopped coming around and I firmly believe he had finally had enough of the Mother-and-Tom games, arguments and fights. I knew it wasn't my fault and often thought one day Mother and Tom would go too far and really do something that they could not undo. There were quite a number of good people I remembered, but soon they stopped coming because of all the fighting. I also wanted to leave, but I couldn't. My heart told me I had to honor my Mother and I tried to take care of her, but my anger towards her grew.

40

MOTHER HAD TOLD ME TO STAY AWAY FROM THE Funeral Home, but I missed my friend Mr. Blakley. So I would sneak over to the back of the Mortuary a couple of times a week and sit in the Embalming Room watching Mr. Blakley work, while he told jokes about the latest body. Our talks always cheered me up.

Mr. Blakley always encouraged me to stay strong. "One day, you'll show them all," he'd say, taking my face in his hand. "Little Mary, take care of your Mother. She needs you, and you'll be blessed for it."

Walking home, hoping I had not been seen leaving the Funeral Home, tears would fill my eyes because thoughts of home depressed me. I knew what I'd find and I felt angry because it just did not seem fair. I had to work so hard for people I disliked so much.

After that last big fight, Tom had sent Ethel to stay with her grandmother again. That left me even lonelier as then I didn't have anyone to talk to. It was about then I recognized I had a love/hate relationship with my Mother. There really is no explanation for it—I loved my Mother and wanted her to love me, yet I truly hated her for her cruelties. The famous Mary Reese, the Queen of Morticians, at home was a real witch. But I would be the witch if I told anyone. No one would ever believe me.

Over the years, I watched all the truly nice people turn their heads and walk out of our lives once they knew what was hidden deep down inside Mary Reese. The alcohol abuse and her avenging angel attitude towards anyone who went against her could not be hidden for long. Those around her who knew, kept it to themselves and that included me.

It seemed that whenever I walked in our front door, all I saw were dirty glasses everywhere and food on saucers left on the floor. What messy friends Mother had and I hated them all, but complaining did no good. Mother's usual attitude towards me was always one of anger and I knew she could destroy me with words. There were times I wished she would just hit me. At least I could forget physical pain as it fades away. Daily I heard the abusive, verbal pain of false accusations, "You ain't shit. I know you're a whore," she would slur. Later on, when she was sober, she would deny ever having said those damaging things. She'd love me for a day and hate me the next.

One Saturday night, Mother came into my room and said, "Be nice to Mr. Grimes, please. He's a nice man, and thinks you're pretty."

She was up to something and I could feel it in my bones, but that evening I did try to be nice to Mr. Grimes even though he was a nasty old man, and told me over and over how much he liked me. He followed me from room to room, like he was my shadow. Evidently from what I figured out, he wanted Mother to come and promote him at his church and also, since he worked for another Funeral Home in South Central, he wanted Mother to come work for the Hill & Hill Mortuary, as their Funeral Director. I was on my best behavior, waiting on all her friends hand and foot, but I had no intention of being any nicer to Mr. Grimes than I had to.

Later, after Mother and Tom had gone to bed and the others had gone home, I was trying to clean up and hoping Mr. Grimes would leave. I thought, "Stay busy and keep moving and then he'll leave." It was after 2:00 a.m., when I felt the hairs on the back of my neck rise and a voice inside saying, "Run!" But my feet remembered the last time I had run and so I just stood still when Mr. Grimes put his hand around my waist. I'll be calm, I said to myself as I pushed his hands away and said, "Please don't!" but obviously that was too polite. He continued to pull me toward him. Where is my Mother? She sleeps while I have to fight off this man. What I need is a big stick.

Instead, what I did was threaten to cut off something very near and dear to him if he tried anything else...and it worked!

"Little Mary, why are you so mean?" he asked in his rough voice, as if under the impression I should like him.

"Listen to me, Mr. Grimes. My Mother is sleeping and everyone else has gone home, so please go home."

"I guess your Mother was wrong. She said you'd be nice to me, and my name is Reverend Grimes to you."

"What kind of Reverend are you, putting your hands on me? My Mother didn't tell you to come on to me, did she?"

I was in shock. She had said be nice, but did she really want me to be that kind of nice? Suddenly my eyes filled with tears and the only answer I had for Mr. Grimes was "No! No! No!"

"I'll buy you anything you want, Little Mary. What do you want?" he said placatingly.

"I want you to get the hell out of my house, that's what I want!" I yelled, pushing him toward the door.

Then he got pissed and his tone of voice changed when he said, "You think you too good for me, 'cause you High Yellow?"

"No! I'm too young!" My heart was racing and I worried what he would do next. I knew Mother was sound asleep and not even a bomb would wake her; therefore, I was on my own. Thinking quickly, knowing not to react and since I didn't want to fight or have him hurt me, I said the first thing that came into my head. "It's two-thirty in the morning Reverend, Mr. Grimes. Aren't you preaching in the morning?"

"Yes, I am. I guess I better go, but I'll let your Mother know how mean you are," he promised as with his head down and acting truly disappointed, he went out the door.

"Yeah, you do that, preacher, and I'll let your church know how you came on to me," I promised right back.

"You're evil, Little Mary, just evil!"

"Well, if you put your hands on me again, you'll see what evil is all about." Suddenly, I realized I was yelling at the top of my voice when I heard those last words coming out of my mouth. I slammed the front door and let out a loud sigh of relief and asked myself, Why? Why does Mother do this to me?

Picking up the glasses, I was so angry I threw one against the wall and then broke down in tears. Crying and mumbling I thought out loud, "I knew I would have to clean up the glass, so why did I do that? I'm not my Mother!"

I cried until my head ached and then when I went to look for aspirin, could only find Stand Back, a headache powder that Mother took, in the medicine cabinet. Deciding to try it, I opened the paper foil and dropped the powder on my tongue before washing it down with water and then said a loud, "Yuk!" It had tasted awful, but within fifteen minutes my headache was gone.

In the living room I went over and over the evening with Mr. Grimes and not for the first time wondered, what is wrong with me? Should I just give in and with her friends; drink, get drunk, and act like a fool? NO! I won't do that just to fit in and belong. I think I hate them all...especially my Mother.

The thought of hating my Mother brought on a bout of guilt and another round-robin of the same old feelings and questions like, how could I have these feelings? Was I truly an awful person? How could I hate my Mother? Death would be what I deserved. Was Preacher Grimes right? Was I an evil person? Sitting on the sofa unable to move, I looked out the window and focused on the houses in the neighborhood. All the homes were dark, the children tucked snugly in their beds, and their parents were there to protect them while they slept. Oh, how I wished I could have parents like that

I did not go to bed, but waited and watched as the sun rose and then got up to clean the living room and kitchen. Waiting for Mother to wake up, I worried about how I was going to tell her what happened and if she would, again, turn on me and cuss me out and accuse me of leading him on. The burden was so much for me to handle, I was willing to take that chance.

The more and more I thought about what had happened, the angrier I got and told myself, "The nerve of Reverend Grimes, and the nerve of my Mother for putting me in that intolerable position!" I had wrestled with the thoughts for hours and had finally decided I wouldn't push this under the carpet—it needed to be brought out in the open, even if Mr. Grimes had gotten angry when I pushed him away.

The kitchen clock read 9:05 a.m., when I heard Mother moving around and then she yelled, "Little Mary, get me some coffee!" It was already made, as I knew her routine. Nervously, I got a cup and saucer, filled the cup with black coffee – strong, just the way she liked it. She had gotten back into bed, as Sunday was her rest day. Even though I walked slowly and carefully, the cup rattled against the saucer because my hands were nervously shaking.

Noticing I was upset, she gruffly asked, "What's the matter with you?"

"Mother…" I began, my voice trembling as I sat on the side of the bed, handing her the coffee. "Mother, Mr. Grimes came on to me last night. I thought he was going to try and force himself on me. He said you told him I'd be nice."

She sipped her coffee as if I had said nothing of any importance. "Mr. Grimes is a Preacher. He's a Godly man, and he would not do anything like that."

"But he did!" I raised my voice for the first time.

"You're lying! Why do you keep trying to start shit?" her forehead wrinkled with frowning disapproval.

"Mother, I'm not lying. He did and he said you told him that I would be nice to him."

"Bullshit! I didn't say that. Girl, you're making that up. Now get out of here! I need my sleep." She pushed the cup toward me and gestured for me to leave.

I wanted to scream at her, but I was afraid she'd really get upset so I stared at her coffee. I was so angry with her because she said she never believed me, yet I was always afraid to argue with her. With my head down, feeling like my tail was tucked under me, I went to my room and fell across my bed, which had not been slept in that night. When I woke it was 6:00 p.m. and I felt as if I'd been drugged.

On Monday mornings I would see Mr. Blakley and tell him all the things that had gone on over the weekend. He was always patient and listened and gave me words of encouragement. We talked about how things were changing, how Lou came and went in our lives, how Mother's drinking was beginning to control her, and how Reverend Lindsey and Mr. Jones were secretly meeting behind her back. At least he listened, even if he couldn't do anything about the situations, and that helped me a lot.

* * *

The parties continued and Mother was in the dark about what was going on. Socializing with her partners was a big mistake because they took her weakness and used it against her. She thought her partners cared about her and were giving her a break when they insisted she take it easy and not work so hard and long at the Mortuary. During parties they'd bring papers for her to sign and blindly she'd sign them, when she had already been drinking. JT tried to tell her she should not sign papers, but Mother believed they were her friends and that belief destroyed her. Reverend Lindsey and Mr. Jones had cunningly bought her out of her own company, right under her nose.

After that, the Funeral Home was really off-limits for me. It grieved me that I would not be able to see Mr. Blakley, or sit in the Embalming Room any more. Also, I would not be able to talk with the dead people. That really bothered me because now I had no one with whom to talk. My hiding place was now lost to me and I missed feeling safe in the Embalming Room and peaceful in the Viewing Room, with the quietness, the soft colors, and the satin comforters that lined the caskets and wrapped the bodies so securely. No longer would I be a part of the funerals, helping people to say good-bye to their loved ones. There was going to be a huge void in my life, and I had no idea how it could be filled.

It was no surprise that after her partners cheated her out of her own Funeral Parlor, getting along with Mother became harder and harder. Naturally she was angry with Reverend Lindsey and Mr. Jones but knowing my Mother, I knew she would get her revenge—it was just a matter of time.

* * *

Now that graduation from junior high was over, I had no idea what I would be doing and it looked like it was going to be a long, hot summer. I was looking forward to going to high school, which was located not too far from my junior high.

I was almost grown now and beginning to feel older, just like Mr. Blakley had said. Getting away from all the craziness was foremost in my plans. The only real way to escape, as far as I was concerned, was to go to sleep for good. The pills I had been hording for some time were stashed away, waiting for when I would wash them all down at once with a big dose of vodka, and then it would all be over. Yet…that same old thought nagged at me, "What about tomorrow? What if something good happened, and if I died, I'd miss it?"

Then I reminded myself I had made a name for myself in South Central. People actually liked me and I had clout—not just because I was the daughter of Mrs. Reese of the J.T. Stone Mortuary, but also because I was Mary Reese, Jr., who had soul and who skated like a professional and danced better than my friends. That was how I had gotten attention and realized I loved every minute of it!

Tremont High here I come! I was excited about being a high school student. Several of my friends who were graduating with me would also be going to Tremont, and that helped to know I would not be alone. I was comfortable about the change and knew my name would have preceded me in the new school, and my reputation of being a "cool" girl would greatly help—I was sure about all that. Also, there would be no more fights because someone didn't like my Color. After all, in high school we were young adults—or so I thought.

41

THE SUMMER STRETCHED OUT LONG, HOT, AND BORING before me as I really had no plans, and since I was unable to go around the corner to the Funeral Home, I became even more depressed. Sleeping late was easy because I didn't sleep well at night due to the fact that the house was usually full of people the majority of the time. I felt tense and on the alert in case something happened. Thus my room became my fortress and that was where I mainly stayed day and night, except when Mother insisted I come out and wait on her company, or she allowed me to go skating. That summer I especially missed Ethel because we were good together. It was nice having a sister around, but Mother took good care of that. I felt as if Mother looked up once in awhile and said, "Oh, it looks like Little Mary is having fun! I'll fix that."

Even though Lenore was at our house every night, neither of us had gotten over what Mother had tried to do to Ilona's baby. One evening while everyone was talking and singing, I leaned over to talk with Lenore and asked, "What made Mother try to kill that baby?"

Lenore was shocked I had said anything and asked, "Why are you asking me that?"

"I don't understand her, Lenore. She's one way with you and JT, and a completely different person with me." Then I told her some of the things Mother was doing, like trying to fix me up with the gravediggers and phony preachers that came in and out of our house, and how scared I was most of the time. "Lenore, I mean she really is trying to get me to be nice to them, if you know what I mean…real nice."

"No!" Lenore looked shocked and disgusted.

"Yes!"

"No!"

"Yes, she is!" I insisted. "That's what I'm trying to tell you. Mother leaves me alone and goes to sleep while I am stuck with these creeps, and they think I'm going to fool around with them. Please help me. Let me come stay with you."

Just then the noise in the room got louder with laughter and Mother was singing, "Oh, Danny Boy." No matter how much talent there was in the room, it seemed Mother always got back to singing her songs.

Lenore looked at me and whispered, "I'll see what I can do."

In my heart I thought maybe there's hope. I would have loved to stay with Lenore, if only Mother would say it was okay.

Later that evening when things had calmed down and most of the company finally left, Mother, Lenore, Tom and I, sat at the kitchen table. I stared meaningfully at Lenore, thinking now was a good time for her to ask Mother if I could go and live with her. I sipped on my Coke and Lenore had another beer. Obviously, she was nervous about asking Mother but she was working up her nerve. But my nerves were shot so I got up and started cleaning, picking up glasses and ashtrays, emptying them, double-checking that the cigarette butts were out.

Tom and Mother began going at it about nothing important, as usual. It had come to the point where we didn't know or care what they argued about because tomorrow they would be calling each other, "Baby," again.

I was frightened as to how Mother would react when Lenore asked if I could live with her and her husband. So badly did I want her to say, "yes." But to be truthful and knowing my Mother the way I did, there was probably little chance but I refused to give up.

There was good reason for my fear. While I was putting glasses in the sink, I heard Mother yell, "What the hell are you talking about?" When I looked, Mother was staring Lenore in the face and her expression had turned downright mean and wicked.

Lenore pushed herself away from the table, standing steady and said, "You don't have time for Little Mary. The house is full of strangers, or fools. Tommy told me that he had to hit Eugene for trying to force himself on her, and where were you? Little Mary said that's not the only time someone has come into her room!"

Mother knocked the glasses and ashtrays off the table with one swoop of her hand, and started cursing at Lenore. "Who the fuck do you think you are? You get the hell out of here!" she screamed like a wild woman.

Tears filled Lenore's eyes and I began to cry. I didn't want any trouble but Mother was pissed, and I knew this would now go on for days. She would stay angry with Lenore and me, and that was not good. Lenore tried to reason with her, explaining the benefits of me staying with her and how she would see to it that I went to school and not get into any trouble. She said her husband would take me and pick me up from school. But Mother refused to listen.

"You're crazy, girl!" she yelled at Lenore. "Little Mary is not going anywhere, and that's that."

Tom tried to interject his opinion by saying, "It might be a good idea, Mary." But that infuriated Mother even more.

Mother turned to Tom and snapped, "You don't say a damn word. This is none of your damn business! She's my child, not yours!" So Tom sat down, lit a cigarette, and smoked while Mother and Lenore argued. The argument was causing their voices to rise and I feared someone would call the police.

"Mother! Please calm down!" I had gently put my hand on her arm, and she yanked it away with force. Her look let me know to back off and I did. Now I knew I'd made a mistake to get Lenore involved. Even though Mother did not want me, she did not want anyone else to want me either.

Finally, after a half-hour or so, they all calmed down and when I saw Mother pull out a cigar and light it, I knew it was time for me to leave the room because I hated the smell of cigar smoke. Cigarettes were cool, but the cigar made me sick. Usually she only smoked cigars when there was a lot of company around, but she was pissed so maybe she felt it would calm her.

Lenore was still upset but she continued to sit at the table drinking another beer with Tom. When we made eye contact, we each knew my leaving and living with her was a losing battle.

When I went to bed I toyed with the idea that this might be the night to take all those pills. After all, life sucked and for me there seemed no way out. Then once again the nagging voice came into my head and kept saying, "Just wait. Maybe tomorrow something good might happen." That night I sang that in a little made-up lullaby and literally sang myself to sleep by repeating it over and over, "Tomorrow something good will happen. I don't want to miss it."

* * *

All summer the evenings were filled with partying, but I hated living like that and wanted to withdraw from life. After midnight I hid in my room and slept during the day. I lost friendships with my schoolmates because Mother didn't like anyone I liked, so naturally they were not welcome at the house. Besides, I really didn't want them to see how we lived, or be exposed to my Mother.

It was not that I didn't have anything to do. No, I had plenty to do, as my "job" was to take care of Mother. Remember, the Bible said to "Honor your Mother..." and that I did, but my heart was full of bitterness and anger and those feeling were my secret. I kept the house clean, ran her bath water every night, washed her back, made her bed, lit her cigarettes, and brought her beer, twenty cans a day. But I refused to rub her feet—that was Tom's job.

About once a week, Mother would have strange cravings. If it were fish, she would fix and serve fried fish and nothing else, just fish and bread. The rest of the time I'd have to find something to eat on my own.

Even at home Mother directed people around as if she were still directing a funeral, and people jumped when she called. She had a way of controlling her friends without them knowing they were being controlled—probably because her charisma charmed them. Can you imagine, her friends thought it was exciting to be around her?

When the evening got started, Mother told jokes and sang, while playing the piano. Then, to top off the evening if no fights broke out, she would read everyone's fortune. She would place a dime in the palm of the person whose fortune she was telling and with the Bible on the table, she would begin telling the person things she "saw" about them. They would be shocked or surprised and say, "How did you know that?"

She'd smile and say, "I know everything!"

Chills would run down my spine because I saw they actually believed her, and I watched in awe. I did not know how she could be so accurate about secrets in other people's lives. But I did know that it made me very uncomfortable.

There was never a dull moment around our house. I only wanted to have a quiet night with no noise and no people in the living room. When the house was quiet, I knew there was no need to get too comfortable, because Mother would soon call, "Little Mary. Come get me a beer," or "Come get me a glass of water," or "Come get me a cigarette."

It didn't make any difference that all these things were at her reach; it was her way of remaining in control. After all, I was her servant and I jumped when she said, "jump" and it didn't matter how high. I wondered what it would be like to wake with everything clean. What a wonderful thought, but it was only a thought. The Reese home was known for entertainment, and guests never cleaned up after themselves. That was my job.

42

THANK GOODNESS SUMMER WAS FINALLY ENDING AND soon I could go back to school, meet new friends, and have time away from home. Then maybe Tom would wait on Mother more and give me a break. With all the late hours, I knew it was going to be difficult to retrain myself to go to bed early. My main concern was how to make my room secure. Repeatedly, I had asked Mother to put a lock on my door, but she refused because she didn't believe in locks; however, a chair wedged under the doorknob did work.

It seemed strange to me that Mother had given up her business without a fight. Mr. Blakley had commented to me before I had been banned from the premises that he didn't understand how she could just walk away. There was a rumor she planned to go and work for the Hill & Hill Mortuary over on 110th and Central Boulevard, deeper into the Inner City, because she no longer wanted the responsibility of being an owner.

Then, out of the blue at the kitchen table one evening, she announced she was selling the house and we would be moving to the West Side. That surprised and saddened us all, especially me. I didn't want to move again and start at a new school. It was scary because I had some friends here and was comfortable in my environment. Begging Mother for us to stay did no good as she had already made up her mind. She said we would be moving before school started and I would be enrolling in the West Side High School.

Even though I was forbidden access to the J.T. Stone Mortuary, every once in a while I would sneak over, watching to see if Mr. Jones or Reverend Lindsey were around. I thought they were the scum-of-the-earth, claiming to be so righteous, standing in the church saying how God had blessed them, while their hearts were evil. They deliberately befriended Mother, socializing and partying with her, and then secretly plotted behind her back. Her drinking had been her weakness, and they had taken advantage of it. Once they had the majority of stock, they bought her out. The businesswoman that had been awarded "Mother of the Year," the woman that had been so respected, was slowly falling. But it didn't seem to faze her that things were changing. She only wanted to have a good time. Frank Sinatra sang, "I Did It My Way," and that was the way Mother was living her life.

It was nice of Mr. Blakley to come over regularly, checking on her, worried that she would do something drastic. When he heard we would be leaving the neighborhood, he was quite upset. He spent hours with Mother, trying to convince her not to make such a move without thinking and planning it through. But, he was talking to a brick wall, because Mother had closed her mind to any reason or logic. She was determined to do it her way regardless of whom she hurt.

To everyone but her, it was obvious she had given up too easily in regards to the Mortuary. JT had also tried to warn her but as much as she respected and loved him, she had been blind as to what was going on around her. Tom reminded her what a fool they had made of her, and this seemed to play on her mind. Even with all the people of influence in her life, she had not seen it coming and blamed herself.

When Mother finally woke up to the fact that she had literally given away her business, her anger toward Reverend Lindsey and Mr. Jones was uncontrollable. Her heart was hard, and she determined she would not rest until she got even or punished them for betraying her. They had taken away the business she had worked hard to build up and what was almost worse, they had stolen the J.T. Stone name.

If her Father could have known what they had done, he would have turned over in his grave. The Funeral Home in Mississippi was the key to success, and people continued to do business with the Mortuary in Los Angeles because they thought J. T. Stone's daughter, Mrs. Reese, still ran it. Reverend Lindsey and Mr. Jones sure knew what they were doing. They had planned the takeover very carefully to get her to sign over her rights and to even use her Father's name.

Mr. Hubert had also kept the Reese name, and his business continued to grow. A family that lost someone would give the body to the Hubert and Reese Mortuary thinking Mrs. Reese was still there, only to later hear she no longer owned the Mortuary—but by then their family member had been buried.

Mother's mistakes were history repeating itself. If she had not been drunk most of the time, she would have never signed away her Father's name.

Late one Wednesday evening when there was no company at our house, which was a rarity, I found it hard to sleep and I guess the quietness had awakened me. Then I heard someone in the kitchen and hoping it was not a gravedigger or a preacher, I quietly walked in and surprised Mother. Immediately, I felt something was wrong. If she wanted something from the kitchen, she normally called me to get it for her.

"Mother. What are you doing? It's late," I said rubbing my eyes and feeling uneasy that she might be up to something.

"Get me a big bag and the sugar out of the cabinet," she ordered.

"Why do you want sugar?" She seemed strange, yet she wasn't drunk.

"Just get it and shut up!" So I got the sugar and the bag and when I went to hand them to her, she had her car keys in her hand and said, "Come with me."

"No. I'm in my nightgown and besides it's late."

She walked out the back door without another word, got in her car and backed the car out of the driveway, very slowly. *Now, that's not the way she normally backs out,* I thought. I wondered what she was up to, yet I was afraid to know. Later I would find out what she had been up to and it wasn't good. I went back to bed. It was 2:00 a.m., and the house was quiet and I did not need to put a chair at the door.

Time was running out. The move to West Los Angeles was a few days away and all the packing was a pain in the neck. This move was a mistake, and I knew it. I was crying and packing at the same time when Tommy came in my room. "Hey, Little Mary, don't cry. It's going to be okay."

"No, it's not!" I cried as if someone had died and I wished it were me.

"Come on, Little Mary. I live not far from where you'll be moving."

My head went up, "Really?" I could count on Tommy. He was gay and not ashamed of it, so he never tried any funny stuff with me. He loved me for me, and I loved Tommy for being the best friend a person could have. There had been so many times Tommy had thrown someone out for trying to force themselves on me that I had lost count. We often laughed at the creeps that came around looking to get free drinks, as they sat around and shot the bull. When the liquor was gone, they were gone.

Tommy had as much resentment for the preachers as I did. "I wouldn't go to their church if they paid me," he'd say.

"I wouldn't either, except for a funeral," I'd answer.

The preachers were something else. Tommy told me their dirty dark secrets. "They're in the closet during the day, but at night they come out."

"Tommy, I don't want to move. I'm tired of moving around," I told him.

"I know Little Mary, but you don't have a choice. When you get older you can go away, make something of yourself, but don't go into the Funeral Business. You're nothing like your Mom. Do something different, like being a doctor or a lawyer. Make a difference."

"I don't want to be a doctor or a lawyer!" For the first time I realized I didn't have any plans for my future because I only thought of dying. I hadn't thought of a future for me. Maybe Mother should read my fortune.

Talking with Tommy was better than talking to the dead people; he made a lot of sense when we talked. Dead people didn't give advice - maybe that's why I liked talking to them. Every time Tommy and I talked, he would tell me how wrong I was for wanting to die. He was the only person with whom I had ever shared my thoughts about my strong urge to kill myself. Afterwards I had been sorry I had told him. Tommy's concern for me was caring and nurturing. We talked about anything and everything.

"Little Mary, if you plan to commit suicide, I want you to stop and think." His sincerity would bring tears to my eyes. He'd say, "What a waste. Suicide is a form of escape. You can't run. You have to stand and fight. Don't let life knock you down, and if it does, get up and fight some more."

His voice would rise, and I'd laugh and tell him, "Now you're sounding like a preacher."

"Yeah. Maybe I am but Little Mary, life has a way of giving you what you ask, so be careful what you ask for."

"Tommy, promise you'll keep coming around. Suppose Mother gets angry at you and you stop coming over?"

"Mary gets angry with everybody, but I know how to handle her."

"Better you than me. I live with her and cannot figure her out at all."

The packing was still a big headache, but Tommy somehow made things seem okay for the time being. The day before we moved, Reverend Lindsey and Mr. Jones stopped by. Reverend Lindsey had a package in his hand. "Mrs. Reese, you're in big trouble."

"What the hell are you talking about?" Mother was upset when she saw them at the door, but now she had fury in her eyes.

I stood in the hallway door, feeling that she might need me to protect her. I knew that if Reverend Lindsey and Mr. Jones were standing in our living room, there was going to be trouble. I hoped Mother wouldn't hit one of them, but she might. They began to argue, throwing words back and forth about who had done what, and how.

Reverend Lindsey shouted, "Listen, this is the second time we've caught you, and now we have proof. We have photos of you putting sugar in gas tanks of the Funeral Home cars."

Just then JT came through the door and asked, "What the hell is going on?"

Mother backed up knowing JT would get them out of there. Me, I just stood frozen in place, not sure what to do, but the feeling of being ashamed of what Mother had done saddened my heart. JT did not want to hear the Reverend because he already knew what Mother had done. He knew she was devious enough to do anything, but JT would stand up for her regardless and lie if needed. The photos made defending Mother more difficult. Reverend Lindsey threatened to call the police, but out of respect he said he would let it go if she promised not to come around him or the Funeral Home again.

JT pushed them out the door and threatened to kill them if they came near his Mother again. Then he turned to Mother cursing, "Why do you do this shit? You know they'll put you in jail for that kind of shit!"

Mother ignored him and the hard evidence and insisted, "I didn't do anything!"

JT was so upset with her I thought a blood vessel would pop in his head. They had photos, yet Mother still denied doing it.

43

WHEN WE MOVED INTO AN APARTMENT BUILDING ON Hobart Avenue on the West Side of town, it seemed as if we had left Los Angeles. It was a big two-story apartment building, and our new living quarters were on the second floor. Upon getting a good look at the stairs up which we had to move all our stuff, I knew it was going to be tough. Then, when I saw how small the apartment was compared to the house out of which we had just moved, I didn't think it would all fit. Actually, we moved only boxes filled with our personal belongings and necessary things like dishes, etc., not furniture. That was because Mother had said, "We are starting over," and had gone out and bought all new furniture. Maybe she was starting over, but I was trying to get started.

Wandering around the empty apartment that first time, I had wondered, *Why would Mother want to live here?* Since I had never been in an apartment before, it seemed very small from my perspective. It consisted only of a large living room and dining room combination, a small kitchen, two bedrooms, and one bathroom. We would be so close to our neighbors, I figured we probably could hear our neighbor's voices through the walls, and hear their toilets flush and showers run. Right away, I knew I wouldn't like it because it was not a house and there would be no privacy. But, the apartment was prettier than the house.

After everything had been brought up the stairs, I took my things and began getting settled into my room. Upon closing the door, the first thing I saw was a lock on the doorknob, and delighted in that one positive as a good thing. Then I looked at the walls and imagined if the room were upside down, would I feel safe there.

Mother and JT decorated the whole apartment. It had tangerine carpet, a white and gold sofa, chairs covered in plastic, black coffee tables, and huge white and gold lamps. A waterfall was in the living room next to the huge glass window, which was surrounded with large plants, giving it a jungle look. Tom and I had not been asked what we wanted, but it actually was quite beautifully and tastefully decorated. So as to protect the carpet, from then on not only did we have to take our shoes off at the door, but also any and all of our guests.

Finally, September 8, 1960, arrived and my first day of high school. It was very frightening for me, but I held my head up and walked tall just as Mother had taught me. "Look people in the eye. The eyes are the window of the soul," she'd say. Also, another of Mother's rules to live by, "Don't let people see you sweat. Keep your cool at all times, and fall apart later if needed." Yes, I knew how to carry myself, but I hoped no one would notice my knees were shaking.

The first thing I noticed as I walked into the huge front entrance to the school was that there were so many White kids. Automatically I looked around for kids of Color but saw only a few Negroes sprinkled here and there. My first thought was, *How will I connect with anyone?* Students hurried around me, knowing exactly where they were going, while I stood in the hallway, lost.

I had never seen such a large school. The bell rang and I had a card that said Home Study, Room, 3D Bungalow. *Where the hell was I, and where or what was a bungalow?* While I just stood there, turning around in confused circles, a White lady approached me and with a nice smile asked, "Honey, are you new here?"

"Yes, and I don't know where 3D Bungalow is," I answered.

With another smile she walked me to an exit door and pointed across a yard that looked as big as the neighborhood from where I had just come. As a second bell rang, the lady said, "You're going to be late. You'd better hurry."

I took off running across the yard, thinking, *Here it is my first day and I am late!* It definitely was not a confidence builder.

The Bungalow classroom was full, and the only seat vacant was right in the front. *Just my luck. Now I have all these kids behind me, and the teacher in my face.* That was probably the longest day of my life. I didn't connect with anyone and if they headed in my direction, I turned and walked away.

Tremont High was where I had really wanted to go because there I would have had friends I knew. They were friends with whom I had fought and who knew I was tough, who knew I was Colored and thought I was cool. At this other high school no one thought I was special; in fact, no one knew me at all! Again, I was alone besides being a fish out of water.

That first day was miserable for me. I didn't want to go home, and I didn't want to be at school either. The end of the day didn't come quickly enough. As I walked to my locker, which took me twenty minutes to find then another twenty to open, the kids hurried around me knowing where they were going. I had never felt so lost before and fear made me want to run, but I didn't know of what I was afraid and just wanted to disappear.

Even though I could have ridden the school bus, I walked home. I had had enough of strange kids for the day and besides, a long walk gave me time to think. *How was I to survive this? I miss not having the Funeral Home to visit. I miss not being able to talk to the dead people. With them I had no trouble making new friends. This neighborhood is like being in a foreign land.*

I got home about 5:00 p.m., and as I walked through the door Mother started yelling, in her loud and angry voice, "Where the hell have you been?"

"I walked home," I answered, confused as to why she was so upset with me.

"I know you're whoring around! It doesn't take two hours to get home!"

"Mother, I walked and it was a long walk…and I was alone. Remember, we keep moving, so I don't have any friends here." Then I went into my own bedroom angry, upset, and feeling as low as the floor, wanting to escape into sleep so I wouldn't have to think and could be alert during the evening and night.

Her calling me a whore was nothing new, but it still made me angry and indignant because it was so unfair and untrue. Never had I done anything to give her cause or reason to accuse or say such hateful things to me. It didn't help me any to know it gave her perverse pleasure to think that I was bad. In fact, her attitude was the main reason I wouldn't let any male get close to me.

Some things never change. For that evening, Mother had invited a few people from our apartment building over for a party. Hearing the doorbell ring several times and hearing more and more voices, I cracked open my bedroom door and cautiously peeked out so as not to be noticed. Surprise, surprise, the living room was packed with people.

Peaking a little later when it was after midnight, I saw that Redd Foxx and some of the showgirls from the Club had come over. The lights were dim, but I could see clearly they had all taken off their shoes at the door. Redd was laughing with my Mother at the table, and I recognized a couple of Mother's preacher friends dancing and holding on tightly to the "girls of the night."

Closing my door quietly, I sat on the bed thinking how nasty they all were and how I hated them! I needed to go to the bathroom but was afraid to come out of my room. Evidently, I dozed off and when I awoke, my clock said 3:10 a.m. Now really having to go to the bathroom, I quietly opened my door so as not to be heard and looked into the living room. What I saw I absolutely could not believe. One of the preachers was actually on the floor, with his pants off with a girl, and another couple was on a chair doing what I did not know could be done that way.

Involuntarily, I gasped in shock and Mother heard me and with an angry glare, hissed, "Go back to your room!" and dismissed me with a gesture of her hand and evil eye. She had not gotten up and then with disgust I realized why. With her dress around her waist and thighs exposed, she was straddling Tom on a chair and doing something I thought was nasty.

It made me feel sick to my stomach and I hurried into the bathroom where I fell on the floor with my head in the toilet, and threw up my lunch. Thank goodness I hadn't had any dinner. It hurt me so much to have seen what she was doing, it just about took my breath away and I wanted to die right then.

Why did she do these things? She didn't even care I had seen her. She waved me off as if I'd walked in on her in the bathroom or something. In our living room there is an orgy going on and it hadn't bothered my Mother that I saw it.

My heart was broken and I hit my head on the floor, crying as if there were no tomorrow. I now knew I had to die and it had to be soon because I did not want to live like this anymore, and I did not want to be around Mother or her friends. The only thing that surprised me was that Redd was not out there. He must have already left.

Creeping back to my own room, I locked the door and once again cried myself to sleep, wishing God would just take me, but that didn't happen. Instead, I awoke late for school. Mother and Tom still slept. The living room was empty, and there was the usual mess left for me to clean.

In a hurry I dressed and since I felt hungry, went and looked into the refrigerator, hoping there would be some milk. My intention was to have a bowl of cereal before I left for school—there was only beer.

With an empty stomach I rushed for the bus, knowing this would not look good if I were late again on my second day of school. Running to my homeroom I slipped in and sat down hoping no one had noticed. To my surprise nothing was said. Evidently when you're in high school, they treat you more like an adult.

It was so difficult to concentrate on anything that whole day because I could not get the picture of people having sex in my living room out of my mind. Now I wondered what I should expect each day. As usual, I dwelled on killing myself and when.

At school I spent most of my time alone, but I did meet a couple of girls who were nice and talked with me. They even invited me to a few after-school things, but I never accepted. After all, I had to go directly home, or I would be called a whore. So I walked around in a daze the majority of the time and really couldn't remember one day from the next. I was there in body, but my spirit was somewhere else.

I wish I could say I came home and had dinner each night, but that was never the case. I'd come home to an empty house, or a house full of people. Either way, I was responsible for myself. If I ate that was fine and if I didn't, it didn't matter to anyone. For all practical purposes, I was on my own. Mother never went to a grocery store that I can remember as food was never a priority for her. In fact, she never went to the liquor store either; she just had everything delivered. There were times I found myself cutting up a candy bar for breakfast and pretending it was eggs and bacon.

Mother and Lenore still went out a lot, but I would be left at the apartment alone. I didn't like being alone, but it was better than being with her drunken friends. For emergencies, if she were out for the evening, Mother would leave the phone number where she could be reached. By 1:00 a.m., I would call and ask her to please come home. She refused and even if I begged and pleaded, it did no good.

Even though I was then in high school, I still wanted her to love me and want to be with me. Since we didn't work the funerals anymore, I missed being with her when she was sober. Those were the wonderful times when she could be fun to be around. To work with her had been an honor. Her business skills and people skills were magnificent. She could have been a preacher herself; people believed in her. That was the Mother I wished I had at home, except at home she was a selfish woman who only thought of her own needs. There was still one child at home and I didn't realize she was already planning how to get me out.

I did well in school, but it did not interest her. Mother did not care if I went school or not, but I went and optimistically hoped my good grades would please her. Feeling proud that I had "A's" in all my classes, I thought they might earn me a reward, maybe a nice word like, "Good! Little Mary, I'm proud of you". Instead, she would see the report card, and tell *me* to sign it. "After all," she'd say, "our handwriting is exactly alike." I'd stand there thinking, *Aren't you proud of me?* But I knew she could have cared less.

I spent way too much of my time trying to prove to her that I was not a bad girl.

Months passed and my Mother made new friends in the apartment building. My nights I spent in my locked room, studying and planning my suicide. Since not being able to talk with Mr. Blakley or the dead people and having no one, I was terribly depressed. Other than school, my only other outing was once a week when Mother allowed me to go roller skating. And there again, I was somebody.

The school year was coming to an end and I knew I faced another long summer. School was a good place for me because there I could get lost in the shuffle and no one knew I had a Mother who couldn't care less about me. That was my secret.

Sometimes I'd sit for hours in my room, trying to remember the good days, when Dad and Ilona were home, times of being a family. There were questions I didn't have the answers to which had always puzzled me—like: Why did Ilona leave me? Why did Dad not let me come stay with him? What had I done to him? Mother said he hated me, why? Then I would think about how Willie Jr. and Ilona had it all and they were family. I envied them so and at times I told myself I hated them for leaving me.

Where had the months gone? Mother had been living off the money from the sale of the Mortuary, but now needed to go back to work in order to have an income. She decided to accept the offer from Hill & Hill Mortuary, to be their Funeral Director, not a Partner. They were counting on her expertise to bring their business into focus. Mrs. Hill's husband had died the previous year, and business was not doing so well. She was drowning in the business and needed help and direction. Mother had a mortician's license, whereas Mrs. Hill didn't.

Mrs. Hill had heard about Mrs. Reese from one of the churches that still had the little fans in their pews. She was both pleased and excited to bring Mother aboard and knew Mrs. Reese's name alone would bring in business. Mother was also excited about going back to what she knew best, directing funerals. I prayed that now I'd get back my Mother who was a real lady, the lady who carried herself like royalty, not the woman who had orgies at her home.

44

THAT FIRST YEAR LIVING IN THE APARTMENT SEEMED like a bad dream. The actual apartment living wasn't as bad as I had first thought it would be, but it didn't stop all the nightlife. Desperate to fit in somewhere I smoked more and I learned how to fake drinking by sipping on one vodka and orange juice all evening. Also, I stayed up later, spending more time with Mother, Lenore and JT. In fact I even got used to them arguing over who would sing and who Mother would favor that evening. I sure knew it wouldn't be me as I did not sing, or care about entertaining her friends. The corner was my domain where I sat and watched and took care of Mother's needs—like seeing to it she always had a drink and a cigarette. Soon, I learned how to put out fires if someone upset her and found I could usually calm her down without it turning into a big incident. Of course not all the time, but enough to feel it was a reason to stick around.

The fighting between JT and Lenore no one could stop. Lenore would interrupt whenever he sang and he'd cuss her out, and then Mother would get angry and cuss them both out, but always took sides with JT. Lenore was like a wounded animal, so then she'd do something drastic to get attention. It was a sure thing, once a week you could count on Lenore trying to commit suicide. She'd get a knife, or take a handful of pills, or run out of the apartment and into traffic. Someone always stopped her but I feared that one time no one would get to her in time. I stopped trying to run after her because I was afraid for myself, afraid to run out into the night.

My heart ached for Lenore because I understood her want and need for Mother to love her. But cruelly, Mother continued to remind her every chance she got that she didn't know who was Lenore's Father. She seemed to enjoy rubbing salt in the wound and keeping it raw. It always was an unsettled issue between them. Lenore only knew one Father, and that was Dad. Bless his heart; he loved her as much as he loved the rest of his children. But that was not enough for Lenore, and Mother's words destroyed Lenore's sense of worth.

"You know you want to fuck him," Mother told her, referring to Dad. The first time Lenore heard those words she was fifteen when Mother woke her up and said them to her. Mother wanted to hurt Dad and she did, but she destroyed Lenore for life.

I wanted so much for Lenore to be able to forget what Mother said. "You know Mother likes to be mean," I'd tell her and give her a hug, but Lenore was afraid to show affection. I kept trying and she'd always push me away. To Lenore, those cruel words shouted at her years before, were tattooed on her heart and in her mind. After that she could never let herself get close to Dad for fear of being accused of such a horrible thing.

Mother's cruelty passed through each one of us, and each of us dealt with it differently. JT was the only one that escaped her cruelty because he knew she loved him and he wasn't afraid to go head-to-head with her. If he was ever hurt, I never knew it. He was tall, dark, handsome, and he did not lack self-esteem by any means. In fact, he didn't care who his Father was; he loved Dad, and he was Mother's first-born. Of course, being named after the great J.T. Stone, in Mississippi, gave him a heritage in which he could be proud. It seemed JT did not need approval from anyone and even though Mother showed her love for him daily, they fought often. To me the love they had for each other was sickening. JT had been treated like he was royalty and everyone else was there to serve him. Like Mother, like son.

Lenore tried to be a good sister to me, but Mother resented that and would tell Lenore and JT bad things about me, all fabricated, but JT and Lenore didn't know that. To JT and Lenore, I was a lazy, selfish girl. Sometimes JT would get angry with me only because Mother had encouraged him to cuss me out for not doing something she wanted me to do. An example: One of my chores was to take the trash out daily, but Mother wanted me to take it out late at night. Since I did not like going into a dark alley alone at night, I took it out in the morning. For some reason, that always kept her upset and JT seemed to enjoy yelling at me about it. Lenore understood Mother liked to stir up trouble and she would defend me. Then she would whisper in my ear, "Little Mary, don't worry about them. You're different. They can't hurt you. You're not like them at all."

I didn't know why she always said that I was different and wondered if it was because I didn't get drunk. Sometimes I wondered if Lenore really understood why it was I didn't drink. Did she remember all the times men had come into my room and I had to fight them off? I had to stay sober, to be on guard because Tommy could not always be there to save me from being raped. Did she know Mother didn't care and that no matter what I did, it was always my fault? Yes, I agreed I was different and always would be. Basically, I was tired of being slapped around, tired of smelling alcohol on men's breath. Being alert and calm, thinking each situation out before reacting, was how I survived—how I talked my way out of men taking advantage of me.

By then, Lenore practically lived with us and our apartment had become her real home. My feeling was she was addicted to Mother, like an addict to heroin. She was there first thing in the morning and stayed until everyone left after midnight. Her husband didn't come around but he respected Mother for the businesswoman she had been; however, he had no patience or tolerance with her when she was drinking. He resented the fact that Mother encouraged Lenore to drink all the time. Basically he gave up the fight, as he knew it was a battle he could not win. Mother always insisted, "There's nothing wrong with us drinking."

Unequivocally, Mother made Lenore into an alcoholic. Lenore would try to wait until noon to drink, but there were days when I saw her start mid-morning. She was such a lonely soul who had absolutely nothing in common with her husband. Their loyalty to one another was something they had agreed upon—they would stay married but live separate lives.

There were times I still thought about Daniel, Lenore's brother-in-law. I had loved him so much. He was now the Father of two children and if I had slept with him, I'd have had two children. But I was glad I had not slept with him, as I did not want to be a Mother. The fear of being anything like my Mother terrified me.

45

THE WORLD WAS CHANGING AND YET THINGS IN THE South were not getting any better. Every day I thanked God I lived in California. There were sit-ins in Greensboro, North Carolina, when college students refused to move from a Woolworth's lunch counter. The television was making the world aware of the problems in the South and I remembered when I had gone to get food for Mother and Tom in Mississippi. That experience had frightened me when I had to pass for White just to get a meal. I prayed I would never have an experience like that again.

The year 1961 was a year that would change the world, change the thinking of mankind. For the first time, there was going to be a televised debate between candidates, Vice President Richard Nixon, and Senator John F. Kennedy. The world watched. The name Senator John F. Kennedy was talked about everywhere I went. He had won the favor of the people, and the Blacks loved him. I loved him.

Even as the world changed, so did I. In a couple of months I would be turning seventeen, school would be out, and I would be facing another boring summer. Listening to the news was one thing I enjoyed because the world's affairs interested me. Maybe that was a sign of maturity that I was no longer a child. I was becoming a young adult by then but didn't have a clue what the future held for me. For me, there were no plans for college—actually, there were no plans for anything.

My life was filled with nightly parties, nightclubs, and sleeping late in the morning. I did not look forward to a future, because I knew one day the nerve would come, and I'd kill myself. Yet…I was still afraid I'd miss something good tomorrow, but all my tomorrows were just like yesterday.

Things didn't change for Mother; she still enjoyed stirring up emotions in order to create chaos in other's lives. Her friends came and went. New friends would be fascinated with her, honored to be at her home only to find in a few months she had used them for her needs and drained their energy.

Mother made a point of arguing with me on a daily basis and then she'd tell me she wanted me to drop out of school, get a job, then get out on my own.

During the summer of 1961, Mother gave a big Gumbo Party to raise money for one of her phony preacher's church. The Preacher, Reverend Andrew, was not one of my favorite people because I believed he probably would buy a new car with the money raised. He was flamboyant with a big diamond ring on his pinky finger and wore brand new suits every Sunday.

The Louisiana Gumbo was a success. It was so good "It would make you want to hit your Momma," that was an expression Mother used repeatedly. Reverend Andrew made over the food and kept telling everyone how wonderful Sister Reese was. Naturally Mother loved the attention and ate up every word. I was happy to see Mother refrained from drinking but I knew she was "working" that party, and when "working," she did not take a drop of alcohol; however, when her job was done, it was "open bar." That social event was to her as if she was working a funeral. She held her head high and encouraged everyone to donate more money. When they passed the bucket for Reverend Andrew's church, people gave much more than they had anticipated.

Actually, I thought Mother sounded like Daddy Grace, "Open up your pockets and give till it hurts. God gave to you; it's your chance to give back." Her voice rose above the music, and someone turned off the record player and Mother began to preach as if she were standing in a pulpit. The people stopped dancing and talking, directing all their attention to her. I was amazed at how she could control a crowd. Her take-charge personality, humor, and charm, would cause people to comply with whatever she wanted. Always the master of ceremonies, she lived her life as though the world was her stage.

I wore a red blouse with white jeans and white sandals. Mother had taught me you only have one chance to make a first impression. So it was important to have everything perfectly matching, to never go out without make-up, and to always wear a good-fitting wardrobe. That night I was confident I looked good.

In a short conversation with Reverend Andrew, he told me how much he appreciated all Mother had done for him and his church. It was obvious the Reverend admired Mrs. Reese; she had helped his congregation grow. Also, he mentioned they would be working together at the Hill & Hill Mortuary, and he would be proud of the opportunity.

All during the event he had been stroking Mother while I avoided being in his presence. The bottom line was, I didn't trust the man. My attitude towards him was negative from the first time I met him. The fact that he was a Preacher said he was supposed to symbolize good, but I felt something evil about him.

Reverend Andrew was dressed to kill. His suit was extremely expensive and he wore a lot of gold. To me, it seemed he moved around the room slowly, like a snake, and his phony smile I likened to one the snake wore in the Garden of Eden when tempting and lying to Eve. I watched him greeting folks—kissing and hugging them. By the time I realized he was walking toward me, it was too late to get away. Having braced myself, I stood there nodding hello to people and tried to avoid eye contact with him. Too late! He was touching my hand and chills went up my arm. I firmly pulled my hand away, without being rude as I said, "That's a beautiful suit, Reverend."

"Thank you, Little Mary. That's nice coming from you."

"What's that mean?" I asked suspiciously.

His voice had been sarcastic and I knew he was not giving me a compliment. "I have to look good for my congregation," he said, ignoring my question.

I couldn't help it and blurted out, "With their money?"

The Preacher just looked at me and walked away. He did not like me and the feeling was mutual. Watching his back as he left, I felt guilty for being so mean to a man who was supposed to love God. Since bad people seemed to gravitate in my direction, I had to trust my gut feelings. But I still felt guilty.

46

MOTHER MET A YOUNG MAN AT THE GUMBO PARTY WHO was nineteen and very handsome. When he had come through the door I also noticed him, but I played it cool since I didn't really think he'd look at me. Remember, I had a hard heart and didn't trust or like anyone, and it showed. But this guy was cute and seemed to have a great personality and Mother liked him immediately. That should have been my first sign to run in the opposite direction, but I thought he might be worth putting down my guard for--a little; also, I had never been on a date with a guy, and I knew Mother was not about to let me start now.

As the day progressed, I learned his name was Eddie but everyone called him Buddy. Buddy sang to me at the party and I melted like a schoolgirl, probably because I *was* a schoolgirl. That was the first party I had ever attended where I had fun. We danced and laughed and I thought I fell in love. In love again, only this time he was the one—because Mother said he was the one.

Even though the Gumbo Party went on into the wee hours of the morning, after it ended, Mother invited Buddy over to our apartment, "And bring your Mother," she told him. I thought she was kidding, but Mother did not kid around. When I overheard Mother and his Mother say something about, "…they would get married." The word "married" caught my ear, and I said, "Hey, we just met tonight. Why would we get married?"

Mother laughed and said, "You guys sure would have pretty children."

"I'm only sixteen, Mother"

"Yes, but you'll be seventeen in a month."

We all laughed, hoping she was kidding. Buddy and I got up from the table and went and sat in the living room. When Mother had asked him to

247

take off his shoes he had a hole in his sock, but he just laughed while I felt embarrassed for him. Buddy was kind. He took my face in his hand and gently kissed me on the lips. We had only known each other a few hours, but after our first kiss I was hooked.

"I'm leaving for Hawaii in a week, but I will write you every day," he promised.

My heart sank as I said, "I just found you and now you're leaving me." We had connected in our hearts and I had hope he was there to save me, to take me away from all the craziness in that house. After Buddy finished his third beer he left. I did not sleep that night, thinking and dreaming of Buddy.

The next week was heaven because I saw Buddy every day. Mother and Buddy sat and drank beer together and I noticed he kept up with her. She would not allow us to go out as dating was out of the question. Then I began to wonder if Buddy came to visit my Mother or me. If she had five beers, he had five. They fried fish and tasted hot sauces to see who could eat the hottest. Mother told him how much she liked him for me. I was blind to what was happening. I was blinded with puppy love. I was still unable to go on a date, but Buddy was patient.

The night before Buddy left for Hawaii, Mother invited Buddy's Mother and grandmother over for a "going-away party." They sat at the table and between the three women, arranged a wedding for Buddy and me. To my amazement, Buddy agreed. I was not sure what to say, but in front of his Mother and grandmother, Buddy asked me to marry him. I glanced around the room and saw everyone smiling at me. Then I looked at Buddy and my heart melted. "Yes," I said.

The room was filled with excitement as a wedding was going to happen. I was going to be a bride but had yet to be out on a date. The thought of Buddy not having a job didn't seem important at the time. His grandmother and my Mother assured us they would help us and that everything would be okay. We had only known each other a week, and the next month he would be out of town.

That next month seemed like an eternity to me. Buddy and I corresponded and we fell deeply in love through the mail. Mother was in seventh heaven. She would marry me off and she and Tom would not have to worry about me any more, as if they ever had.

The wedding date was set for two weeks after Buddy returned from Hawaii. Mother would sign for me and Buddy's Father would sign for him. Later I found out Buddy's Mother thought Buddy was marrying into a rich family, and my Mother thought Buddy's family was rich.

At night I'd sit in my room thinking of the coming event. Everything had been rushed and I had really not had a say in anything. So used to not speaking up and defending myself, I was afraid to say, "Stop." Then, once the invitations were already delivered, I felt caught and that it was too late.

Of course, I had no say in where the wedding would take place either. But Mother took me to Saks Fifth Avenue to buy the prettiest wedding dress the mind could envision. Why wasn't I happy? I did not feel the same excitement Mother felt and was actually afraid of marrying Buddy. Yes, I loved him, but I didn't really know him. In fact, Buddy and I had never been alone in the same room, but there was no turning back as we were both caught up in the avalanche of our Mothers' making. Mother kept insisting, "I know he is so right for you..." So at her urging, I dropped out of school without a second thought.

Mother was so happy I was getting married she even agreed to let Ilona be in my wedding, and said I could ask my Father to give me away. Good thing, as I did not want Tom to give me away. He and Mother had fought so much he had finally moved out but we all knew he would be back.

To all appearances it seemed her heart had softened. I didn't know how long it would last, but knew there was no way Dad and Mother could be in the same room together as they would end up killing each other. I knew Mother would never be able to control her temper so why was she being so nice? My gut instincts said to be careful, but this was one time I was not paying attention to my instincts.

Happily, Ilona and Lenore were there every day to support me. They explained to me about my first night when Buddy and I would make love and how I would probably bleed, that it would hurt, but that it would get better after that. The thought terrified me.

I worked up the nerve to visit my Father and ask if he would give me away at my wedding. Lenore and a friend drove me to my Father's business. Naturally, I was a little nervous as I had not visited or talked with him for three years, since the awful night Mother fought with him and the night I had made the mistake of running down the street. It was a nightmare that still haunted me.

For some reason, I was nervous about seeing my Dad. No longer a child but a young adult about to be married, I had hoped when he saw me walking up he would run out, grab and hug and kiss me, so happy to see his baby girl. When I walked toward the open door to his building, my heart beat faster with every step.

As I approached, I heard a man's voice say, "Willie, I think that's your daughter coming up." Dad did not turn around so I touched his shoulder. Seconds seemed like minutes before he turned to face me.

"What are you doing here?" he asked with a puzzled look on his face.

Feeling out of place, I said, "Dad, I'm getting married."

I heard! "You're going to be just like your Mother! A bunch of kids and a drunk!"

He was being mean; this was not the man I remembered. My eyes filled with tears and fighting the urge to cry and run away, I stood tall and looked him straight in the eyes, and said, "I thought you'd be happy for me."

"Why would I be? You're too young, and you'll be just like your Mother."

When he said that again, I became angry. "I'll never be like Mother!" My voice rose above his. With blood rushing to my face, I asked, "Why are you being so mean? I came to ask you to give me away." My words scrambled together. A knot formed in my throat.

"I don't want to have anything to do with it. You're making a mistake, and I won't be part of it."

I ran to the car where Lenore was and my heart stuck in my mouth. His attitude had been cold and I could still feel the chill of his voice. My Father was not happy to see me and I left crushed.

The wedding went on in spite of what my Father thought or said. There were hundreds of people in attendance, and I did not know any of them.

As weddings go, it was a nice wedding with bridesmaids and groomsmen, and the reception party lasted until after midnight. Buddy had more fun than I did—probably because he drank all evening. When we reached the apartment, he passed out.

There would be no honeymoon as we had no money and nowhere to go, and we had to stay with Mother. I will just say our wedding night was nothing like I thought it would be. For the first month we lived with Mother and Buddy still did not have a job, and he never went to look for one. He and Mother drank every day, all day, till late evening, and then Buddy would pass out.

After a month, Mother said she was tired of paying for Buddy's liquor and literally threw us out. With nowhere to go, Buddy and I slept in his car for a few nights behind a grocery store. While Buddy slept, I kept watch, too afraid to close my eyes. There were no words to describe the fear I felt. All the promises his grandmother and Mother had made about giving Buddy a job had suddenly been forgotten.

47

I LOVED BUDDY, BUT OUR MARRIAGE WAS NOT WHAT I had expected. The many episodes of Ozzie and Harriett on TV, which I had watched, were of a real family and nothing like mine. So naïve, I honestly thought my life would be like Ozzie and Harriet's. Buddy would work, come home and I'd be waiting for him at the door with dinner on the table and a wonderful smile as I'd say, "How was your day, dear?" That was the life I had dreamed of having—my own home, with a white-picket fence, a dog, and a swing on the front porch. Then later, if I were to change my mind about having children, I would love and protect my kids with my life.

Instead, there I sat in a parking lot in a 1954 Pontiac, hoping no one would see us. It was about four o'clock in the morning and Buddy was asleep in the backseat. Wanting to close my eyes but fearing bad things might happen in the dark, I watched every moving thing near the car and waited for daybreak. I was frightened and cold and didn't know what to do about it. Here I was with my husband who had promised to take care of me. So how could he fall asleep in a car?

I decided when Buddy woke up I would tell him we had to find a place to stay because I couldn't continue living in a car! As I assessed my husband's character I realized nothing bothered him. He felt life owed him everything, and he was not giving anything back. As it was given to him he took, but working was not in his plans. His family had always supplied him with liquor and food, but not money.

But, when Buddy finally awoke, I was too afraid to say anything, so we remained living in our car.

My thoughts of dying were more frequent than ever. Real peace was lying in a casket, surrounded with satin comforters and people grieving that

I was gone. Then there would be no more sorrows, no more tears, and most of all, no more fears.

It was quite something for an immature, seventeen-year-old bride to realize she had absolutely nothing in common with her husband. Sure Buddy was good looking, but I found all too soon that was all he had on the positive side going for him. Soon I saw that after several beers his mean streak surfaced. In fact, he was worse than my Mother. Shock of all shocks, I had jumped out of the skillet and into the fire!

Buddy's verbal attacks turned into physical attacks and I never knew what would set him off. I had experienced Mother's wrath when she'd get drunk but knew how to calm her down, but nothing seemed to work with Buddy. He enjoyed hitting me and soon convinced me I deserved it. Crying was meaningless and lost on him. My tears, my sadness, belonged to me. My days seemed as dark as my nights and from somewhere deep inside, my survival instincts kicked in and led me to look for a job, any job. I found a waitress job at a barbecue joint, not in the best area but they hired me. Without a diploma I didn't have any marketing skills other than working at a Funeral Home. But that was out since Mother had lost her business and was living high on her own money.

The waitress job wouldn't pay much, but at least I would be making money and that meant no more sleeping in the car. When I shared some of my troubles with my new boss, he was willing to help me. He said I was a nice young girl, and sleeping in a car was a disgrace and I could not have agreed more. Nice man that he was, he gave me one week's advance, fifty dollars. I was loaded!. Now I could rent a room for us. His kindness was appreciated, but in my heart I kept guard.

I found a boarding house that rented out rooms at twelve dollars a week. The bathroom was down a long hallway, and it was shared with the other tenants. To me that was disgusting, but not as scary as the car. The furnished room was not anything I would have chosen if given a choice. I hated the dingy, dark furniture. In addition, the room smelled as if the window had never been opened, and I did not want to think about who had slept in the bed before me. One thing, we had to supply our own sheets and I was glad for that. Among the *few* wedding presents Mother *allowed* me to keep were a set of sheets.

At seventeen I had my own place and a job. I knew it did not have the same prestige as working at the Funeral Home, but at that point I did what I had to do to keep from sleeping in the car. There would be no more kissing Buddy's parents' behinds, or begging them for help. I could take care of us as it had become quite obvious Buddy didn't know how to take care of us because he couldn't even take care of himself.

Ilona knew of my troubles and generously gave me money once in a while. I didn't like feeling like a loser, but that's what my life was all about at that time. I had made a big mistake by quitting school. Then I had let myself be railroaded by Mother into a quick marriage with a lazy loser. And on top of all that, I had no plans for the future. For being so foolish I began to believe I deserved my beatings.

Living with Buddy had not bettered my life—all I had done was change my address. Naturally, Buddy spent all of his time with his friends and they all were heavy drinkers, so once again I was in a situation where I did not belong. After work my evenings were spent in that one room, playing solitaire with no telephone and no food other than junk food because one of the Boarding House rules was no cooking. We were not even allowed to have a hot plate, so I ate crackers and peanut butter for breakfast, lunch, and dinner. Who knew what Buddy ate, or where.

My pride would not allow me to ask for help. Ilona had a good life and I did not want to burden her, and Lenore had so many of her own problems one more would have pushed her over the edge.

There was something inside me that insisted I wanted more. Daily I had pity parties but no one ever showed up except me. The silence I felt by being alone was deafening with no TV, just a bed and a chair. It was a box and felt like a coffin—only I was alive, not dead. I just had to do something! But what could I do? Buddy was now my worst enemy. The love we had was not love; it was an excuse to get away from Mother, only I ended up trading one trouble for another.

My infatuation with Buddy was soon crushed under the weight of a heavy dose of reality and it died. Now, I didn't trust him and his constant drinking and running around drove me crazy. If I fought with him he won, because he fought with his fists. There was no peace in my life. I cried all the time and was afraid to leave the room for fear Buddy would beat me up for going out.

Working was my only outlet. I would get up at six o'clock in the morning while Buddy still slept and I dressed, in the dark, trying so hard not to make a noise because if I awakened him he would get angry and slap me around. Constantly I tried to appease him because I was tired of going to work with black eyes or busted lips but then again, sometimes Buddy would walk in and slap me just for the hell of it.

There was not a day or night that passed when I didn't try to figure a way out of my dilemma; how could I get away? Buddy threatened he'd kill me if I left. I wanted to die, but I didn't want to be killed. For some reason it was important that I be the one to make the choice of how I would die. Sometimes I'd sit and try to will myself to death so I could fade away. I truly believed no one in this world loved me because I was not lovable, and agreed with my Mother that I should never have been born.

Because my boss began flirting with me and wanting me to work late at night, I quit working at the barbecue place. In his back room was a bed, and he said when business was slow I could feel free to go lie down. Now I was a fool for getting married and quitting school, but I was not stupid. I knew men played games with your mind and mainly there was only one thing they wanted.

When I brought my check home, as Buddy always insisted, and told him I had quit, he was pissed. Fearing his anger, I left out the whole truth about my boss flirting with me. Buddy began cussing me out for not having a job and kept telling me how no good I was. I told myself if I didn't argue with him he'd quiet down and go to sleep, but I knew he would probably not be satisfied till he had knocked me around, but hope springs eternal and I secretly hoped he would pass out.

Buddy stayed awake long enough to slap me around, and when I wouldn't cry he told me to sleep on the floor. I hurt so much I wanted to die and could feel my lip throbbing. From the salty taste, I knew I had blood in my mouth. It was not the first time I had tasted my own blood. Desperately I needed to go to the restroom down the hall, but Buddy forbade me to leave the room. I stayed sitting on the floor so that he couldn't slap me down again, and I held myself while he brought over a bucket. His reason for bringing in a bucket was that late at night he wouldn't have to go down the hall.

With my knees up, holding them tightly to my chest and my chin resting on them, I rocked myself back and forth while sitting on the floor. I kept wondering, *Why was he so mean? Why did he like hurting me? One day, he'll come home and find me dead and I hope that really hurts him.*

Keeping my head down, I tried to muffle my crying. If I cried he'd really get upset and I didn't have many tears left anyway. I remember Mother telling me, "If you keep crying, you won't be able to urinate. You'll use up all the fluid in your body and the pain of kidney failure will be awful." I fought to hold my tears.

I thought Buddy was finally asleep when I felt him pulling my arm, lifting me off the floor. "I'm sorry, Little Mary. I didn't mean to hurt you," he whispered as he began to unbutton my blouse. His breath was sour and he smelled of sweat but being in bed with him was better than being on the floor. After he finally rolled off me he smiled and said, "Now, back on the floor."

"Why?" I was in shock. He had just apologized for being mean and had made love to me and now he wanted me back on the floor. I stayed on the bed, hoping he was only teasing me but he grabbed my arms and pushed me onto the floor.

"Sleep on the floor!" he snapped.

I fell to the floor and crawled to the chair, but Buddy jumped off the bed and pushed me away from the chair. "No! You sleep on the floor! That way next time you quit your job, you'll think about where you'll sleep."

He turned off the lamp and my heart raced. I was so afraid there might be bugs on the floor. I tried to crawl as quietly as I could toward the bed, but Buddy was not so drunk that he couldn't hear me. He yelled, "You better keep your ass down there."

On the floor is where I stayed, afraid to fight back. Into a fetal position I curled—afraid to cry, afraid to die. Holding myself tightly, shivering and praying for the daylight to come through the window, I waited for the longest night of my life to end. But my mind worked constantly and I tried to make plans, the first of which was get another job and second, find a way to run away from Buddy. But how and when were good questions, with no immediate answers coming to mind.

When daylight came Buddy stayed in the bed, while I lay on the floor. I didn't hate Buddy. I actually felt sorry for him, and I didn't know why.

48

ONE AFTERNOON AS I SAT IN THE ROOMING HOUSE playing solitaire, I heard a car's horn blowing and blowing. Leaving my solitaire game, I got off the bed and ran out of the room. For some reason, which I didn't understand, I had the feeling that horn was blowing for me. To my surprise, it was my Father. It had been several months since our last meeting, and he was the last person I expected to see. My heart welled up with excitement as I ran out the front door of the rooming house. My Father was getting out of his car and the first thing I saw was his big, beautiful smile and my heart jumped with joy. I was so happy I thought I would burst and with tears running down my face I ran into his open arms. When my Dad held me I melted into his arms, hoping to gain his strength and the love that was missing from my life.

"Baby, I heard how you're living and I had to come. What can I do?" his words rang in my ears. He cared! He loved me! Somebody loved me! Now this was the best day of my life.

As I continued to hold onto him, I realized we were still standing in the street. "Come on, Dad. Come inside," I pleaded. I felt like a little girl as I held his hand and thought it strange that I couldn't remember ever feeling like a little girl. This was a moment I would always remember—I finally knew my Dad really loved me.

"Baby, why are you living like this? Why didn't you let me know you needed help?"

"Dad, I really messed up, huh?"

"Yes, you have. I told you, but you're like your Mother; you wouldn't listen."

My blood ran cold and my face became stern as I snapped back, "I'm nothing like Mother! Dad, I'm nothing like Mother; please don't say that."

"I didn't mean it like that—I meant you have a strong will."

"I don't understand what that means, but I made a mistake and I don't know how to correct it. Dad, Buddy beats me up, and when I called and told Mother, she said it's my fault."

"Then why don't you leave?"

"Where can I go? Mother won't let me come back to her; can I come stay with you?"

"Well, no. I've got Willie Jr. and Ilona and her husband. There just isn't enough room for anyone else."

I knew Willie Jr. had one of the duplexes, and Ilona and Norman had the other. I guess it hurt Dad to tell me I couldn't live with him, but it hurt me more to hear it.

"I brought you some money and I'm working on getting you a car," he told me, trying to make me feel better. "Here, take the money," and he held out two twenty-dollar bills.

I needed the money, but I was too proud to take it. "I can't take your money, Dad."

"Yes, you can," he stated, taking my right arm and pushing the money down into the palm of my hand. I closed my hand around the twenties, feeling ashamed for accepting it but so glad to have some money that Buddy would know nothing about.

We talked for awhile and I inhaled each word, thrilled to talk with my Father after such a long time. Eight years had passed since we had been together, and I had forgotten everything about him. He was like a stranger, a stranger coming into my life to give me hope and I prayed Buddy would not come home and steal my few moments alone with Dad. Buddy was like Mother in many ways; he loved to be the center of attention.

Finally, Dad told me that he had to leave. He hugged me, brushed my forehead with his lips and I watched him drive away. Now I no longer felt lost; my life would change now and somehow I would overcome—I had hope. If I had killed myself that past night, I would have missed my Father today. It was then I decided I was going to hold onto life no matter how bad things got. "I'll wait for tomorrow. Something good will happen. It just has to."

Going back into that rooming house I wore a smile as big as the Grand Canyon, walked to my room and locked the door. When I fell onto the bed, looking up at the ugly-gray cracked ceiling, I didn't care about being in that small, dark room because I now knew my Father loved me. Thinking of all those wasted years believing he didn't love me just because Mother told me he hated me, nearly broke my heart. He loved me and really hated *her*! Finally I now understood what had been going on—Mother had to control everyone around her and she had brainwashed me into believing I was unlovable. Maybe she didn't love me, but Dad cared and that was a wonderful revelation to me.

During our little visit he had made it clear he did not like my getting married and as long as I was with Buddy, he would not do much to help me. "Oh, I'll give you a few dollars every now and then, but that's it," he had told me.

Yes, the money was nice, but it wasn't what mattered because I had only wanted to know I was loved. Wanted to know someone in my family was "normal." To me "normal" was Dad. He didn't drink or smoke, had a nice home, and sat down and ate dinner at the same time every night—there was order in his life. Also he had standards of what was right and what was wrong by which he lived. It gave me a new sense of pride that there was one good man in this world, and it was my Dad. That little bit of happiness I would tightly hold onto every day. Now I was a new person and I was going to prove to Dad I would be somebody and never be like my Mother.

Hugging these happy thoughts, I lay on the bed for hours until my stomach said, "Feed me." My thoughts of the man who tried to kill me kept crowding into my mind, trying to steal my happiness. I had hoped the fear would pass if I continued to think about my Father, but when the sun went down, I began to get tense. Every sound outside was a threat in my mind and I was not going out for anything. I decided to just drink water while waiting for Buddy to come home.

It was no secret Buddy spent more time at Mother's house than with me since that was where he could get free liquor. I thought, *At least I am on the bed. Maybe he won't come back at all tonight, but I won't be that lucky.*

Enjoying my thoughts I sat alone in my room and turned on my small radio. It had bad reception but I could make out the news and it was all about President Kennedy. He was making changes for the Black race and I was proud he was the President of the United States. *I guess there are two good men in this world,* I told myself.

The newscaster talked about Fidel Castro in Cuba, who was always trying unsuccessfully, to cause trouble. Listening to the news around the world helped me realize my troubles weren't so bad. I could have been living in Cuba or Mississippi.

There were Freedom Riders from Washington, D.C., and across the deep South, to protest segregation. I even toyed with the idea of running away and joining the Freedom Riders. When I heard Martin Luther King, Jr. on the radio or television I had been mesmerized by his speeches. He taught love, not hate, and when he gave his speech "I have a dream…" that was when I became a believer that there was a real God. Martin Luther King, Jr. had love that passed all understanding He believed that all men were equal, and to Martin Luther King, Jr., I said, "Amen!"

Thinking it was a time for the Black people to be proud of their race, I suddenly and gleefully realized I now had three men I could believe—my Father, President Kennedy, and Martin Luther King, Jr. To me it seemed they had so many things fighting against them and that each time they'd take one step forward they would be knocked back two.

What a shame being Black meant you had to fight for everything. I was proud to be Black and it ticked me off whenever I had to tell people I was Black and not White.

I turned the radio dial looking for music and the song, "Money, That's All I Want" came on. Jumping off the bed I started singing and dancing and thought, *No more pity parties for me. I don't need Buddy or Mother. I will make it! All I need is a plan*

After "Money" finished, an old doo-wop group, the Moonglows, began to sing "Sincerely." I lay down on the bed and silently cried myself to sleep.

49

THE DAYS AND WEEKS AFTER MY DAD'S FIRST VISIT passed quickly, yet so many of the days seemed worse than the day before. I spent my days looking for a job, but I didn't have a high-school degree so anything that paid a decent salary was almost surely out of the question for me. In spite of being turned down each time I applied for a job, I was determined not to give up.

The meetings with Dad I kept to myself, and once in awhile Buddy would take me to see Ilona. I envied her life because she ate dinner with her family, had a home, a television, and they played games together. It was obvious Norman adored Ilona and their baby. He worked two jobs so that Ilona could stay home and raise their child and they were a happy family, which was something I doubted I would ever have.

There were times I wondered why life was so complicated for me and what was it I had or had not done to deserve such unhappiness? A fatalistic attitude settled into my soul and I concluded happiness was for only a chosen few and I was not in that group. When the cards of life had been dealt, my hand had said, "You ain't worth shit." So with that attitude I walked with my head down; no longer proud to be the daughter of Mrs. Reese, the Queen of Morticians. I was just Buddy's wife, and he thought slapping me around would inspire me to do better—better at what I did not know.

* * *

One evening when Buddy was gone to Mother's, I heard a knock on our door. I was afraid to open the door so, I stayed quiet hoping whoever it was would go away. As I stared at the door I saw a piece of paper being shoved under it. Still terrified to move to see what the paper said, I stayed where I was until I heard footsteps moving away from our door. Then I tiptoed to the door, picked up the paper and broke into tears when I read we were being kicked out of the rooming house. Evidently Buddy had spent whatever money he made and the money I made on liquor, so our rent had not been paid. All I could think about was, *What are we going to do? We have nowhere to go.*

Two days before our landlord was going to literally throw what little we had into the street, Buddy's grandmother said we could stay with her for a month—one month and that was all! Buddy's grandmother ran a home for retarded men, most of whom were in their forties. They had the minds of children and were treated like children. I was afraid of them, but then I was afraid of everyone. Though they seemed truly harmless, his grandmother was someone to fear.

During the day I walked around in a daze and at night Buddy's grandmother would locked me in our room to keep me safe from the retarded men. "Here's a port-a-pot if you have to go," she had said when she first showed us where we would sleep. I lay in that room, night after night, not understanding anything about life. I knew why his grandmother locked me in, but I hated it with all my heart. I had no control over my life and that was the worst part.

Buddy climbed out the window and went out, but I had nowhere to go. I was too ashamed to let anyone know what was going on. I never thought about praying anymore because for me it didn't seem to work. So many times I lay face down on the floor with my arms and legs spread out, crying out to God to help me, but He never answered. He never gave me the peace for which I longed and I was convinced my prayers never went any higher than the ceiling.

Our month stretched into three and on my eighteenth birthday, I knew I had to do something. I had no car, no job, and I wasn't allowed to eat or drink anything without Buddy's grandmother's permission. She only allowed me to eat the leftovers from dinner—*after* she had served her patients, so I lived on the little bit of leftovers and on fruit for three months.

Finally, the day came when I said I would no longer live like that. I called Ilona and told her how my life was, how I was locked up in a room at nine o'clock at night, and that I hadn't had a glass of milk in months. Ilona was shocked and immediately said, "I'm coming to get you," and she did.

After fixing me the first good meal I had had in months and letting me cry on her shoulder, she had to take me back but before she did she gave me some advice. "First, you have to leave Buddy. He is not taking care of you anyway and obviously doesn't know anything about love. I love you, but I have a husband and a baby in this tiny house and there just is no room for you. It will have to be for you to figure out how to get out, I can't do that for you."

There it was plain and simple with no magic door to go through that would easily let me out of my miserable world. On the drive back to Buddy's grandmother's house, I once again allowed my mind to go down the destructive path of self-pity and began planning my own suicide. Over and over I re-thought how to accomplish the feat. It seemed to be the only thing I could think about. In my imagination I had Buddy find me dead, and that would be his punishment for being so mean to me. In the state I was in I didn't care if I would miss something tomorrow as I had lost faith in today. For me the word love had no meaning but the word hate was the real word in my life.

After Ilona left me off, I sneaked through the window to our room. Around 2:30 in the morning, I heard someone climbing through the window and fearing a prowler, my heart almost stopped. But it was Buddy, drunk as usual and he was happy for a change, with a drunken grin on his face. "I got a job, Little Mary, and found us a room in a Boarding House not far from your Mom's."

I threw my arms around his neck and screamed, "Are you for real?" My excitement was more than I thought I could feel as I had purposely stopped trying to feel anything for fear of being let down. Buddy's job was for real and we would be moving the next day. My heart was ecstatic and now I'd have my own place. It would only be one room, but it would be ours and his grandmother wouldn't be able to lock me in ever again.

It didn't take long to move, since we hardly had anything and I welcomed the new room as if it were a Penthouse. It was mine! Then I realized something about myself: When we moved from Buddy's grandmother's house to our one room, it hadn't taken a lot to make me happy.

Buddy started his new job but can you believe it, after one week his Mother and grandmother took him liquor on his lunch break? So again Buddy was unemployed.

I continued to search for work but door after door was slammed in my face, or at least that was how I felt. All that time I knew I needed to go back to school but, "How" was the $64,000.00 question.

Four weeks after moving into our room at the boarding house, Buddy and I were locked out and had no choice but to sleep in the car. Actually, Buddy really didn't care as he would be so drunk he'd pass out and not remember a thing until the next day. During those waking hours I felt so lost and wondered, *Why had I walked down this road with Buddy again?*

That was it! I determined I would find a job and only depend on me. I was eighteen-years-old and my future was dark, but I could not stand living like that. What and where was the peace that all the "low-down" preachers talked about? At least they weren't sleeping in cars. My plan was that I would beg Mother to let me come home—at least that had to be better than sleeping in a car. I also knew that as much as Mother loved Buddy, she did not want to take care of him or me; therefore, I determined not to give up and set myself a goal that by the end of the week I would be working.

Since we were still living in Buddy's car, I went to Mother's home every day to clean up and dress, still determined to change things. But each day was a dead end. Even as my hopes were fading into my mind came the words, "There's always tomorrow. Something might change."

Then I received a phone call from Ilona that Dad knew where I could get a job. "When asked, just say you graduated from high school and no one will know," she told me.

The job was a telephone answering service for Hollywood movie stars. Since I had only worked at the Funeral Home and as a waitress for a short time, this would be an entirely new experience for me. Feeling frightened about what would be expected, I decided to wear a black jacket, white blouse, and a black skirt with high heels. Hoping to give myself a more mature appearance, I wore my pearl earrings. One thing Mother had taught me, whenever in doubt, always wear black and white because it always looks very professional. I don't know what did it but I passed the interview with flying colors.

My hours would be from 6:45 a.m., to 3:30 p.m. Since I had had no previous experience with a PBX Board, my first week was training without pay. Surprisingly, I loved answering six to ten calls at a time; putting people on hold, and being in control. I was good at that job because I loved what I was doing. The people I talked with every day weren't sad all the time so I began to smile again. There was no need for me to console anyone—I just took the calls and connected them to the person to whom they wished to speak.

The clients loved my service, and within the first three months I moved up to the "Top Operator" position. In fact, I even received thank you notes for my services from our customers and once in awhile, even flowers. I made people happy and while I was at work it was the only time I was happy.

Mother finally gave in and allowed only *me* to move in with her as long as I paid rent. That was okay by me and I worked as much overtime as my boss would allow. It was a good feeling to be able to save what was left of my money after rent and expenses. Even though Mother's nightly parties continued, I no longer cared. If a fight broke out, I didn't get involved unless I thought she would really get hurt.

Buddy was back living with his grandmother. He wanted us to get back together and pressured Mother to convince me to come back to him. Though I hated living with Mother, I was now older and knew how to fight off her friends more effectively. My feelings were that any place was better than living in Buddy's car.

* * *

November 22, 1963, was a typical day for me and I liked that more and more. I was feeling good about myself and owed this to working and loving what I was doing. Now I even had friends who liked me for me. That day I had just sat down at my desk when my boss burst from his office with tears in his eyes. "President Kennedy has been fatally wounded," he announced to us. I looked at the PBX and all the lines on the switchboard were lighting up, but I just sat there stunned. I couldn't believe the words he had just said. *Not President Kennedy! No!* my heart and mind begged it not to be true.

Time seemed to stop for all of us sitting at our switchboards, with all the phone lines ringing and ringing. I was unable to speak and stood up, unhooked my headset, and walked out. Tears were running down my face as I walked home, still in a daze and heartbroken. President Kennedy was a man I never met but loved from the bottom of my heart. That man never knew but he had given me a hope and strength. Everywhere I saw tears in the eyes of the people in the cars as they passed and people on streets were openly crying. Unaware of my steps I just kept walking. That was a moment when time seemed to stand still and not just for me. Hearts skipped beats, pulses slowed, and the whole Nation was numb with grief and seemed to have filled the air we breathed. Oh, how we had loved him!

To me, he had been a man of great honor and I felt the world would never be the same without him. My biggest fear was that the Black man would be in trouble again. Who would stand up for what was right? Who would say, "Do not ask what your country can do for you; ask what you can do for your country?"

It boggled my mind and I kept asking myself, *Why would anyone want to kill my President? What kind of man could kill a man like President Kennedy? Would I ever understand mankind?*

Once again my life was full of unhappiness as I grieved for the loss of President Kennedy as if he had been a family member. I felt such a deep sorrow and pain at losing one of the three men I truly admired and in whom

I had believed. That was when I fully realized how final death was because this time it was someone close to my heart.

It would take years for me to heal from that terrible loss. Lyndon B. Johnson was sworn in as President, but he did not have the charisma or the power President Kennedy had. The world was changing again, and I was a witness.

50

SOMEHOW BUDDY CONVINCED MOTHER HE WAS WORKING and would not hit me any more. Though I felt sorry for Buddy, I had reservations about returning to him. I was making good money by then and really felt I wanted to have a place of my own. I agreed to give Buddy another chance and try again at homemaking. Buddy decided since I made more money than he did, I should give him my paycheck—and for some reason, I agreed to do so.

Our apartment was a big improvement over the boarding house. It was considered a bachelor apartment because it was a large room with a bed that pulled out of the wall, had a small kitchen, and our own bathroom.

I was so excited and proud of our new apartment that many times I invited Mother, Lenore, and Tom, to come over. They would all get drunk so the evenings would be a disaster and I'd end up being hurt, so I finally stopped inviting them over.

My landlady became my best friend and even though she was old enough to be my Mother, she treated me like her own daughter and I loved her. I called her Jonesy instead of Mrs. Jones. Jonesy spent hours with me, teaching me how to cook, how to use personal hygiene, and how to have faith in a God, that I had trouble believing existed. To me she was an angel and I wished she could have been my real Mother.

I remember telling her, "If you had reared me, I could have been a doctor, lawyer, or even a judge."

Jonesy's reply was, "It is never too late, Little Mary. You can do anything your mind thinks it can." I knew I couldn't get away from Buddy or Mother because they were my family and I was stuck with them.

One of Jonesy's favorite sayings to me was, "Little Mary, when you have had enough, you'll know it. You can't let a man hit you all the time and then say he loves you and then hit you again. That's not love. When you have had enough, no one will be able to make you go back to him."

Jonesy was wise, and I was a fool. She was my mentor—full of life and energy. I'd hug her and tell her, "Give me some of that energy," and we would laugh.

We played cards together and talked for hours, the same way I had talked with the dead people. In the same way, she was safe and I knew our conversations would stay just between us. Jonesy would never betray or hurt me. Her words were always encouraging and I drew on her strength.

* * *

My job was my lifesaver and meant everything to me and I never missed a day of work. I worked other shifts for my co-workers because I liked being at work—probably I liked being needed and I was the best Operator there. My co-workers teased me about looking so White, and that I should pass for White in order to get a better job, but that only irritated me. I had worked at that job for less than two years and I was making more than any other Operator. Also, I worked well with the other employees, but I never went out with them after work. Buddy didn't want me going anywhere with my friends so I always went straight home. Another thing, my paycheck could only be opened by him. Even though I really needed some personal things, Buddy restricted me to lunch money only.

At the end of one particularly long day, one of my friends suggested we go shopping. It was payday and there was a sale at May Co. I wanted to go, but I was afraid of what would happen if I did. Dottie, a large White girl, said "Mary, girl, you're a fool to let that man keep your money. You work fifty, sixty hours some weeks. Go buy yourself something; you deserve it." She would not let up and insisted, "Come on. I'll go with you and then I'll take you home."

My mind said, *You shouldn't,* but my heart said, *come on, you do deserve it. After all, it's your paycheck.* Knowing I would be late, I asked Dottie to stop by my apartment so I could leave Buddy a note and then we went shopping. It felt like Christmas! I walked up and down the aisles, looking and touching everything. My eyes fixed on clothes that I was afraid to bring home. *How could I justify buying myself anything?*

Dottie kept saying, "Come on, you can get yourself something. What is Buddy going to do? Beat you up?"

If she only knew, I thought.

Buddy had been self-absorbed lately and had not hit or yelled at me in months, so I pushed down my fears and bought myself three pairs of panties and three bras. Mother had taught me to always wear pretty underwear just in case you were ever in an accident. If your underwear was dirty or ragged, people might talk about you.

Dottie dropped me off at home, and my heart was in my mouth. I trembled as I entered our apartment fearing how Buddy would react when he found out I had spent some of my paycheck. *What would I say? What excuse did I have? How could I justify opening up my check and then cashing it without him?*

In our apartment I took my newly-purchased items from the bag and looked at the beautiful underwear but there was no longer any joy in how pretty they were, only fear filled my heart. Guilt flooded my soul as if I had done something wrong and knew Buddy would be angry.

So, pacing the floor, I practiced what I would say to Buddy. *Maybe I could say,* "Buddy, I came home and you weren't here. I wanted to go shopping and get some underwear; I really needed them." *No,* I thought. *I've got to do better than that. How about,* "Buddy, Dottie took me to May Co. and I saw this sale on underwear, so I bought a few things."

As that thought left my mind, I heard Buddy at the door. "Hi there," I said trying to smile as he walked through the door. Suddenly I realized I had left the May Co. bag on the bed when I saw him looking at it. "Buddy," I began, and that was the last word that came out of my mouth before Buddy's hand struck me across the face.

"I've been calling and calling and you weren't here! Where the fuck have you been?" He turned and picked up the May Co. bag. "What the fuck is this?"

Still in shock over being slapped so hard, I stammered, "I went shopping with one of my friends from work. You weren't home, and I needed some underclothes."

"That's bullshit," he snarled. "You don't need anything, and why the hell did you cash your check without me?" Buddy was not big on listening, so I didn't get a chance to answer his question. He started kicking and throwing whatever he saw lying around. Then he took my new underwear and tore them up in front of me, snatched my purse off the floor and took all the cash I had, and then slammed out the door.

I don't know how long I lay on the floor crying, but I finally managed to pull myself off the floor and struggle into the bathroom. My nose felt as if it was broken and I prayed that it wasn't. Looking in the bathroom mirror I saw my eye was swollen and my lip was bleeding so I splashed cold water on my face, patted it dry as gently as I could and then went to the refrigerator to get ice for my eye. Tomorrow I had to go to work and I knew I looked a mess. When Buddy returned in the early morning hours, I pretended to be asleep.

The next day when I went to work everyone kept asking what happened. I lied and said I had walked into a door. My boss took me into his office and said, "Mary, I know your husband did this. Why do you stay?"

I fought back tears knowing crying doesn't do any good and asked, "Where can I go?"

"Mary, you're taking care of Buddy. He needs you, but you don't need him!" It sounded good, but I was afraid. "Call your Mother," he told me. " I'm sure she will help you."

I called Mother and told her that Buddy had beaten me up again and asked if I could I come stay with her for a short time. All she said to me was, "You must have really done something to him, for him to get so upset."

"Mother, I spent twenty dollars on myself."

"Well it's your fault!" she replied, and I could hear a voice in the background.

"Mother, who's with you?"

Buddy's voice came through the telephone line, "It's me," he laughed, and slammed the phone down. I just stood listening to the dial tone.

My boss was looking at me as I hung up the phone. "What's wrong?" he asked.

I stood there frozen in time. "My Mother says it's my fault. Buddy's there with her."

He looked at me with pity in his eyes, and I felt as though I was sinking into quicksand. I thanked my boss for caring and went back to work. I heard the other employees whispering about how my husband had beaten me up but they acted as if it was some kind of joke, but I was hurting inside. Once again no one cared—I was a fool and knew it. But I didn't know what to do.

Times did not get better and Buddy lost control and was beating me on a regular basis. There were times I thought Buddy would kill me and actually hoped he would. Maybe he would do what I did not have the nerve to do myself.

* * *

By 1964, there were more job opportunities for Blacks. Blacks were being put in Front Offices where they could be seen. The Aircraft Industry hired Black engineers. Times were changing and I hoped I would be able to get a better job. Even though I loved my present job, I needed to make more money. I applied at several doctors' offices for a receptionist position on my way to my Operator's job. Even though I knew I would have to lie about my education on any application I filled out, I thought I could fake it and I did. The only problem I had when I was interviewed was that I was too light-skinned! "Sorry," the interviewer would say, "We are looking for Black people who look Black." A receptionist's position was visible to the public, and I would not be recognized as a Black young lady. I thought my lack of education would have been my problem but no, I was denied a job because I was not dark enough. I knew if given the chance I could learn anything as I always caught on quickly, but I didn't get that chance.

51

BUDDY AND I MOVED SO MANY TIMES I HAD TROUBLE remembering one address from the next. Then one day, Buddy came home drunk as usual. I did not like having sex with Buddy, especially when he had been drinking, but he forced himself on me and then laughed about it. I hated the fact I had no control or power over my life, but I was afraid to step out on my own.

A couple of months passed and my period did not come. I knew I was pregnant. *Oh, no! Why did this happen? I didn't know anything about having a baby. What would Buddy do? Would he be upset?* There was no doubt in my mind he would be upset as he didn't want kids, at least not yet.

In a panic, I called Mother and as usual she only made me feel worse. "What the hell did you let that happen for?" she yelled over the phone.

I never thought I would get pregnant because actually Buddy and I hardly ever had sex. We hadn't had sex since the day he forced himself on me, so I knew the exact day I got pregnant. Another problem was that Buddy was not working and I was, plus we had no insurance and no room for a baby.

I became so depressed and unable to do my work that my boss decided to lay me off and I collected unemployment. He offered to pay for me to have an abortion if I wanted to come back to work, and Buddy felt that might not be a bad idea. I knew I was not ready to be a Mother and even though I had thought of killing myself many times, I would never even consider killing my baby.

Months went by like hours in a day and I felt the life inside me kicking and pushing to come out. I'd rub my big stomach wondering how a baby was born because I had never learned about childbirth. Also, I had not taken any classes on how to care for a baby. Basically, I was scared to death. Buddy didn't respect the fact I had a living person inside me so if he got angry about something, he'd slap me and say he just had to hit someone. I'd yell at him but then he'd get worse, so I stayed in my room and hoped he'd go away.

While rubbing my big belly I talked to my child and assured it that somehow we would make it. I also promised that I would never let him be around his grandmother and lied that his Father loved him. Buddy was owned by alcohol and he could only love one thing at a time, but I told my baby not to worry, I had enough love for him.

In my sixth month, Mother said I really should see a doctor, so she introduced me to a Black doctor on the East Side of Los Angeles. He was tall, dark, and handsome, and knew it. He spent more time flirting with me than examining me.

My first exam terrified me. It was the first time I had been to a doctor except when I had been seven and my appendix had ruptured. I was so embarrassed when he told me to put my legs in the stirrups, move my hips to the end of the table, and spread my legs. I didn't know my legs could open so wide.

The handsome doctor put me on vitamins and told me I was not only healthy, but that he thought I was beautiful. I could not imagine someone saying that I was beautiful especially when I couldn't even see my own feet. I did notice that during each of my appointments when the doctor examined me, he would gently rub my thigh with a smile and would insist on rubbing my breasts. That always made me uncomfortable. I hoped his nurse would stay in the room, but he would nod for her to leave. I wondered, *Why did he have me coming in once a week. If I'm so healthy why can't I come back in a month?*

During my last exam, when I was a little over seven months along, I felt so uneasy with the exam that I said, "Doctor, please stop!"

He rubbed his hand up my thigh and said, "You know there is no woman as pretty as a pregnant woman. Are you having sex?"

Quickly, I pulled my feet out of the stirrups and with difficulty tried to sit up. He grabbed my hand and helped me. "You are as pretty as you will ever be and sex is good for you," he said still holding my hand. I tried to cover myself and felt my face flush. I did not like to talk about sex. Buddy and I hadn't done anything in months, and I was too afraid of hurting the baby.

"Mary, I'm going to be straight with you, I want to make love with you right now! I've wanted you from the first day you walked into my office. I've dreamed about you."

"Oh Doctor, no! This is wrong," I told him, pulling myself off the table, longing to feel the cold floor on my feet.

"No one has to know." He was calm and not ashamed of his thoughts about me.

I grabbed my sheet and wrapped it completely around me and said, "Please call the nurse in. This will never happen! Doctor, you're a married man. What is wrong with you?"

I tried to keep myself from over reacting, not knowing if I should consider this as flattery, or that he was just a fool. The thought of having sex when I was so big was disgusting. Then I wondered how many other patients he had solicited. The doctor had five children and now I knew why. He loved having his wife pregnant and now he wanted even more. I hated the thought that I had to go to him, but he was cheap and Mother would pay his bill. For now, I was stuck between a rock and a hard place. The rock and hard place was my life.

The baby inside me wanted out and sometimes he kicked so hard tears filled my eyes. For awhile Buddy and I had an apartment in the building where Mother lived. With Mother so close I thought she would be of some help, but that was a joke.

During my seventh month, Buddy and I were evicted out of our apartment. Buddy drank up the rent money, so we were homeless again. Through a friend we found a place about a mile from Mother. The apartment building only had eight apartments, nice and clean, with two bedrooms upstairs. This was really a nice place, the best we had in our three years together.

Buddy got a job as a bus boy at the Pancake House. I begged him not to let his family know when he went to lunch, but my begging was in vain. Buddy and his family were co-dependent on each other. They were proud he was taking hold of life, working and paying his rent, this one time. After a few weeks, Buddy's friends on the job gave him a baby shower and Buddy was excited for the first time. He finally realized that this was a real person I was carrying—his baby, and he was going to be a Father. I began to relax in my mind, so tired of worrying all the time. Now Buddy was serious about having a family and making it work. Since I also wanted so much for it to work, I cooked and cleaned and kept the apartment immaculate. Buddy had nothing about which to criticize me.

October 17, 1964, a baby shower had been planned for me and I was excited. I spent so much time alone that I was looking forward to being around the family and my few friends.

My only contact with anyone, as I stayed alone in our apartment, was The Helms Bakery truck driver. He came down my street every day like clockwork. I lived on cream puffs. My first line of credit was my charge account with Helms Bakery. Sometimes, the loneliness I felt was unbearable.

I missed my friends at the Funeral Home but working at the Funeral Home seemed like a lifetime away.

I talked to my baby, who pushed and turned around inside me, and told him I would protect him for the rest of his life. Also, I would love him and he would never be afraid, as I knew fear could destroy you if you allowed it; so, I fought to hold onto the thought that tomorrow would bring something good into my life.

One evening Buddy came home drunk. He had been sober for a couple of weeks and it had been wonderful. His complexion had cleared, his eyes weren't red, and I was proud of him for staying sober. But I should have known it wouldn't last and hated myself for believing in him - I hated him that evening. In response to my attitude, he slapped me a few times and I grabbed the bottom of my stomach as if the baby would fall out and yelled at him, "What are you doing? I'm pregnant, you can't hit me!"

Buddy slurred his words and didn't make any kind of sense. There was no reason for his anger, no reason for him to hit me. He finally managed to slur out that he felt like it and that was that.

The phone rang and I ran to get it before Buddy. It was JT on the other end. Surprised to hear his voice, I started screaming that Buddy was hitting me. Then all I heard was a dial tone when Buddy snatched the phone out of my hand. I tried to run into the bedroom and he grabbed me by my hair. The names he called me weren't fit for a dog. I had finally managed to lock myself in the bedroom when I heard JT banging on the front door.

"Open up the fucking door," he yelled at the top of his lungs. JT had a loud voice and I'm sure the people down the street heard him.

Buddy opened the door and JT charged in, pushing Buddy against the wall and knocking over the lamp on the table near the hallway. It seemed he easily lifted Buddy off the floor as JT was over six-feet tall and Buddy was only five feet, eight inches.

"If you put your hands on my sister again, I'll kill you! Do you understand?" He had his face right in Buddy's face and since JT had Buddy by the throat, Buddy shook his head as best as he could. I stood there in amazement. JT had never come to my rescue; he had never stood up for me, not to Mother, not during all the times he had heard that men were molesting me. I didn't think JT knew I was alive, but this evening would go down in my mind. I had a big brother who had said, "Don't hurt my sister." Of course Mother would have said it was my fault.

Buddy did not talk to me for days and for the life of me I don't know why I felt sorry for him. I knew he had a sickness and that my husband was not an Ozzie Nelson and never would be. Drinking controlled his life; it took over his body and I could not help him. But I sure hoped that JT had put the fear in him that it was not okay to hit me.

The day before the baby shower Buddy and I went to visit my Mother. Mother decided it was time to tell me about childbirth. Actually, I think she looked forward to scaring the hell out of me! She seemed get a perverse pleasure out of explaining to me how a baby was born, how it would hurt like hell and that before it was over I would want to die from the pain. Then she explained that when my water bag broke, if and when I saw blood, the baby would be coming in a short time.

Sure enough she scared me half to death with her graphic descriptions. She knew I hated pain and to me it seemed with relish she assured me there was no way to get out of my situation. The realities of being pregnant hit me as I dealt with the fact the baby had to come out of my body and for the first time in my pregnancy I was afraid. I had stopped going to the sex-maniac doctor, but I knew I still had a couple of months to go. When she continued to describe in graphic detail all the worst parts of having a baby I finally said, "Okay, I have the picture and I don't want to hear anymore."

What made the situation worse for me was that we were not alone when Mother gave me the blow-by-blow gory details of childbirth. Tom, Mother, Buddy, and a few of her friends from the church were also there, and were sitting around drinking and laughing at me. For some reason, they thought it was funny.

I wasn't laughing. I wanted to go home and asked, "Buddy, could we go home now?"

He turned and said, "When I'm ready."

I sat on the sofa and waited, not wanting to argue and watched the clock on the kitchen wall. At 9:00 p.m., I knew Mother would be going to bed because when she had funerals on Saturday, she would not get drunk on Friday night.

Again I said, "Buddy please, let's go home."

Buddy had too much to drink and his mean streak was rising to the surface. "Okay, let's go," he finally said, smiling at everyone as we said our good-byes.

"Buddy, why don't you let me drive?" I said, but he ignored me. "Buddy…" I reached for his arm, gesturing for him to give me the car keys.

He pushed my hand away and all he said was, "I'll drive."

I was so nervous because I knew he should not be behind the wheel of the car. It always amazed me he had never been arrested for drunk driving. But since I had no choice but to get in and shut up, I just prayed we would not have an accident.

Once again, I had to deal with the fact I had no control of my life and that made me feel weak, but I was weak. I was married to a drunk who hit me when he felt like it, and I allowed it. That's what my boss had told me and his words played in my mind on a daily basis. But there I was, seven-and-a-half-months pregnant and things just kept going from bad to worse.

That night the drive home was a nightmare and it is a miracle we were not killed. I remembered the old saying, "God takes care of fools and babies." Well, a fool was at the wheel and a baby was in my stomach, and I thanked God for small favors.

Parking the car in the garage was a challenge for Buddy, but with a few tries he managed to get it inside. By then my nerves were shattered and I felt so tired that I asked Buddy to help me out of the car. As we walked to the front of the building, I looked at the stairs ahead of me and thought it would be like climbing a mountain so asked, "Buddy, please get behind me and push me up there." And drunk as Buddy was, he could see I was having difficulty in walking, so he helped me up those steps.

All I wanted to do was get in my bed. Buddy helped me into our bed and I swear as soon as my head rested on the pillow, I was out like a light.

At 11:30 p.m. I woke up thinking I had to go to the bathroom. Since I didn't want to wake Buddy, I quietly moved around in the dark. Something wasn't right but I didn't know what was wrong. I sat on the edge of the bed for a moment and lifted both legs at the same time and a gush of liquid ran out of me. I panicked and screamed, "Buddy, I'm bleeding to death!" But it was not blood but water, and my stomach became hard as a rock. The contractions started and terrified I grabbed Buddy and started shaking him and yelling, "Wake up. Wake up!"

Buddy stretched, groaned, and sleepily asked, "What's wrong?"

"I don't know! Water is running out of me. What should I do?" I was known to always be cool in any crisis, but this was not one of them. I hurt and I let him know it.

Buddy was trying to stay calm as he rushed around the bed looking for the doctor's phone number. "Mary, you're not due yet; the baby can't come now," Buddy said.

I looked at him like he was crazy. "I know it's not time but something is wrong," I moaned. "My stomach is balling up like a hard rock, and I hurt. I'll call Mother while you look for the doctor's number."

Tom answered the phone and I yelled, "Tom, I need to talk to Mother. Now!"

"Little Mary, you know she's asleep, and nobody wakes her for nothing."

"Let me talk to my Mother!" I screamed.

A woman's voice came on the phone and said, "This is aunt Georgia. How are you, child? I just got in town, and your Mother won't get up for me."

"Aunt Georgia, I think my water bag burst. Please put Mother on the phone," I begged.

"I can't wake her; you know she gets really mad if you wake her when she has funerals on Saturday."

I could hear laughter in the background and my blood was rushing to my head. I handed the phone to Buddy and Buddy started yelling at aunt Georgia, then Tom was on the phone and Buddy threatened to come back over there if they didn't get Mother. While Buddy argued, I kept running to the bathroom, trying to dry myself off. Buddy hung up on Tom and dialed the doctor.

Doctor Hughes answered the phone after about fifteen rings and Buddy in a panic said, "Doctor Hughes, this is Buddy and Mary is losing a lot of water. What should we do?" I could see Buddy was scared and that didn't make me feel any better.

"Have her lay on a towel. She probably has a little leak and it will stop," he said in a calm reassuring voice.

Nudging Buddy I said, "Tell him I think I'm having contractions."

Buddy told him but he said it was too soon. "Lay flat with a towel and call me tomorrow," and then he hung up.

My contractions became harder, and harder. Buddy timed them and they were five-minutes apart. I could not stand feeling so wet, so I went to the bathroom to clean myself again. As I wiped my legs with a towel I saw blood. Remembering what my Mother had said, I screamed in fear thinking the baby was falling out of me. Buddy ran in, saw all the blood, and rushed to call the doctor again. This time all he got was an answering service. "This is an emergency, get the doctor!" His voice was frantic. He slammed down the phone and called Mother again. When Tom answered he yelled that I was bleeding furiously.

"Buddy, I can't wake her," I could hear Tom yelling through the phone.

Buddy helped me up and said, "I'm taking you to the hospital." He had sobered up in a hurry and now took charge. My towel could not hold all the blood I was losing, so we left a trail of blood as we headed for the car. The contractions were getting closer together, which made Buddy speed through the streets and break every traffic law there was. The hospital was on the East Side of town, normally a thirty-minute drive—we were there in ten. Rocking and crying, I was trying not to yell as Buddy turned into the driveway of the private hospital.

I saw Mother standing in front of the hospital and when she came over to the car she angrily said, "I heard Tom and Georgia talking about you going into labor, and they wouldn't wake me. I cussed those sons-of-bitches out!"

My Mother had come! I had my Mother there. Was this her way of saying I love you? I hoped so very much that it was true.

Buddy banged on the front of the hospital door, but the people inside the hospital would not open the door. They told us they could not let me in because I was not registered there. Mother threatened to burn the place down if they didn't let me in, but they still refused. It was now, 2:30 a.m., and it was total chaos. JT had shown up with Lenore, and he started banging on the door of the hospital. I fell down, unable to stand, with blood running down my legs, and I really thought I would die right there on the sidewalk.

"Call Dr. Hughes!" Mother screamed, and within two minutes the lock on the door turned and an orderly brought out a wheel chair. A nurse met us in the lobby and Mother started cussing her out. A Japanese male nurse came over to take my pulse.

The contractions were unbelievable; I had never felt such pain. I cussed and screamed and even tried to get up and run because I didn't know what to do. I fought every time someone touched me. All the while I was wondering, *Why hadn't the doctor come? He had been called hours ago!*

Finally, I was wheeled to a room and after helping me into a bed, the two nurses tied my arms down to stop me from hitting them. "Breathe," they kept saying. "Pant." I didn't do anything, they said. Then I started to push. "Don't push," they ordered, "Pant." I pushed harder. Then I heard the male nurse say, "The baby's coming and we have to get her into the ER now!" *Where was the doctor?*

The two nurses would not let anyone come into the room with me, and I continued to fight them and push as hard as I could. I wanted to get that baby out!

With me fighting them every inch of the way they finally were able to place me on a gurney and roll me into a room that looked like an Embalming Room, only there was a mirror directly in front of me that ran from the ceiling to the floor. Lifting me was difficult because I kept hitting them, so they tied my hands with leather straps to the side of the table.

Panicked, I pleaded with them, "Talk to me, tell me, what is going on?" But they said nothing to me and only talked to each other. "Where is Dr. Hughes?" I demanded.

The clock on the wall read 6:30 a.m. I had been screaming and fighting since midnight and the male nurse was over at the sink washing his hands, while the other nurse stood at my head. "You need to pant," he instructed me. "Don't push. Your doctor should be here soon." I had heard that over and over, but he wasn't there and I thought I was losing my baby.

They put my feet in the stirrups and it seemed as if they spread my legs across the room. I wanted to feel ashamed but I was in so much pain I didn't care. The mirror in front of me was the scariest thing I had ever seen. I saw the top of the baby's head and I leaned and pushed with all my might. It was as if a balloon popped and out came my baby with such force that one nurse screamed, and the male nurse ran from the sink. He barely managed to catch my baby before he slid off the table.

I fell back in total exhaustion; so relieved he was out. The male nurse cut the cord and took the baby out of my sight, but I could hear him crying. I had no strength left, not even to lift my head. While the nurse untied my hands she said, "I'm sorry, but you could have hurt yourself and the baby the way you were fighting." All the rage and anger had left. I had fought the fight and I had won. I had a baby.

The male nurse was concerned. "He's small, a preemie," he said to the other nurse.

"What's a preemie?" I asked panicky. "Is he alive?"

"Oh yes, little lady," the nurse said with a smile. "Your baby is fine—just got here before he was supposed to. He weighs five pounds. That's good for a preemie." Then he walked over and placed my baby on my chest as he said, "He's a fine little boy."

"It's a boy?" I was too tired to really care what gender my baby was, as long as he was healthy. To me that was all that mattered.

Out in the waiting room there had almost been a fight. Buddy's Mother and grandmother had come and when they heard the baby was a preemie, my Mother said it wasn't from her side of the family. They thought that since he was a preemie he must be deformed, or dead. It was then explained to them that although the baby was a month-and-a-half early, he was as healthy as a nine-month baby. They were all relieved! He was small but healthy.

When I next looked at the clock it was 7:15 a.m., and the nurse was still cleaning up when in walked Dr. Hughes. I watched his feet as he walked toward the table.

"It looks like your baby didn't want to wait," he said with a grin. I wanted to reach up and slap him but I didn't have the energy. Dr. Hughes had on his house slippers, and when he leaned over me I could smell old alcohol on his breath. He told the nurse he would take over and clean out the afterbirth.

"What after birth?" I wanted to know. Unable to move, I watched him wash up and position himself between my spread legs and reach inside me, pulling something. I thought I was having another baby.

281

"You have torn some, so I'm going to put in a few stitches, you'll be fine." He was gentle, and I only wanted to sleep.

I would miss my baby shower, I thought, *but that is okay. I now had my own baby. This is going to be a life-changing event.* I just didn't realize how much. I drifted off, not caring what the doctor did to me.

When I awoke, Mother, JT, and Lenore, were all standing around, talking about how they couldn't believe I could have a baby and that he was so cute. I still only wanted to sleep but they would not leave.

When I noticed strangers walking outside my room, looking in and staring, I asked Mother, "Why are people staring at me?"

"You tore this hospital up last night," she answered, laughing as she rubbed my forehead. "You screamed so much people couldn't believe you were having a baby; they thought someone was trying to kill you." Mother was in a good mood. "They keep looking in here 'cause they want to see who was making all the noise. They keep asking how someone as little as you could have made so much noise."

I didn't care what the people thought of me. I was a Mother now. What was I going to do with this new life? When my family left, I sighed with relief; I needed to think.

Life is no longer about me; it is about the baby. I have tolerated Buddy and Mother's abuse because for some reason I was made to feel I deserved it and that it was normal. But is this the kind of life I want for my child? I am twenty years old and feel fifty.

52

FOR THE FIRST TIME I COULD EVER REMEMBER, I FELT the compassion of a Mother's love. Mother insisted the baby and I come stay with her for the first couple of weeks. She knew I did not have a clue as to what to do with my baby so she taught me how to hold him, change his diaper, feed him, and to understand his cries—if he was hungry, or wet. Those two weeks made all the difference in the world to me. It was during that time I learned that at one time in her life, Mother did know how to be a loving parent but for some reason had kept it hidden.

Like a typical grandmother, she was proud because my little boy was adorable. She would tell me, "I told you, you guys would make a pretty baby." Yes, the baby was pretty but his Father had ugly ways, and I had to do some serious thinking about what the future would hold for my precious little boy.

With pressure from Buddy, we named our baby after him, Eddie, which was Buddy's real name. Our son's full name was Eddie Saco III. Even though Buddy was half Hawaiian and half Black, under "race" on my baby's birth certificate I had put "Black." I was thankful his skin color was a little darker than mine so that maybe he would not have to explain his heritage as often as I did.

I called him Eddie, since I refused to call him Little Buddy, as I did not want him to be anything like his Father. Instinctively, I knew his life's challenge would be not to be like his Father; just as I had to fight not to be like my Mother. That little bundle of humanity meant the entire world to me and I held my baby with all the love heaven could cast down.

For two weeks I fell in love with Mother. She was wonderful, and even her parties didn't bother me. I kept expecting the real Mother who had reared me and had been so cruel to show up, but for those two weeks she was the Mother of which I had always dreamed. Each night I would lock Eddie and me up in our room, and he would sleep through the noise of Mother's parties.

I knew I had to go back to Buddy and it was depressing, but my hands were tied. I had no job and Mother's kindness would not last and I didn't want to push my luck. She always said, "Fish and company smell after a few days." It was better we leave before the real Mother appeared again.

The night Buddy came to pick us up, I noticed immediately he had been drinking and was probably on his way to being royally drunk. Instead of leaving, he decided to have a few more drinks with Mother and soon he was really drunk.

"Let's go," he slurred. I did not want to ride with him and the hairs on my arms actually stood up, but Mother said, "It's okay. Go home with your husband."

On that drive home he terrified me and I promised myself it was the last time I would get into a car with him. Also, the drive proved Buddy was a sick man. "Damn," he said. "I should have gone to the bathroom before we left."

"Why don't you stop at a service station?"

"It's too late. I couldn't hold it," he laughed. I looked at his lap and could see he had wet himself and he showed no sign of shame or of being uncomfortable. Holding tightly to Eddie, I prayed to God to get us safely home. God did see us safely home, and I kept my promise never to ride with Buddy again.

* * *

Six weeks after Eddie was born, I called and asked my boss if I could have my old job back. He welcomed me with open arms. With no car of my own and having to take Eddie to a baby sitter, the only transportation I had was the bus because Buddy was always suffering from hangovers and I could never count on him.

Eddie always seemed to be sick and I knew it was the early morning cold air that caused him to get colds so often.

Even though each day was a struggle, I never depended on Buddy for help. If he worked that was fine and if he didn't, I didn't care. I made enough money to take care of us. Things were tight, but I knew we would survive.

Life with Buddy became more difficult every day. I hated his drinking and was beginning to hate him. Even though I'd wake up in a good mood, Buddy would do his best to change it. Then he became jealous of Eddie, and started fighting with me again. After a while my energy level was so low it was a struggle to get up in the middle of the night with the baby while Buddy snored.

My baby loved life and wanted to be awake day and night, and the joy he brought to my heart was all I needed to keep me going. But there were days I would actually fall asleep on the job, which was hard to do with hundreds of phone lines buzzing. The weariness I felt began to show on my face and finally, I literally passed out at work from pure exhaustion.

My boss must have been the most understanding man in the world. He told me for my own good he was going to lay me off and allow me to draw unemployment for a few months. "Get yourself together! You can't work all day, get slapped around, and get up with the baby all night," he said.

I knew he was right, but I felt trapped. No one would help me as long as I was with Buddy and I was trying to be the best Mommy to my baby. Knowing my tears would upset my baby, I hid my tears from him because I loved him so much.

One afternoon after being laid off I was trying to get Eddie to take a nap and as I stood over his crib I knew he wanted me to pick him up, but I had to be strong because he needed his nap. I tried gently patting him on the back to help him go to sleep, all the while thanking God for this beautiful life he'd given me. It was hard to believe at nine-months old he was already trying to walk. He would probably wear me out and never get tired.

When I heard the front door open I knew Buddy had come home. He'd only been on that job a couple of weeks. Since it was too early for him to be home from his job, I immediately knew he'd lost that job too.

I continued rubbing Eddie's back, leaning into his crib while fear ran through my veins. Something felt wrong and instinctively I knew something bad was going to happen. I hated that feeling, because it was usually correct. Just as I turned and looked up I saw Buddy walk into Eddie's bedroom, and had just a moment to realize his hand was open and he slapped me across the face. Startled, Little Eddie looked up, and even at nine months I realized he was aware something was wrong.

"Why did you hit me?" I cried, trying not to show the tears, not wanting to scare my baby. Buddy was drunk. It was 1:30 p.m. and he was already drunk.

"I felt like it," was all he said. As usual he never gave any other explanation for what he did to me. The blood rose inside me and my head began to throb, but I continued to pat the baby trying to reassure him things were okay and to go to sleep.

Buddy went into the living room as if nothing had happened, while I stayed until Eddie fell into a deep sleep, then I kissed him on his soft head.

When I walked into the living room I felt as if I was in a trance. Being a good housekeeper I had been vacuuming earlier but when I had to stop and take care of Eddie, I had left the vacuum cleaner sitting in the middle of the floor because I had not finished.

It seemed as if I were moving in slow motion as I picked up the long hose by the metal end. Buddy was sitting at the dining room table drinking a beer, without a worry in the world when I softly said, "Buddy." He turned and looked at me. "If you ever lay your hands on me again, I'll kill you." Then I hit him across his head with the metal part of the hose and continued to hit him, again and again, until he ran out the front door screaming.

There were knots swelling on his head and a little blood coming from the corner of his mouth as he ran away from me. I felt like a heavy weight had been lifted off of me. No longer was I going to be a victim but from that moment on, I was going to be victorious. I realized I loved my child more than myself. I had taken control of my life. It was then I determined never to allow my son to witness or feel pain as I had. I would not let him grow up with a Father who would slap his Mother in front of him and he would *not* grow up with drunks in his life.

That day I am sure I would have killed Buddy if he had not run from the apartment. Buddy knew that and so did I. After that, I would not let Buddy back into my life and explained to him he should be afraid to go to sleep around me, for who knows what I might do to him while he slept.

My baby was my world and I had to stand guard at the gate of his life. The bitterness I had harbored toward Buddy turned into hate and as for Buddy, he could not believe I had actually hurt him and could beat him up. From somewhere I had finally found the strength I did not know I had. With an instinct for survival and self-preservation, from that day forward, I determined to protect myself—and my child I would protect with my very life if, necessary. It was a new day and a new life! I would never be alone! I didn't need to talk to the dead people anymore! I didn't need anyone! I had my baby! Finally I had a reason and someone for whom to live and make it all worth the effort.

After that night, when I remembered the times I had wanted to commit suicide, I would think that if I had killed myself, I would not have had Eddie. My hope was that one day life would give us a break.

* * *

Little Eddie and I first went to my Mother's house and then we rented a one-bedroom apartment. I determined not to move back in with my Mother. Now that Buddy was out of my life, Dad and Willie gave me a car and free gas. This was a great blessing as it made it much easier for me to get back and forth to work. Often Willie would slip money into my purse, or pocket, and then walk away quickly before I could thank him. Although no one could really help me, it did wonders for my self-worth and morale knowing that Willie cared.

Having only been around my family, "dysfunction" was a way of life with which I had learned to live. I wanted to be normal, normal like all the White families I had seen on TV and I wanted my child to know what a real family was like. The trouble was, I really did not know myself.

53

THE DAY FINALLY CAME WHEN I KNEW I HAD TO GET A divorce from Buddy. I needed more money for Eddie and a divorce would force Buddy to give me financial support; otherwise, I knew I would never get any help from him. By then I had very little money saved, so I decided it was time to call on my friend Johnny Cochran. Phoning his office was easy, but getting an appointment was tough as Johnny was always very busy.

Thank goodness he was not too busy to help a friend and we made my first appointment after work. I walked into his office and saw Johnny sitting at a huge desk with folders stacked high. His framed law degree was hanging on the wall near him, along with other certificates.

"Little Mary, it's good to see you," he greeted me as he stood and walked around from his desk and gave me a big hug. "Have a seat" he said, and then gestured toward two high-backed chairs facing his desk and walked back to his desk. Feeling small in the big chair, I sat on the edge. It was different seeing Johnny as a man of power and not as a teenager who hung out with my sister. We talked about family and about the Funeral Home, how his parents were, and then we got down to business. At first Johnny encouraged me to consider staying with my son's Father, if at all possible.

"Johnny, he beats me up, all the time, and the last time I wanted to kill him. That is no way to live, is it?" My voice was trembling and tears were forming in my eyes, as I couldn't help feeling so beaten down. Dropping my head I hid my face while I fought back the tears.

Johnny's compassion was more than I expected. He had known me most of my life and now I was crying in his office, asking him for help. "Don't you worry, Little Mary," he said and seemed so in control. "No, we can't have any man hitting on a woman, especially you. I'll handle everything," he assured me as he stretched his arm across his desk, handing me a Kleenex. "Come on, it's going to be okay. How long have you and Buddy been separated?"

"Almost a year now, and I'm really struggling. How much is this going to cost me?"

"Do you two have any property or any assets to split?"

I laughed. "Oh, Johnny, we don't have a pot to pee in. I'm working overtime a lot and I can probably pay you in payments."

"How old is your baby now?"

"Almost two, and he gets into everything."

Johnny smiled with such assurance that I knew I had someone on my side. "Little Mary, don't you worry. I'll take care of it. Is Buddy working?"

"Yes, but I'm not sure where."

"That's okay. I'll find out what I need. Do you have his social security number?"

"Yes, and the address where he lives. He still lives with his grandmother."

"How old is he?"

"Twenty-four going on twelve."

"I'll see that he pays you child support and have the court take it directly out of his paycheck—no matter where he works. You'll get some money for your baby."

My heart was full and I began to cry again as I blubbered, "How can I thank you?" Of course another good question was how could I pay him?

Johnny stood again and walked over to me, taking my hand, "It's going to be okay. Trust me and don't worry." Yes, I trusted Johnny and believed he was a man of his word and that he would not let me down. He was a man of character and I felt safe with him.

He never did tell me how much but whatever it was, I didn't have it. The gratitude I had in my heart was overwhelming. Walking out of his office, I thought, *What a wonderful friend.* Actually, I felt like I had a Godfather, someone who would fight for me.

Buddy would not contest the divorce because he neither had the money or the love to keep us together. Sometimes it was disheartening to realize Eddie and I would always be last with him because alcohol was his only love.

Several months passed before Johnny called to tell me I had a court date. I was on my way to being a divorced woman, and thrilled about it. It made me want to celebrate and I went to Mother's and told her all that Johnny had said.

"I think you should go back to your husband," she snapped, her words dripping with attitude.

"Why? So he can beat the shit out of me when he feels like it?" I had lost my cool.

Mother jumped up and screamed, "How dare you cuss at me, girl!"

"I'm sorry, but you always defend Buddy, and I'm the one with a black eye or busted lip. Why haven't you ever cussed him out for that?" My voice was shrill as I was so tired of her always trying to put me in the wrong.

Then she said, "You are being disrespectful to me and God will punish you for not honoring your Mother." She kept up her verbal abuse as she followed me from room to room as I gathered my things. By then Eddie was in tears because Mother's rage scared him, and I could not move fast enough to get out of her apartment.

It was such a stupid argument and trying to make amends I later called to tell her how sorry I was, but I was now on punishment. Since I was the one who had offended her and had made her angry, she now would not let me forget it until she was good and ready to forgive me. Every time I called she would hang up on me because I had hurt her feelings. If anyone could put a person on a guilt trip, Mother was a professional at it. So, after calling her about ten times, I gave up.

One evening, several days later when Eddie and I were sound sleep, the ringing of the phone startled me awake. Glancing at the clock I wondered who would be calling me after eleven. Anyone who knew me knew that I went to bed early. Eddie was sound asleep in his bedroom with the door half-open; I could hear his steady breathing. The sofa bed left something to be desired. I longed to have my own bedroom with pretty curtains and a bedspread, and I knew that my day would come. I had to be at work by 7:00 a.m., which meant getting up by 4:30 a.m., getting breakfast for Eddie, dressing him, then getting ready to take him to the babysitter. God willing, the car would start. Triple A and I had a good understanding.

Startled by the phone ringing, I rubbed my eyes and feeling like my teeth had on pajamas, I answered the phone. "Hello?"

"Baby, you don't need me! Nobody needs me! I'm going to kill myself!" Then I heard a gunshot and the sound of the receiver as it dropped. It was Mother, and she had sounded extremely distressed.

Terrified, I jumped out of bed saying, "Oh, my God! Oh, my God!" as I visualized a gunshot wound to Mother's head with blood gushing out all over. I knew it was all my fault. Quickly I ran around my small apartment grabbing my coat, car keys and purse, then I snatched up Eddie and wrapped him in a blanket. He moaned in his sleep as I placed him down on the backseat of the car.

I drove as fast as I could, praying all the while she would be okay. When I reached her street I could see her apartment window was dark and the street was quiet. I pulled behind her car in the parking stall, and turned off the ignition as I turned to make sure Eddie was asleep, which he was. As quietly as possible I got out of the car and locked the doors, leaving Eddie still asleep on the backseat with the windows cracked part-way open. I argued with myself whether I should take him in or leave him sleeping. I left him.

As I raced up the stairs, I tried not to think about what I would find in Mother's apartment. Arriving at her door, I started banging on it but there was no answer. Quickly I ran to the apartment of one of her friends and as I banged on their door I was screaming I thought Mother had shot herself. Half asleep, Bill answered the door in his pajamas and asked, "What's wrong?"

By then I was in a total panic and Bill tried to calm me as we ran over to Mother's apartment. This time the door was unlocked and as I pushed it open and ran into her bedroom, with Bill two steps behind me, there sat Mother on the bed, laughing. She was smoking a cigarette and a glass of Scotch was on the bedside table. The gun lay on the bed next to her.

Bill said, "What the hell is going on?"

I was too tired to say a word. Mother looked at me with a gleam of joy in her eye. "I wondered how long it would take you to get here."

"Mother, why would you do that to me? Why would you scare the hell out of me like this?" Even though I was pissed, I was relieved she hadn't killed herself. That was sure something I did not want to have on my conscience.

Bill turned and walked out, cussing and saying, "Mrs. Reese, you're crazy." I heard the door close behind him. Unable to understand anymore of that, I walked out and drove home. Eddie never woke up.

54

Y EARS PASSED AND TIMES WERE TOUGHER THAN I could have ever imagined. Eddie knew I loved him but my life was beginning to affect him. I worked long hours and left him with babysitters a lot because I did not have a choice; but when you're a child you don't understand any of those things.

Mother continued playing her mind-games on JT, Lenore, and me. Her desperate need for attention evidently led her to let Ilona back into her life. I was making decent money and while my apartment was small, it was mine.

Why I continued to allow Mother to control me, I don't know. At the time I guess I felt she needed me. She still made friends but they never stayed for very long. Part of her control over me was that I was haunted about what might happen to me if I didn't go when she called. Then I would be blamed for her pain and the thought I would be punished for not honoring my Mother was a heavy burden, and so I was not willing to take that chance.

She continued to work at the Hill & Hill Mortuary but only did Saturday funerals. Once in a while I would go and ride along just to keep her company.

JT was in and out of our lives but Mother still tried to control him. She'd call him late at night playing the, "I'm killing myself game," and he'd just say, "Go ahead." He knew she was bluffing but I was always afraid that she might actually do it. I would go to her no matter what time it was. Mother fought for JT's attention because he was now married and didn't need her like she needed him. She would attack his wife, call her names, and talk about her Momma.

Lenore had become numb to the mind games but still fought for Mother's love, while I played middleman. Unfortunately, Lenore was hooked on alcohol and self-destruction.

Living alone seemed the best for Eddie and me. I still had problems with the night and Mother knew that. It was always during the night when she wanted me to come over to the apartment.

Finally she bought herself a dog, a little Black Chihuahua, and then she named him after her husband, Tom. Now I love dogs, but that one was mean. Naturally Mother loved that little critter and upon observation I believed she probably loved that dog more than she did her own children.

One night about 1:00 a.m., she called me crying that Little Tom, the dog, had gotten out and she couldn't find him. She demanded I come over quickly before something happened to him. Once again I gathered up Eddie and we drove over to look for her dog. After searching the entire neighborhood, I returned to her apartment only to find she had never lost him. It had been her cruel way of getting attention from me and in Mother's mind, seeing me upset made her happy. She knew she could get away with it because I had been programmed not to disrespect her, and that I would jump when she called. So, she frequently tested me. To her it didn't matter how far I had to go— she demanded and knew I would come. It was a mean game but at the time I felt I had no choice but to play.

Mother had asked many times for me to move in with her now that I was an adult and working, because she hated being alone. When her so-called friends would leave, there was no one to wait on her hand-and-foot. She had to make her own coffee and wash her own back. Actually, she wanted and needed someone to order around and as I was the weakest child and loved her unconditionally, she knew it was easy to control me. Even though I understood that, I still allowed it. After all, she was my Mother, and I had to honor her so my days would be long upon this earth. That's what the Good Book said.

I liked living on the West Side of town even though running back and forth over to South Central was a pain, but I did it for Mother. Mainly, I wanted to keep Eddie in a good school and there was no doubt the best schools were on the West Side. True, the rent was higher there but if necessary, I was willing to work two jobs.

It definitely was not Beverly Hills but a median residential neighborhood with only a few apartment buildings. I coveted my neighbors' homes, always trying to peek in their windows to see how they decorated. "One day, we'll have a house, bigger and better," I'd tell Eddie.

I always hoped that one day things would change. Eddie depended on me and was my inspiration. We would sit and play together and I'd tell him stories of the big house that I lived in as a child. Stories about the house being haunted fascinated him but I assured him they were friendly ghosts. "I think they're angels," I'd say. "I always felt that they were there to protect me."

"Mommy you should write a book," he would often tell me. He was a good reader and loved books, probably because I read to him so often. Then he'd read to me, only making up his own story.

Buddy didn't come around very much and when he called he made promises to Eddie, like promising to pick him up, take him to the park, and spend time with him, but each time it would be the same thing—he'd never show up. I'd watch Eddie sitting on the steps outside the apartment for hours. He'd wait so patiently and Buddy never came. My heart would break when Buddy called and told Eddie, "I promise this time; I'll be there." But Buddy's friends always came first. He'd get drunk and forget.

One time I even threatened to hurt Buddy if he called Eddie again and did not show up. "Don't make a promise to our son that you aren't going to keep," I told him. "Eddie needs his Father to show him he loves him. You are breaking his heart, and his spirit." But Buddy had good intentions and that's all they were. So many times I watched Eddie pack a bag, excited to spend a night with his Daddy but each time his heart would break, and he'd run in crying saying that his Daddy didn't love him. The only comfort I could give a five-year-old child was my own love but I could never replace the love of his Father. I tried to love him enough for both of us but I knew he was missing something. Buddy was missing even more but he was too dumb to know it.

Then against my better judgment, I moved into a house with Mother. She convinced me we would be partners in the house. It was on the West Side, built by Nancy Wilson, and it was fabulous. There were two huge master bedrooms and a large backyard. Oh, the backyard was the sweetener for me. Eddie needed to have a yard to play in and that was the only way I could afford to be in a house. Tommy, the good friend that he was, still came around and said if I moved back with Mother he would buy Eddie a swing set for the yard. I was sure Ozzie and Harriet Nelson had a swing set for their kids. This would be as close as I would ever get to giving my child a real home.

Can you believe it, Mother managed to convince me her partying days were behind her and that she was only going to drink beer, and no more hard alcohol. She was going to straighten up her act, she promised.

She had run Tom off long ago and had married and remarried several times, but they never stayed long enough for me to get used to any of them. I knew they would not last because she really loved Tom, but he had given up on her. He was fed up with all the fighting over nothing.

For her it was always about control. She would marry and then after a few months kick her husband out. This was her way of hurting Tom and as she did not believe in shacking up with a man, she had to marry him, even if it wasn't "till death do us part."

Surprisingly, Tom loved her but he refused to react the way she hoped. Also, he had stopped drinking and had become a much nicer person, and Mother hated that. So, the final blow she dealt him was to marry his brother and that did it! Tom was out of her life forever.

Eventually Tom married again, to a woman who looked so much like Mother they could have been sisters. Not only did she look like Mother, she also had five children. My stepsister Ethel and I lost contact after she married and had a child. I'd heard she was happy.

The saying, "Water seeks its own level," was apropos in my Mother's choice of men who seemed to come from the bottom of the barrel, but now she wanted to change and needed my help. She wanted us to buy that house together and all would be well. Dumb me, I agreed, hoping for the best.

As you probably have already guessed, the move turned out to be a big mistake on my part. Mother continued to control me and bring strange men into the house and I slipped back into my role of being her servant—she went back to Jack Daniels. The hard liquor is what brought on her mean personality. Mrs. Reese, the beautiful and respected women got buried deep inside her and then the real Mother surfaced.

Lenore and JT came over on a regular basis, and Tommy and his Significant Other were there most nights. Tommy had become my son's Godfather and he showered us with gifts. If there was a need, he filled it. He was a good friend, and I loved him. I always had reservations about his lifestyle but I did not want to judge him. In my heart I felt it was wrong and so never left him alone with Eddie or allowed him to babysit. It was not my intention to hurt Tommy's feelings and I believed he understood my position. It was his financial help that kept me going for a long time. I appreciated his friendship more than words could express because he was always there for us…except for one horrible night when he left early.

I had let my guard down and for some reason, why I don't know, I had not locked my bedroom door. That was the night I learned never to expect anyone to save me. I could only depend on myself but this night I failed.

When Eddie and I had gone to sleep, I felt comfortable because Tommy was in the living room and no one had tried to bother me in a long time. Feeling relaxed I went to bed without any concern—after all I had a child in the bed next to me. My room was safe, or so I had thought.

Mother had a lot of company that night and they were all sitting around playing cards, talking loud, and drinking their "fire water," as I liked to call it. Tommy and his friend left early that night, also forgetting what kind of friends Mother had in her house. I woke to a man's hand over my mouth and then his body dropped down on me. Eddie was in the twin bed next to me and my mind began racing as to what to do. *If I fought and screamed, Eddie would wake up and be terrified and I didn't want him to be afraid of the dark.* So I lay there while whomever the man was rubbed and fumbled my body. I tried to stay calm as my pulse beat ever so fast trying to figure out what I should do. I kept still, trying not to make a sound. The man's voice was cold and heartless. His breath reeked of alcohol and his words sounded like screams in my ear.

"It's gonna be good. Don't fight me if you know what's good for you," he threatened. I did not know who it was as it was dark; I could not see his face and did not recognize his voice. Forcing my head to turn and look over at my precious little boy, I saw he slept like an angel. I prayed, *Somebody please help me!*

By then the man had his other hand under the covers and had begun to touch and hurt me. I wanted to cry out, bite his hand and scream, but he kept putting one hand over my mouth. Desperately afraid to even let out my groans, I knew if Eddie woke up he would never be able to forget the sight and fear of seeing someone hurt his Mother - I couldn't let him witness that. I remembered all the times I'd seen Mother in fights and since it had hurt me, I wouldn't let Eddie get hurt.

The man seemed to take pleasure in my pain. Seemed to know why I would not cry out my dilemma. He whispered what he would do if Eddie woke up. So I pretended it did not hurt and refused to accept the pain. I stopped feeling anything and did not give him the pleasure of seeing me cry or flinch from his cruelty. My baby was okay and I knew it would be over soon. So I stepped outside of my body.

When it was over, I watched the man leave and I did not know who he was. I knew I would have to come back to the reality of what had happened and when it did, the pain was excruciating.

There was no noise coming from the living room, so I put a chair at my door but it seemed silly at that point. It was my fault that I had not put a chair at the door before Eddie and I went to bed. So many thoughts ran through my mind of what I should have done. I wanted to fight but I did not have the courage to fight anymore. I was tired, so tired of fighting. Tommy could not protect me that night, no one could. No one knew and I never knew who the man was. All the bad things happen in the dark.

Quietly I went into the bathroom and lay in the tub, cleaning myself over and over trying to wash away the filthiness I was feeling. I spent the rest of the night in the tub. Eddie never woke up, and I thanked God that he would never know.

* * *

For weeks after I cried during the nights and during the days when Eddie was not around. I was so depressed and despondent and felt so unworthy of life, but Eddie needed me. He knew nothing of what was going on while I silently died inside. As usual, when I finally told Mother I had been raped by one of her "friends," she accused me of making up the whole story.

I became a shell of a person but knew my only purpose was to raise Eddie and make sure he knew how important he was to me. In return, I received the love of my child, and that alone made my life worth living. Sometimes I wondered how I could show him love when I didn't know what love was. I only knew I loved my child and he was my gift, a gift that no one could take from me.

* * *

I kept plugging away at going to school, hoping to get the education I'd need in order to get a job that would pay me the money I needed to make life better for us. There were offers to work at the Hill & Hill Funeral Home, but I had seen too much. When I went into the Embalming Room one day I found Reverend Andrews fondling a dead-man's penis. I yelled, "What are you doing, Reverend?," instantly becoming sick to my stomach. I wanted him to know that I had seen him. He quickly started explaining but there was no explaining about what he was doing. There was not anything he could say to make that right.

It seemed that the way the world was going everything wrong was being made right, and everything right was wrong. When I told Mother what I had witnessed, surprise, surprise, she told me to mind my own business and that I should not have gone in there in the first place. Then she ordered me not to tell anyone.

I hated all of them. I hated their wickedness and knew I had to get Eddie away from those people before he was old enough to understand what was going on around him. To me it was imperative to not let him know how dark and cruel people could be. I wanted him to be a good man and I knew I needed to get him where there were only good men, only I didn't know where any good men could be found. Evidently, they were already married, or dead.

55

Each day I planned to move away because I knew all the bad things in my life would continue to happen if I didn't. I knew I needed to find a way to leave the past in the past and that living with Mother was not a healthy environment for my child, or for me. But while going to night school and working full-time and also some overtime, I needed help; also, I understood Eddie's never wanting me to leave him.

Life has a way of helping you make choices. I'm thankful for all of the ugly things because they allowed me to know how to make a right decision. Even if it's wrong, I can choose again and again until I get it right. Procrastination was my enemy and it would lead me to make my last mistake with Mother. My only wish was that I had moved one-day sooner. But I took a chance hoping to finish out the semester. I know that there is always a plan, even if it's not yours.

One evening after night school, I drove up in front of our house. The feeling of something being wrong came over me and as I quickly looked at the house while parking my car, I immediately noticed the drapes were hanging crooked. Feeling a chill and knowing something was seriously wrong, I jumped out of the car and ran to the front door. I turned the knob, and the door opened. *Why was it not locked?*

Suddenly Eddie came running to me crying, "Mommy, Mommy, you should see all the blood. Auntie Lenore, auntie Lenore!" I grabbed Eddie and picked him up and hugged him with the assurance that Mommy was there. Then I saw a lady sitting in the living room, someone I'd never met.

"Who are you?" I demanded in an agitated tone.

"I'm Vera. Your Mother asked me to stay with Little Eddie here."

"Why? What happened?" I looked around noticing that the drapes had been torn down and there was glass on the floor. Then Eddie climbed from my arms and pulled me by the hand toward the bathroom. As I walked down the hall, fear rushed from the top of my head to the bottom of my feet. In the doorway of the bathroom my eyes zoomed in on the mirrored medicine cabinet that was shattered, and the shower curtain torn and hanging off the hooks. Blood was splashed on the floor, in the sink, and on the door and my heart raced as though I were running a race.

Eddie was still holding my hand tightly and he said, "Mommy, Mommy," he stuttered, "auntie Lenore all cut up."

Not sure of the best way to handle things I picked him up again and said, "I want you to go to bed. I'm sure auntie Lenore will be okay. Did someone take her to the hospital?"

"Yes, Mommy, the police and an ambulance."

I hugged Eddie. "It's going to be okay. Don't be afraid, Mommy is here." Then I lay beside him in his bed and rubbed his forehead until he fell asleep. I did not want him to be afraid even though he had reason to be scared to death.

The anger I felt inside I knew I had to control. I could visualize what had happened. It was always the same scenario. Lenore had probably tried to kill herself again after she and JT had a fight, which was always instigated by Mother. Making sure Eddie was sound asleep, I quietly left the room and went to talk to Vera in the living room.

My suspicions were right-on and as I was sitting talking with her, Mother and Lenore came through the front door. Lenore had bandages on both wrists; she looked as if she had fought a war and lost. I had so much anger in me that I walked into the kitchen and got a big butcher knife out of the drawer.

When I came back into the living room Lenore and Mother were sitting on the sofa as if they had just come back from a stroll. I walked in and stood over Lenore. Her hair was messed up and her black eyeliner was smudged on her face from her tears. Mother was telling Vera that the doctor had said Lenore needed psychiatric help and I could not have agreed more.

I showed Lenore the knife and waved it in front of her face. She looked up at me in surprise as I promised, "If you ever try to kill yourself in front of my child again, I'll do it for you! Do you understand me, Lenore?" I never blinked my eyes as I stared directly into hers. Her pain did not faze me; I did not raise my voice. I was very calm as if I were greeting her with a nice welcome, but the look in my eyes told Lenore she had screwed up with me. She knew exactly the point I was making. I wanted her to know never to hurt my child with her craziness. Lenore got the picture.

Mother leaped up to push me out of Lenore's face and started telling me how wrong I was and that Lenore had problems. "Who the hell do you think you are?" she yelled.

That night I told her who I was. "I am Eddie's Mom and don't you ever forget it!" And then I let out the years of rage and hurt that had been building in me. The words flowed out of my mouth like water rushing from a dam that was destroying everything in its path. I also told Mother what I thought of her and that if she ever tried to kill herself, don't call me. I meant every word.

* * *

My old friend Jonesy had said, "When you have had enough no one has to tell you, you will know." I knew that this was it; I had had enough. I was moving on. My life was going to change and I was going to be the one in charge. All the fears of being under Mother's control disappeared. I felt an inner strength that said, *You'll make it.* The prison gates had opened. My mind was free, the chains of guilt broken for the first time in my life

I realized I had not made all the bad things happen but I had allowed them to go on because I didn't believe I could live without my Mother, because her control was all I knew. But the moment I broke the chain of dependency, I felt the freedom flowing through my whole body. I would come out fighting and no one would ever have a hold on me again. My child would **NOT** grow up thinking he deserved to have bad things happen to him.

Lenore was in deep trouble and that night I realized just how much. I did not want to end up like her. I loved Lenore. She had a beautiful heart but unless she took control of her life, one day alcohol abuse would kill her. It hurt me to realize that although she too had a wonderful son, she did not see him as her way of escape. Now she had gone to a point of no return and I realized I could not help her, the same way I realized I could not look for Tommy to protect me at night. I had to protect myself. Life's lessons can be hard and it's an education most people don't get. The human behaviors of wicked people are real, even though sometimes they hide behind the cloth and they disguise themselves as righteous, or as your Mother.

My Mother had serious problems that she would never face or admit. But I was no longer responsible for her. I had taken as much as anyone could. It was Mrs. Reese I loved with all my heart, standing tall and respected by so many people—people that only knew her as Mrs. Reese. My love for Mother was never appreciated or accepted and she had used her knowledge of people's nature to break a person's spirit and tear them down with words that cut to the heart.

At every opportunity she had told me how I would never amount to anything. If I disagreed with her about her men friends, or if I refused to entertain her friends, she would tell me I was not normal. When I refused to play her games, it caused her to be creative in her ways to win me back. She spent years lowering my self-esteem. Threatening me that if I did not wait on her and honor her, God would punish me.

That day I was transformed from the dark to the light. Eddie's fear of seeing auntie Lenore acting crazy woke me up. I was responsible for him and I would never let him go through a night like that again, or go through life the way I did. I vowed to make his life better and no matter what it took, I would die trying. In my mind I had been walking a line and knew if I ever crossed over the line, there would be no coming back. Every day I fought to hold onto what was right and had to really fight not to cross the line in my mind. It had been hard to believe in Heaven or Hell because Hell was where I had lived. Mother had governed my life for so long that when she told me who to like or who to hate, I had believed her. I had been locked up and held prisoner. Mother had the key but the night Lenore attempted suicide, she lost it.

It was liberating to realize that no one has the right to control another human being. Life should be free, free to love and receive love. The little person in my life, Eddie, became the biggest gift I had ever received. I had believed I had no belief, but that was how the darkness tried to take over. There is a dark world out there *only* if you accept the darkness. I decided that I hated the darkness and from that day forth my mind would only walk in the light.

There are all kinds of people, some good and some bad. Unfortunately, I had had more than my share of the bad ones. Now I know that only the strong survive and I am a survivor! Throughout my life I prayed to a God whom I thought never heard my prayers and that my prayers had only gone as high as the ceiling. Today I am a witness that God **is** real and He **does** hear our prayers. He is obligated to answer your prayers when you believe in Him. It's not always the answer we want but He always answers. There are no explanations for my past and no more sorrows. I lived in the past and now live in the present. Each day is a new beginning.

I had made wonderful friends at work and learned that the White people I worked with were nothing like the people of the South. They became my mentors and helped me make my transition from under Mother's thumb. As I watched how they treated their kids, I learned things I could never have learned at home. Before I had given them the cold shoulder for fear they would hurt me but when my boss shared what I had been through, they all came to help. One friend named Dorothy said, "If you need help, just ask."

For me that was a novel concept, as I had never thought to ask anyone for help because I expected and feared rejection. But now I was ready for anything. I could handle rejection; after all, I had handled rejection all my life but this was a new beginning. Eddie would be okay because he knew his Mother loved him. He would learn to be a healthy productive person. I would keep him in a good school and teach him not to hate anyone because of their Color. God did not make any mistakes in making us and I was going to be a living witness. I left my Mother's house without any guilty feelings. Knowing Mother would not believe me, or let me go, I learned to be tough with her. I stopped running every time she called. My heart pushed me on occasion to go, but now it was my decision, not hers.

56

My CONFIDENCE WAS GROWING AND I HAD BEGUN feeling empowered with self-assurance. I thought I could handle almost anything until one day I made the mistake of rushing to pick Eddie up from the babysitter. As I backed my car out of the driveway at work, I thought I had looked both ways when I heard a man screaming at the top of his lungs. I had knocked him down and his screams sent terror up my spine. He was cussing me and threatening to put me in jail. When I had frantically jumped out of the car, I was deathly afraid I had done him serious harm. The way he screamed I thought he must be under my tire or something but no, he was standing and continued to call me names as he brushed off his suit and pointed to his pants leg that had been torn. He was okay; there was no blood. I was relieved to know he was not seriously hurt and I silently thanked God. All my apologies meant nothing to him. He just kept yelling that he was going to sue me for everything I had but I only had Eddie.

Still knowing I could handle anything, I called my friend Johnny Cochran. Again I would need his help and again I had no money for his services. As busy as Johnny was, he always took my call.

"What's going on, Little Mary?" With my trembling voice I told him what had happened and that I really didn't have any money to go to court. He asked for all the information and told me not to worry, he'd get back with me. Two days passed and I was so nervous I couldn't eat or sleep. All I thought was that I would lose my child, and visualized he would be put in a foster home and I would have to go to jail. I was terrified at the thought. With no car insurance or medical insurance at the time, I would probably be put in jail.

A week passed and I had a difficult time hiding my fears but I was afraid to tell anyone what had happened. I kept wondering what I was going to do because I was in big trouble. I was at work when one of the telephone operators told me I had a personal call. Quickly I took the call, relieved to hear Johnny's voice, but afraid to hear what he had to say.

"Little Mary, Johnny here."

"Hi there," I whispered.

"Little Mary, I talked with the man, and he was really upset."

"But Johnny, I barely tapped him. He didn't get hurt!"

"That's not the point. You hit him with your car and you don't have insurance."

"I know. What's he going to do to me?" I watched the office door, thinking the police were on their way to get me.

"I convinced him you didn't have anything to sue for and that you were rushing to pick up your kid. It took some heavy talking but he wants you to pay for his suit, one hundred and seventy four dollars. Do you think you can do that?"

"Oh, yes," my voice went high and I could not believe what I was hearing.

"Little Mary, the next time you hit someone, make sure it's not an attorney!"

"I hit an attorney?"

"You sure did and he's a tough son-of-a-gun. Get that money to me ASAP."

"Johnny, I'll bring it over today."

"Good." I could tell he was probably smiling because he knew he had saved my butt again.

"Thank you Johnny. I don't know what I would have done without you."

"Well you don't have to do without me, just stay out of trouble, okay?"

I felt so excited, I unplugged myself from the switchboard and knocked on my boss's door. After a long explanation of what had happened and that my Attorney Johnny Cochran had really come through for me, my boss agreed to advance me the money.

Before I reached the door to leave his office, my boss said. "Give me your attorney's phone number. I want him when I get in trouble." We both smiled as I walked away.

I had another chance to make my life right. I was free again, free from fear. I had found that there is always a solution to every problem, if you know who is in your corner. Johnny Cochran was the Godfather I always wanted and he let me know that friendship meant something to him and he did not let his friends down. Oh, I was ever so grateful.

57

MOTHER CONTINUED TO WORK FOR MRS. HILL OF HILL and Hill Mortuary. Having been a widow, Mrs. Hill then married Reverend Andrews, who knew that she had inherited everything from Mr. Hill. It was obvious he had married her for the money since everyone knew he liked boys but like Mother said, it was none of my business.

When I had caught him fondling a dead man, it had turned my stomach and I could never be in the same room with him after that; of course, I never told Mrs. Hill, who always seemed to be walking around in a daze. Her attitude was, "I don't want to know so don't tell me." Mrs. Hill seemed to be a good person but I had to question her character when she married Reverend Andrews. I felt she needed to know how evil he was. I accepted that it was not my place to say anything.

Reverend Andrews was getting a reputation around Watts; he was known to lure young boys with drugs and then take advantage of them. The neighborhood in Watts was low-income. The kids did not have places to go and nowhere to channel their energy, except to get into trouble. Once these children got hooked on drugs, it was a no-win situation for them. They did whatever it took to keep up their habit.

For years, several of the well-known preachers were getting a reputation for their deviant ways. They preached, pretending to be righteous, while taking advantage of their own congregation, using the church money for expensive cars and jewelry. While they lived high-on-the-hog, their congregations blindly continued to give and to believe they were men of God, but I knew better. They were a lot like Reverend Andrews, maybe not as bad, but they were bad. I could count on one hand the few preachers that were sincere in their beliefs and in their hearts.

Hill & Hill Funeral Home was on the border of Watts, in Los Angeles. The word had spread about what the preachers where doing and some of the neighborhood teens resented these preachers with a passion. They decided to take matters into their own hands and a "hit list" of the preachers' names that they wanted to get rid of had been circulated in the Hood, and I do mean get rid of permanently. Reverend Andrews was on the list because one of the teens in the Hood had found out that his little cousin, who was thirteen-years old, had been drugged and taken advantage of by the preacher. Mother had heard about the list and feared her name might be on it, and was quite nervous during that time. Her name was not on the list but as the Bible says, "Bad company corrupts good morals." She was no saint but she also was not a Reverend Andrews.

* * *

I no longer was involved with Mother's friends or the Funeral Home. My life was free from all the craziness that went along with her lifestyle. Somehow I knew evil men would be judged and Reverend Andrew's time came up. Reverend Andrews was eventually murdered and died a horrible and cruel death. But that is another story in itself.

The only satisfaction I had was knowing that one day the wicked will be judged. My hate toward Reverend Andrews and the other preachers tore at my heart. I had to stay away and remove them from my mind. I became the "outcast," as Mother referred to me. I did not want to be around when lightening struck them, as I knew it would.

I became more involved with my own church, where there were wonderful programs for kids, like the summer camp Eddie loved. The church never allowed me to pay for any of the programs, or summer camps, as they were aware of my circumstances and worked with me to raise my son. Being a single Mother was a struggle from the moment I got up to the time I went to bed. But I did not feel lonely as some thought I should. Being alone was my best friend. I enjoyed coming home to an empty, yet clean home, with no strangers coming in and out.

For years I read self-help books on the psychology of human behavior, like the birth order in your family and how it affects you. I learned to think for myself. From the time I can remember, Mother always told me the Bible says that I should honor my Mother so that *her* days would be long upon the earth (Ephesians 6:1-4). My Mother had misquoted. When I read further, the next line said, "Parents, do not provoke thy children unto wrath."

I no longer feared what God would do to me if I did not respect and love my Mother because I no longer feared God, because God knew me inside and out. There could be no secrets from Him. Determined to live the rest of my life in the light, I let go of all the fears concerning people judging me. The dark past was just that—it was in the past. I would only live in the present. I had spent years of feeling guilty to the point of wanting to die. The Funeral Home had been my refuge. I had found peace in the Viewing Room and the dead people had what I did not. They slept without fear. Now the Funeral Home was part of my past. I no longer had the desire to be in the presence of the dead. I enjoyed being with the living.

As years passed, I still made many mistakes. I fell down many times, letting men into my life who would use me or take advantage of my weaknesses, but I always got up again and again to start over, never giving up. If life were designed to live each day free from mistakes, I would not know when I was on the right track. I still refused to go backwards in life, only forward.

Each job I got was always better than the last. I continued to take classes on neuro-linguistic programming, a self-improvement course, because I was determined to learn who I was.

The first and most important thing I had to learn was that I was not my Mother. The two personalities of Mother almost cost me my life. But I learned my social skills from her; I learned poise and vanity. I walked tall, no matter what the circumstances were. I represented the Hubert and Reese Mortuary, and the J.T. Stone Funeral Home, the most respected Black business in the South, and in Los Angeles. I was proud to say, "I am the daughter of Mrs. Reese," because she was a woman who was respected. I was always going to be Little Mary and that was okay. I wanted to be the best I could be.

As I continued to work on my self-improvement skills, I became a Mother of whom Eddie could be proud. I studied the Bible from cover to cover because I wanted to understand its history, why and for whom it was written. It helped me be prepared for false preachers, as I didn't want any preacher to deceive me. Also, it helped me know immediately if they were quoting the Bible incorrectly. Sad as it may seem, so many preachers that came across my path had never read the Bible.

The journey ahead of me was going to be a long one. As Carlos Castaneda's Don Juan said, "It is important to know if the path before us has a heart. A path without a heart is never enjoyable." I would have to work hard to stay on the path but on the other hand, a path with heart is easy.

Self-esteem is not something with which you are born. You have to create and maintain your self-esteem. No one can give it to you. My Mother had taken away my self-esteem and my self-confidence as a child. Only I could rebuild and become the person God wanted me to be. Many years have passed and I am still learning and growing.

Yes, I continued to care for Mother but always kept her at arms-length. I set my mind to be positive and not negative toward her. When I saw her as a sad woman, who had lost everything, it helped. The fact that she lost it all because of her foolishness was not the point. She was alone until Lenore let her son live with her.

Darin, at the age of ten, was happy to stay with Mother at first because Lenore left him alone so much he only wanted someone to be in the house with him; however, it was a huge mistake. Darin became Mother's servant and she treated him poorly. At the age of thirteen, Darin told Eddie, who was ten at the time, that he was going to run away to a Catholic Church and work for his keep. Eddie could not keep this a secret; he loved his cousin and told me the plan. I could not allow my nephew to live this way and invited him to come and live with us. He did, and we made it work.

It was so rewarding to see Darin happy for the first time in years. He had a family—Eddie and me—and he became an "A" student and went on to college, graduating with honors. Today he is a fine and prosperous young man.

Lenore was grateful I was there for both her and Darin. Eventually she realized she was helpless and lost in Mother's world, which had made her unable to be a good Mother to her own son. Though Lenore dearly loved Darin, her addiction to alcohol and Mother kept her from being a responsible person. My sister had a heart of gold and I am thankful I was able to love her in spite of her faults and weaknesses.

* * *

How fast time passes and life keeps happening even if you are not paying attention. Mother became meaner and meaner with each year. Her bitterness continued to rip the family apart as she played her games, turning each one against the other, sisters and brothers fighting constantly. Where was the love one should feel for their siblings? It was not there. Somehow Ilona and I maintained a close relationship and were able to get back to the same relationship we had before she married and went away. All the instigating Mother has pulled on us has only brought us closer.

Mother's lifestyle finally caught up with her as she neared her death. She was left with only a few friends and her children. Ilona and I took care of her. JT lived on the outskirts of Los Angeles, at least a two-hour drive away and Lenore did not drive, never had and never would. Ilona and I took turns going back and forth to the hospital. There were many times when the nurses would call and complain about how Mother fought them and would run down the halls late at night. Evidently, she fought sleep because she was fearful of dying. The sleeping medication didn't work—she had a strong determination to stay awake. Yet, without sleep, she carried on like a madwoman.

In August of 1980, at the age 67, my Mother died alone, in a hospital in Beverly Hills. I'll never forget the phone call. I hung up feeling stunned and slowly sat down on the sofa thinking, *It's over.* I realized I was neither crying, nor grieving—just feeling a sense of relief—and then I felt ashamed. After making the necessary phone calls, I drove to the hospital. Ilona and I reached the hospital at the same time. One of the nurses came over to us, sharing her condolence and led us to the room where Mother had died.

We weren't sure about going in because Mother had said she did not want anyone to see her dead but I had to see her. We pulled the sheet from her face and the fear I saw on my Mother's face was truly the look of torment. Ilona and I stood there not saying a word. Ilona had tears in her eyes but I watched and wondered why I had no tears. With my head down, I walked out and then looked around. It was so strange. I had just lost my Mother and everyone was going on about his or her business as if nothing had happened.

When we told JT about looking at Mother's body, he was furious with us and for days cussed us whenever he saw, or talked with us. Her wish for no funeral was ignored by JT; he staged an elaborate funeral. It was more like a parade than a funeral. On top of the hearse was a gigantic picture of Mother for everyone to see as the procession slowly moved down the streets of South Central Los Angeles. Every Black-owned Funeral Home sent one of their Cadillacs and hundreds of people showed up for her funeral to show their respect to an, "Extraordinary Woman." The Black radio stations announced her passing and where her body was to be buried.

Yes, Mrs. Reese made a difference to many people and was loved by those who knew her. My heart wept for Mrs. Reese but not for my Mother. The Black Community had lost a role model, a Black woman with power.

58

My WORLD HAD TRULY CHANGED. THE CORD HAD finally been cut and I had been released from Mother's control for good. Even though she was dead, I knew the past could still control me. The words of the past that had been imprinted on my heart and in my conscience, I would have with me forever. All the self-help books in the world could not erase the pain and hurt that Mother had caused me. I live each day saying I forgive you but how can you forgive a person who believed she was never wrong? My final step in healing Little Mary was to write my Mother a letter and take it to her grave. There, alone, I read the letter and then set a match to it, burning it over her grave and spreading the ashes, letting go of all the pain. The words I wrote said it all—I had hated her, yet I loved her with all my heart. The healing finally began and I began to grow, allowing myself to enter into freedom.

Most of us think we know the importance of a positive mental attitude and what it takes to get through tough times. I have been tested and sometimes failed but I have now begun to realize that attitude is everything. I cannot change the things of the past, just as I cannot predict my future. I had no control over Mother and there was nothing I could have done to change her. I had to accept who she was and make sure I did not become like her. When they buried her, I was reborn.

* * *

A couple of years after Mother passed away, Buddy died at the age of forty-two from colon cancer. Several years later, Lenore's life was taken suddenly at the age of fifty from a massive heart attack. Dad died a few years after Lenore.

Although I visited him nearly every Sunday, when he died I did not grieve as a daughter should for her Father. Again I felt ashamed that I did not have a lot of tears for my parents. My heart had become hard and although I tried to remember the good times, I couldn't. All the losses of my family only taught me that life is for the living. I let them go, with all the memories that I wanted to forget. It was natural to want to pretend I had parents that really loved me but I would only fool strangers, not myself. All the phony preachers had long passed on. Reverend Andrews's murder and death made the news and it shook up the preachers in Watts. At least I hope it did.

* * *

Physically, Mother died some twenty-years ago but as is usually the case with either good or bad parents, she still lives on in the hearts of each of her children. Through the years JT and I worked on having a more positive relationship and for the most part I think we have succeeded. Willie, bless his heart, I have never doubted his love; he has always been there for me. Although Ilona and I have always been close, we have major differences in regards to memories of our Mother. She prefers to remember that Mother was good to her when she was a child—up until Mother pistol-whipped her. Somehow, I seemed to have missed that good part of Mother. Could it be the four-years difference in our ages gave Mother time to change into the person about whom I have written?

It is unfortunate that to this day all my siblings cannot peacefully be in the same room together due to Mother's lingering spirit that still has the power to stir things up for us. It never fails that whenever she is mentioned in a conversation, all the old hurts and angers from the past will surface and all hell seems to break out in our midst. She still seems to negatively intrude on our lives.

It has taken some time but I have finally come to the realization that my siblings and I will never forget the past, because they cannot stop talking about Mother as though she were still alive. I have been able to let her go but for some reason they still want to keep her alive; therefore, we can never come together, loving each other for who we individually are—sisters and brothers. Ingrained bitterness for one another is alive and well and keeps us separated—just, as I believe, Mother intended.

Each new day I live as if it were my last. I make sure I say "I Love You" to everyone I know. I do not want to miss the opportunity to tell people what they mean to me. My lonely journey has been with 'Hind's Feet,' and my inward journey was to learn not to blame my struggles on anyone, to pioneer my own new life with high expectations for myself. I believe that I can accomplish anything I want. I am not afraid of hard work.

Eddie has grown up to be a man of whom I am very proud. He has always been my inspiration to do more. He gave me strength to keep going, to keep moving towards my goals. If I studied for exams, he was there to quiz me. As you can imagine, time was not standing still - it was flying by me and when Eddie was grown and no longer needed me, I grew depressed. With Eddie on his own, I felt emptiness, a void in my life. I had to believe that through it all there would be an answer to my prayer of "What next God?"

The decision to make a career change came to me in the middle of the night. At forty-two, I wanted to be an entrepreneur. My friends and most of my family thought I was crazy to leave a good job in a Media Buying Service. I was told starting a new career at that age was ridiculous. People kept asking, "But what will you do?"

That was a good question and I had no immediate answer, but I was tired of working hard for someone else. My desire to work for myself was strong and I explored what I could do to make a lot of money in a short time. I knew I did not have forty-some years ahead of me like I had behind me, so I had to move quickly.

What would be my unique talent? Again, I got my answer in the middle of the night. "Become an insurance agent." I struggled with this thought but it seemed attainable.

The years passed quickly as I moved into my new career. I filled the void I had after Eddie had moved away with helping others. The best way to take your mind off yourself is to help someone else. I loved working for myself and it was easy to sell something in which I believed. Educating people on the importance of life insurance was my unique talent and it felt good to be helping them while they were living. My experience in the Funeral Business was one of the keys to my success because I could give families first-hand information on what it is like to lose someone, and then have to pass the hat for money to bury them. My past was contributing to my future success. I never would have thought things would work that way.

* * *

I had no hope of ever having a healthy relationship with a man because I had decided I would not know a healthy man if he came up and stood on my foot. God had given me the gift of being able to live alone and love it. I had no desire to have a man in my life.

317

My clients were all the social life I needed and I was thankful I never allowed myself to stay depressed for long periods. Whenever I felt low, I'd spend a day alone and tell myself to shake off the dust and move onto something new. The voices of the past—Mr. Holmes, uncle Bud, and Mr. Lary in the Embalming Room, were my inner strength. Their words of encouragement that I would be someone important one day, always stayed with me.

"There's something special about you, Little Mary." "There's light in your eyes." "Don't you ever give up." Those words had been music to my love-starved ears. The voices of the past were also branded on my subconscious.

Quitting for me was never an option. I had overcome challenges, especially my fears of the night. There was a plan for me and I had a purpose and would not question it anymore. I accepted the place where I was and I chose not to complain, for God had brought me through the fire and out of the ashes to be a woman-of-means.

I have come to understand the awful things that happened to me in the past have taught me not to judge circumstances by their appearance. What often seems to be a tragedy is for our own good and it can turn out to be a healing for someone else. Learning to be content does not come easy, it's natural to always be wanting more, not out of need but out of greed. *Things* can never fill your heart. In all my years of working in the Funeral Home I learned, as I once heard someone say, "You'll never see a U-Haul truck behind the hearse."

I found that "time does *not* heal all wounds," only God can heal. Time can push the memories deeper into the mind but one tiny memory can bring it all back up to the surface, and it never leaves. My quest for happiness was to be content with things just the way they were and that is when life surprises you. I believe God is monitoring your every step along your path.

To say, "I will never," is an excuse for saying "I'm afraid." When one is truly content in the state he is in, that's when the unexpected happens. My favorite line was, "I'll never marry again; I'll never trust a man, not in this lifetime." I was putting on a good front—so good I really believed it. I thought as strong as I was I did not need anyone in my life to make me happy because I was happy with me. After all, I had set goals and I had accomplished each goal I set for myself. But the One who monitors my life did have a plan and when I let go of all my burdens of the past and accepted the freedom He had given me, He put his plan in motion. Unbeknownst to me, my life was about to change.

For years I had run from any man I thought would like me or become serious about me, since I cherished my freedom. I did not intend for my joy to be taken away. I did not have to care about any man's feelings or needs. It was all about me now and I did not want that to change.

God works in mysterious ways. After an enormous amount of persuasion from Ilona, I agreed to meet a man named Verne Smith. Ilona's husband had become acquainted with Verne and felt we would enjoy getting to know each other. I loved Ilona and often did what she wanted, so to keep the peace between us I agreed—but only for breakfast.

My plan was to have a short and sweet breakfast, be nice, and after he left to go on his way I would spend the rest of the day delivering insurance policies. But there was another plan, a Divine Plan in motion over which I had no control.

That morning I walked onto my sister's patio and Verne stood and shook my hand; it was electric. He smiled at me and I thought I saw a glow from behind him and just like that, I melted like a schoolgirl. My well-laid plan was erased and we ended up spending the entire day together. When the time came for him to leave, I was filled with genuine sadness as I did not want him to leave. I tried to tell myself I was being foolish. After all, he lived in a different city, in a different state, and I had my career. Long-distance relationships never work out.

Nevertheless, it was God who dropped this man into my life, a very special manly man. He was everything that represented strength and he lived by the standards and beliefs that all things work together for good. Verne Smith of Sedona, Arizona, came into my life like a lightening bolt streaking through the sky. Since I had never heard of Sedona, I knew this would not be the man for me. But who was I to change a plan that had been designed for me?

Verne did not waste any time courting me. I received a dozen roses a couple of days later and I called to thank him. Not only was I smitten, so was he. His voice would light up my life whenever he called.

When I first met Verne that morning of July 20, 1996, it had been quite an awakening for me. It was with surprise that I realized my heart was not the cold stone I thought it had become. I did have feelings and I did want to be loved. My life had been safe up until then because I believed as long as I was alone, no one could hurt me. But now the doors to my heart had been unlocked and thrown wide open.

On his way back from a business trip, Verne made a special trip to Los Angeles, in order to have breakfast with me. In the few hours we spent at breakfast, we knew fate had brought us together and he asked me to marry him. He told me that if I married him and moved to Sedona, I would meet some of the best friends I would ever have in life.

319

I surprised even myself when I showed no hesitation and told him, "Yes." To marry this man I had only known a few weeks, I knew that I was willing to take a leap-of-faith, and I wondered if the light I saw in Verne's eyes was the same light Mr. Lary, Mr. Holmes, and uncle Bud, had seen in my eyes? When I was in Verne's presence, I felt peace - I felt safe, a feeling I had longed for all my life.

We set December 21, 1996, as the date we would marry, five months after our first meeting. I married a total stranger, who is now my best friend. The life I live, is the life I dreamed about. Ozzie and Harriett Nelson have nothing on me.

My soul-companion that God sent me is the most honest, ethical man I've ever known.

He has taught me how to appreciate all living things, from bugs to trees. The circle of life is around us and it has a lesson for us all; if we watch the seasons change or watch the stars that hang in the sky. They are all gifts for each of us—if only we accept them. Albert Einstein said, "I want to know God's thoughts…the rest are details."

Sometimes I wonder where I would be if I had not met Verne. At fifty-two years of age, I was sure I would live the rest of my life alone and that was okay with me. But, that was not the Plan and I thank God everyday for the life he has given me. I'm thankful when I wake each morning. I wake and I breathe and it's because He gave me breath. Death is final and I would have missed this life if I had given up. I cannot stop thanking my God for my past and for what it was; it made me the person I am today.

I quote from an unknown author:

> **The past is history; the future is a mystery,**
> **And this moment is a gift,**
> **That is why this moment is called the present.**

I will live in the present, knowing that the past cannot hurt me. I am a soul survivor and proud of it.

Printed in the United States
20884LVS00004BA/46-402